Security, Data Analytics, and Energy–Aware Solutions in the IoT

Xiali Hei
University of Louisiana at Lafayette, USA

A volume in the Advances in Web
Technologies and Engineering
(AWTE) Book Series

Published in the United States of America by
    IGI Global
    Engineering Science Reference (an imprint of IGI Global)
    701 E. Chocolate Avenue
    Hershey PA, USA 17033
    Tel: 717-533-8845
    Fax: 717-533-8661
    E-mail: cust@igi-global.com
    Web site: http://www.igi-global.com

Library of Congress Cataloging-in-Publication Data

Names: Hei, Xiali, editor.
Title: Security, data analytics, and energy-aware solutions in the IoT /
  Xiali Hei, editor.
Description: Hershey, PA : Engineering Science Reference, an imprint of IGI
  Global, [2022] | Includes bibliographical references and index. |
  Summary: "While the recent rapid proliferation in hardware, software,
  and communication technologies have facilitated the spread of
  interconnected sensors, actuators, and heterogeneous devices to collect
  data for offering a new class of advanced services characterized by
  being available anywhere, at any time and for anyone, this book
  addresses these topics across multiple abstraction levels, ranging from
  architectural models, the provisioning of services, protocols, and
  interfaces to specific implementation approaches"-- Provided by
  publisher.
Identifiers: LCCN 2021031865 (print) | LCCN 2021031866 (ebook) | ISBN
  9781799873235 (h/c) | ISBN 9781799873242 (s/c) | ISBN 9781799873259
  (ebook)
Subjects: LCSH: Internet of things--Security measures.
Classification: LCC TK5105.8857 .S445 2022 (print) | LCC TK5105.8857
  (ebook) | DDC 004.67/8--dc23
LC record available at https://lccn.loc.gov/2021031865
LC ebook record available at https://lccn.loc.gov/2021031866

This book is published in the IGI Global book series Advances in Web Technologies and Engineering (AWTE) (ISSN: 2328-2762; eISSN: 2328-2754)

British Cataloguing in Publication Data
A Cataloguing in Publication record for this book is available from the British Library.

For electronic access to this publication, please contact: eresources@igi-global.com.

Advances in Web Technologies and Engineering (AWTE) Book Series

ISSN:2328-2762
EISSN:2328-2754

Editor-in-Chief: Ghazi I. Alkhatib, The Hashemite University, Jordan & David C. Rine , George Mason University, USA

MISSION

The **Advances in Web Technologies and Engineering (AWTE) Book Series** aims to provide a platform for research in the area of Information Technology (IT) concepts, tools, methodologies, and ethnography, in the contexts of global communication systems and Web engineered applications. Organizations are continuously overwhelmed by a variety of new information technologies, many are Web based. These new technologies are capitalizing on the widespread use of network and communication technologies for seamless integration of various issues in information and knowledge sharing within and among organizations. This emphasis on integrated approaches is unique to this book series and dictates cross platform and multidisciplinary strategy to research and practice.

The **Advances in Web Technologies and Engineering (AWTE) Book Series** seeks to create a stage where comprehensive publications are distributed for the objective of bettering and expanding the field of web systems, knowledge capture, and communication technologies. The series will provide researchers and practitioners with solutions for improving how technology is utilized for the purpose of a growing awareness of the importance of web applications and engineering.

COVERAGE

- Human factors and cultural impact of IT-based systems
- Strategies for linking business needs and IT
- Web systems engineering design
- IT readiness and technology transfer studies
- Web user interfaces design, development, and usability engineering studies
- Ontology and semantic Web studies
- Competitive/intelligent information systems
- Security, integrity, privacy, and policy issues
- Quality of service and service level agreement issues among integrated systems
- Knowledge structure, classification, and search algorithms or engines

IGI Global is currently accepting manuscripts for publication within this series. To submit a proposal for a volume in this series, please contact our Acquisition Editors at Acquisitions@igi-global.com or visit: http://www.igi-global.com/publish/.

Titles in this Series

For a list of additional titles in this series, please visit:
http://www.igi-global.com/book-series/advances-web-technologies-engineering/37158

Emerging Trends in IoT and Integration with Data Science, Cloud Computing, and Big Data Analytics
Pelin Yildirim Taser (Izmir Bakircay University, Turkey)
Information Science Reference • © 2022 • 334pp • H/C (ISBN: 9781799841869) • US $225.00

App and Website Accessibility Developments and Compliance Strategies
Yakup Akgül (Alanya Alaaddin Keykubat University, Turkey)
Engineering Science Reference • © 2022 • 322pp • H/C (ISBN: 9781799878483) • US $225.00

IoT Protocols and Applications for Improving Industry, Environment, and Society
Cristian González García (University of Oviedo, Spain) and Vicente García-Díaz (University of Oviedo, Spain)
Engineering Science Reference • © 2021 • 321pp • H/C (ISBN: 9781799864639) • US $245.00

Integration and Implementation of the Internet of Things Through Cloud Computing
Pradeep Tomar (Gautam Buddha University, India)
Engineering Science Reference • © 2021 • 357pp • H/C (ISBN: 9781799869818) • US $245.00

Design Innovation and Network Architecture for the Future Internet
Mohamed Boucadair (Orange S.A., France) and Christian Jacquenet (Orange S.A., France)
Engineering Science Reference • © 2021 • 478pp • H/C (ISBN: 9781799876465) • US $225.00

Challenges and Opportunities for the Convergence of IoT, Big Data, and Cloud Computing
Sathiyamoorthi Velayutham (Sona College of Technology, India)
Engineering Science Reference • © 2021 • 350pp • H/C (ISBN: 9781799831112) • US $215.00

For an entire list of titles in this series, please visit:
http://www.igi-global.com/book-series/advances-web-technologies-engineering/37158

701 East Chocolate Avenue, Hershey, PA 17033, USA
Tel: 717-533-8845 x100 • Fax: 717-533-8661
E-Mail: cust@igi-global.com • www.igi-global.com

Table of Contents

Detailed Table of Contents

Chapter 1
Hengshuo Liang, Towson University, USA
Lauren Burgess, Towson University, USA
Weixian Liao, Towson University, USA
Chao Lu, Towson University, USA
Wei Yu, Towson University, USA

The advance of internet of things (IoT) techniques enables a variety of smart-world systems in energy, transportation, home, and city infrastructure, among others. To provide cost-effective data-oriented service, internet of things search engines (IoTSE) have received growing attention as a platform to support efficient data analytics. There are a number of challenges in designing efficient and intelligent IoTSE. In this chapter, the authors focus on the efficiency issue of IoTSE and design the named data networking (NDN)-based approach for IoTSE. To be specific, they first design a simple simulation environment to compare the IP-based network's performance against named data networking (NDN). They then create four scenarios tailored to study the approach's resilience to address network issues and scalability with the growing number of queries in IoTSE. They implement the four scenarios using ns-3 and carry out extensive performance evaluation to determine the efficacy of the approach concerning network resilience and scalability. They also discuss some remaining issues that need further research.

Chapter 2

Sidi Mohamed Sidi Ahmed, Independent Researcher, Mauritania

The internet of things (IoT) is one of successive technological waves that could have great impact on different aspects of modern life. It is being used in transport, smart grids, healthcare, environmental monitoring, logistics, as well as for processing pure personal data through a fitness tracker, wearable medical device, smartwatch, smart clothing, wearable camera, and so forth. From a legal viewpoint, processing personal data has to be done in accordance with rules of data protection law. This law aims to protect data from collection to retention. It usually applies to the processing of personal data that identifies or can identify a specific natural person. Strict adherence to this law is necessary for protecting personal data from being misused and also for promoting the IoT industry. This chapter discusses the applicability of the data protection law to IoT and the consequences of non-compliance with this law. It also provides recommendations on how to effectively comply with the data protection law in the IoT environment.

Chapter 3

D'Tron James, University of Louisiana at Lafayette, USA
Md Abdullah Al Momin, University of Louisiana at Lafayette, USA

Biometric sensors are becoming more commonplace in today's world. These biometric sensors are especially common in today's smartphones. Billions of smartphones use these sensors for security purposes, and these are slowly but surely replacing traditional forms of password authentication. Biometrics are commonly used to unlock devices and also for purchases. In this chapter, the focus will be on the most common types of biometrics featured in phones along with the sensors associated with them. Next, an analysis of the security risk of these sensors along with common attacks to exploit these risks are discussed. Lastly, various ways to patch and combat these various risks will be discussed.

Chapter 4

Jie Lien, University of Louisiana at Lafayette, USA
Md Abdullah Al Momin, University of Louisiana at Lafayette, USA
Xu Yuan, University of Louisiana at Lafayette, USA

Voice assistant systems (e.g., Siri, Alexa) have attracted wide research attention. However, such systems could receive voice information from malicious sources. Recent work has demonstrated that the voice authentication system is vulnerable to different types of attacks. The attacks are categorized into two main types: spoofing attacks and hidden voice commands. In this chapter, how to launch and defend such attacks is explored. For the spoofing attack, there are four main types, such as replay attacks, impersonation attacks, speech synthesis attacks, and voice conversion attacks. Although such attacks could be accurate on the speech recognition system, they could be easily identified by humans. Thus, the hidden voice commands have attracted a lot of research interest in recent years.

Chapter 5

Michael Arienmughare, University of Louisiana at Lafayette, USA
Andrew S. Yoshimura, University of Louisiana at Lafayette, USA
Md Abdullah Al Momin, University of Louisiana at Lafayette, USA

This chapter will provide a survey on cyber-physical systems security related to automobiles. In modern vehicles, there has been discussion on how automobiles fit into the world of cyber-physical systems, considering their interaction with both the cyber and physical worlds and interconnected systems. With many modern vehicles being connected to the outside world, there are many vulnerabilities introduced. Modern cars contain many electronic control units and millions of lines of code, which, if compromised, could have fatal consequences. Interfaces to the outside world (e.g., in-vehicle infotainment) may be used as a vector to attack these critical components.

Chapter 6

Md Fazle Rabby, University of Louisiana at Lafayette, USA
Md Abdullah Al Momin, University of Louisiana at Lafayette, USA
Xiali Hei, University of Louisiana at Lafayette, USA

Generative adversarial networks have been a highly focused research topic in computer vision, especially in image synthesis and image-to-image translation. There are a lot of variations in generative nets, and different GANs are suitable for different applications. In this chapter, the authors investigated conditional generative adversarial networks to generate fake images, such as handwritten signatures. The authors demonstrated an implementation of conditional generative adversarial networks, which can generate fake handwritten signatures according to a condition vector tailored by humans.

Currently, the vast majority of smart devices with LEDs are on the rise. It has been observed that the lights emitted by each LED have unique spectral characteristics. Despite the fact that there are a number of methods out there to generate fingerprints, none seem to explore the possibility of generating fingerprints using this unique feature. In this chapter, the method to perform device fingerprinting using the unique spectrum emitted from the LED lights is discussed. The generated fingerprint is then used in device pairing.

The laser-based audio signal injection can be used for attacking voice controllable systems. An attacker can aim an amplitude-modulated light at the microphone's aperture, and the signal injection acts as a remote voice-command attack on voice-controllable systems. Attackers are using vulnerabilities to steal things that are in the form of physical devices or the form of virtual using making orders, withdrawal of money, etc. Therefore, detection of these signals is important because almost every device can be attacked using these amplitude-modulated laser signals. In this project, the authors use deep learning to detect the incoming signals as normal voice commands or laser-based audio signals. Mel frequency cepstral coefficients (MFCC) are derived from the audio signals to classify the input audio signals. If the audio signals are identified as laser signals, the voice command can be disabled, and an alert can be displayed to the victim. The maximum accuracy of the machine learning model was 100%, and in the real world, it's around 95%.

Chapter 9

Technology has greatly increased the availability of medical procedures in remote locations that are difficult to access, such as battlefields. Teleoperated surgical robots can be used to perform surgeries on patients over the internet in remote locations. A surgeon can remotely operate the robot to perform a procedure in another room or in a different continent. However, security technology has not yet caught up to these cyber-physical devices. There exist potential cybersecurity attacks on these medical devices that could expose a patient to danger in contrast to traditional surgery. Hence, the security of the system is very important. A malicious actor can gain control of the device and potentially threaten the life of a patient. In this chapter, the authors conduct a survey of potential attack vectors a malicious actor could exploit to deny service to the device, gain control of the device, and steal patient data. Furthermore, after the vulnerability analysis, the authors provide mitigation techniques to limit the risk of these attack vectors.

Chapter 10

Anthony Triche, University of Louisiana at Lafayette, USA
Md Abdullah Al Momin, University of Louisiana at Lafayette, USA

Launched in 2017 to widespread publicity due to the involvement of tech magnate and outspoken futurist Elon Musk, Neuralink Corp. aims to develop an advanced brain-computer interface (BCI) platform capable of assisting in the treatment of serious neurological conditions with longer-term goals of approaching transhumanism through nonmedical human enhancement to enable human-machine "symbiosis with artificial intelligence." The first published description of a complete prototype Neuralink system, detailed by Muskin the company's only white paper to date, describes a closed-loop, invasive BCI architecture with an unprecedented magnitude of addressable electrodes. Invasive BCI systems require surgical implantation to allow for directly targeted capture and/or stimulation of neural spiking activity in functionally associated clusters of neurons beneath the surface of the cortex.

Chapter 11

Md Abdullah Al Momin, University of Louisiana at Lafayette, USA

Implantable medical devices (IMDs) are miniaturized computer systems used to monitor and treat various medical conditions. Examples of IMDs include insulin pumps, artificial pacemakers, neuro-stimulators, and implantable cardiac defibrillators. These devices have adopted wireless communication to help facilitate the care they provide for patients by allowing easier transferal of data or remote control of machine operations. However, with such adoption has come exposure to various security risks and issues that must be addressed due to the close relation of patient health and IMD performance. With patient lives on the line, these security risks pose increasingly real problems. This chapter hopes to provide an overview of these security risks, their proposed solutions, and the limitations on IMD systems which make solving these issues nontrivial. Later, the chapter will analyze the security issues and the history of vulnerabilities in pacemakers to illustrate the theoretical topics by considering a specific device.

Preface

The Internet of Things, commonly abbreviated as IoT, refers to the connection of devices (other than typical fares such as computers and smartphones) to the Internet. The devices are usually interconnected sensors, actuators, and heterogeneous devices to collect data to offer advanced services. Like wireless sensor networks, IoT networks collect, store, and exchange a large amount of heterogeneous data. It has already shown promising outcomes in providing potentially critical services (e.g., safety applications, military, healthcare, manufacturing), but it raises many challenges related to the security and limited resources of the performed operations and provided services. Accordingly, research on the sensor/user data analysis and security of IoT is attractive to both industry and academia. Thus, this book's central theme is to report novel methodologies, technologies, techniques, and security solutions for IoT and Cyber-physical systems.

Writing a book in the area of security and privacy stemmed from my desire to improve the security of current technologies that contribute to making human lives efficient by reducing the time and complexity of the tasks performed. A lot of security issues are present in emerging technologies. The task of the researchers is to prevent misuse of these technologies by discovering novel approaches to exploit these technologies and to propose efficient preventative measures. A myriad of scientific articles is published each year in which the researchers present their approach to attack the technologies and the solutions. Compared to the published scientific articles, a book is a more organized version from which future researchers and students can learn about the different types of security flaws present in state-of-the-art technologies and shape their ideas on resolving the issues with novel approaches.

The book results from my years of experience working as an apprentice researcher when I was working as a Ph.D. student in Computer Science at the Temple University in Pennsylvania, USA, through becoming and working as an assistant professor and a researcher at the University of Louisiana at Lafayette. My main research interest lies in the area of security and privacy. Through my experience, I noticed that I often need to refer to different books as reference materials while imparting knowledge in a classroom setting and the novice researchers planning to tread on the exciting path of scientific research. The students can learn from the novel security risks and the solutions to those problems. In turn, they can become more responsible users of the latest technologies by becoming aware of the security and privacy risks associated with the emerging technologies. After acquiring knowledge about the security flaws and the solutions, they can become interested in security research. Through their research works, they can contribute to the development of a world with fewer security issues and improve the lives of the users as a whole.

In this book, the authors discussed the basics, as well as complex security flaws present in different technologies. Chapter 1 discusses about the challenges involved in designing efficient and intelligent Internet of Things Search Engine (IoTSE). Chapter 2 discusses the IoT from a legal perspective. In Chapter 3, the authors analyzed various cell phone biometric sensors and the security risks of those sensors. In this chapter, the authors discussed the fingerprint and the facial recognition process, the hardware, and the algorithms needed for these recognition systems. Later the authors discussed the types of attacks that can be performed to spoof these recognition systems and the countermeasures. In Chapter 4, the attacks on voice assistant systems are discussed. The authors of this chapter first provided the idea of different types of attacks based on hardware non-linearity, obfuscated, and adversarial attacks and discussed the solutions. In Chapter 5, a brief survey of automotive cyber-physical systems security has been provided. The authors of this chapter briefly discussed the cyber-physical systems and then discussed them in the context of automobiles. Then they discussed the security threats in different layers of automotive cyber-physical systems, such as threats in sensing and communication layers. Chapter 6 discuss the method to spoof handwritten signatures in electronic check using Conditional Generative Adversarial Network (CGAN). Chapter 7 reviewed handwritten signature spoofing with generative adversarial networks. In Chapter 8, a deep learning approach to protect voice-controlled devices from laser attacks is presented. Chapters 9 and 10 discuss the security of teleoperated surgical robots and attacks on brain-computer interfacing devices. These chapters will give a brief idea about the attacks that can be mounted on these technologies and the preventative measures to the attacks presented in the book. Chapter 11 discusses Implantable Medical Device (IMD) security. This chapter first presented the types of attacks that can be mounted on IMDs, and then presented pacemakers as an example for the case study.

In editing this book, I incorporated the ideas disseminated by different authors. I thank all the authors who helped me write the book, my family and colleagues for their continuous support through difficult times, and all of my students for assisting me with the research works. I look forward to making regular improvements to the book so that it becomes a primary source of refined knowledge of security and privacy. I spent a very long time calling for chapters and encouraging the authors to complete and revise their book chapters. Since the impact of book chapters is limited compared to the conference and journal papers, I have to push the authors to revise the chapters many times.

The readers should start from the content and choose the chapters more related to their work to read. The book chapters reviewed and covered many perspectives of the IoT and cyber-physical system related security topics.

The book will help the communities composed of educators, researchers, faculty members, industry practitioners, graduate students, etc. Besides, the same would be proved to be beneficial to the professionals working with smart devices, government policy-making tasks and planning, government enforcement agencies, legal and regulatory services, and with business enterprises to understand the practical aspects of next-generation IoT and Cyber-physical systems and future research directions. Further, it would help them secure the IoT systems in the various sectors where attackers' susceptible activities are detected. The general nature of the book will attract a large number of enthusiastic people who are actively related to IoT and Cyber-physical system security research and would like to move in their direction.

Introduction

This book aims to provide specialized knowledge about the vulnerabilities and methods to exploit the vulnerabilities of modern devices and technologies. Each chapter in the book discusses how these devices and technologies can be attacked and controlled and the defense mechanisms to prevent such attacks. To improve the robustness, these technologies are continually being studied to improve security. In addition, this book discusses recent works on making some of the most important technologies secure that involve interacting with humans.

The first chapter discusses the Internet of Things Search Engines (IoTSE) as a platform to support efficient data analytics. Internet of Things (IoT) has been emerging as the next big thing in the world. It is envisioned that billions of physical things or objects will be outfitted with different kinds of sensors and actuators and connected to the Internet via heterogeneous access networks enabled by technologies such as embedded sensing and actuating, radio frequency identification (RFID), wireless sensor networks, real-time and semantic web services, etc. IoT is actually cyber-physical systems or a network of networks. With the huge number of things/objects and sensors/actuators connected to the Internet, a massive and, in some cases, the real-time data flow will be automatically generated by connected things and sensors. It is essential to collect correct raw data in an efficient way, but more important is to analyze and mine the raw data to abstract more valuable information such as correlations among things and services to provide a web of things or Internet of services. This is where IoTSE comes into play. IoTSE is a platform to support efficient data analytics. There are a number of challenges in designing efficient and intelligent IoTSE. The first chapter focuses on the efficiency issue of IoTSE and designs the Named Data Networking (NDN)-based approach for IoTSE. At first, a simple simulation environment is designed to compare the IP-based network's performance against Named Data Networking (NDN). Then four scenarios tailored to study the approach's resilience are created to address network issues and scalability with the growing number of queries in IoTSE. These four scenarios are implemented, and extensive performance evaluation is carried out to determine the approach's efficacy concerning network resilience and scalability.

With the arrival of the information age, the concern about data security is gradually becoming more important. Even when digital technologies were not around, humans used to collect data manually to analyze it later and reach efficient decisions. In recent times, the method of collecting data has been replaced by digital media and smart devices. As a result, a lot of different ways are present by which data theft can happen. This is caused by the usage of different types of smart devices, which have many vulnerabilities since these devices are still being investigated to improve security. Chapter two discusses IoT from a legal perspective and the concern about personal data. IoT technology has penetrated almost all sectors of modern life, such as transport, smart grids, e-health, environmental monitoring, logistics, etc.

Moreover, IoT can collect pure personal data through a fitness tracker, wearable medical device, smart watch, smart clothing, wearable camera (Mardonova & Choi, 2018). Hence, it has become crucial to ensure the integrity of these systems. This chapter discusses the protection offered by data protection law to personal data and the applicability of this law to personal data in the IoT environment. The concentration of the chapter is on the protection of personal data from a legal viewpoint and what IoT stakeholders could do to meet the legal requirements. To achieve this objective, Section 2 of the chapter provides a brief discussion of data protection development and its relevance to the information age. In Section 3, data protection law will be surveyed and analyzed to know its relevance to the IoT industry. This section is the most important component because it points out the applicability or inapplicability of data protection law to personal data flow in the IoT environment and also discusses the so-called data protection principles that are at the heart of data protection law. Part 4 focuses on the importance of compliance with data protection law in the IoT sphere and the consequences of overlooking such matter from the legal perspective. Especial attention will be paid to such consequences on data subjects and data controllers. Section 5 suggests solutions and makes recommendations in light of data protection principles. Finally, Section 6 summarizes the main points discussed in the chapter and provides concluding remarks.

Smart devices have been prevalent in recent times. The most common devices are smartphones and personal computers. Smart devices are an integral part of our day-to-day life to facilitate the work process and maintain effective communication. These devices often employ different biometric sensors to secure personal information and prevent intruders from accessing personal data. Every individual has certain unique features. Often the features are a combination of elements from different sources such as iris, fingerprint, voice, face orientation, etc. Chapter three discusses two primary biometric recognition services, namely, fingerprint and facial recognition systems. This chapter briefly discusses these two biometric recognition systems and the hardware requirements to employ the recognition systems and the algorithms. Then the possible attack scenarios along with the countermeasures are discussed.

One of the most common smart devices that have become an integral part of our daily lives is voice assistant systems. Voice assistant systems made our lives easier by providing us the opportunity to control information flow by giving commands through our voice. Voice assistant systems work by first recognizing the user. If it fails to recognize the valid user, then it will not process commands. But it is possible to attack these smart devices and make them work even though the user providing the command is not a valid user. As a result, a malicious user can gain control of the voice assistant and assume himself as the valid user and can cause harm to the actual user of the device. To prevent malicious users from gaining control over the voice assistant system and causing damage to thc valid user, it is crucial to ensure the robustness of these systems. Chapter four first discusses voice assistant systems, automatic speech recognition, and audio processing mechanisms. Then the chapter presented three types of attacks on voice assistant systems: spoofing attacks, hardware non-linearity attacks, obfuscated command attacks, and adversarial command attacks. The chapter then discusses how to exploit these attacks to gain control on the voice assistant systems, and then defending mechanisms to prevent such attacks are presented.

In our daily life, we rely on automobiles to transport ourselves from one place to another efficiently. Automobiles have been around for quite a long time. In the early days, automobiles mainly were a medium to transport goods and humans, just after its inception. But with the development of digital technologies, automobile manufacturers have started to integrate smart devices and electronics into automobiles in order to make them more efficient and luxurious for travelers so that the travels can reduce travel fatigue and enjoy their journey at the same time by listening to music. Moreover, smart electronic devices are integrated into the vehicles to provide the user more control over the vehicle. These smart devices often enable the user to see crucial vehicular data such as wheel rotation, torque, vehicle speed, etc. The intelligent electronic devices that provide such critical vehicular data are also connected to the internet. Hence the name Cyber-Physical systems. With many modern vehicles being connected to the outside world, there are many vulnerabilities introduced. Modern cars contain many electronic control units and millions of lines of code, which, if compromised, could have fatal consequences. Interfaces to the outside world (e.g., in-vehicle infotainment) may be used as a vector to attack these critical components. The structure of this chapter is as follows. First, the definition of Cyber-Physical Systems will be discussed briefly. Then different components of automotive will be discussed and why they are considered CPSs. Finally, after understanding the different components of automotive CPSs, the security and threats of various components of modern vehicles will be discussed.

Modern economic systems cannot be imagined without banking systems. In earlier times, the bank process was performed using physical documents and paper checks. With the advent of digital technologies and smart devices, banking systems are digitalized so that banking and transactions can be performed electronically and instantly. Before the arrival of digital technologies, people used to send and withdraw money using paper checks. But due to the availability of modern technologies, people often deposit checks electronically. Deposit of electronic system uses two potential information written by the account holder on the check. The account holder needs to write down the amount of money and the unique signature that the banks will check when updating the system after depositing for verification (Pennacchi et al., 2006). Every individual has a different handwritten system that can be identified using the character pattern and the pressure point of any handwritten materials. By using this concept of difference in handwritten systems, banks like Chase bank introduced Chase QuickDeposit. In the prospect of forgery, an adversary can spoof the amount written in the check or spoof the signature using the deep learning approach and specifically using Generative Adversarial Networks (GANs). This chapter discusses the threat model to spoof an electronic check using GANs. The chapter also discusses the implementation and limitations of the approach.

When two devices need to pair with each other, the first thing the devices do is to recognize the other device. In order to do this, some unique characteristics of each device are considered so that the device can be identified correctly. Extracting the unique features is known as fingerprinting. In Chapter seven, fingerprint generation from unique spectral characteristics of LEDs to perform device pairing is presented. The chapter first claims the ubiquity of LEDs; thus, the authors proposed the conceptual model to perform device pairing. The chapter also presented captured images from different LEDs, the method to preprocess the images and extract special radiance patterns from the images. Then Convolutional Neural Network is used to classify the data to perform device pairing.

Due to their effectiveness and ease of use, smart voice assistants are ubiquitous. With the advent of voice assistant technology, devices such as Amazon Echo, Google Home, Apple HomePod, and Xiaomi AI became more prominent. The need to make these devices more secure and safe to use comes along with the emergence of these devices. Because voice assistants are widely used in smartphones and IoT devices, attackers can attack voice-controllable systems using various sources like laser light (Sugawara et al. 2020), long-range attacks (Roy et al. 2018), ultrasonic waves (Zhang et al. 2017), solid materials (Yan et al. 2020), electromagnetic interference signals (Kune et al. 2013, Tu et al. 2021), etc. The chapter discusses voice reply attack, operating system level attack, hardware-level attack, machine learning level attack, etc., and then describes the use of Mel Frequency Cepstrum (MFC) to detect train a deep neural network model to differentiate and detect a malicious signal to prevent the attack.

In recent years, teleoperated robots are making their way into the conventional surgical room to replace and reduce the number of human surgeons. These robots are complex electronic systems consisting of a wide variety of sensors and are connected to the Internet to perform surgery remotely. The sensors and the network can be exploited to mount various attacks on teleoperated robots. Stealth attacks, replay attacks, covert attacks, DoS attacks, eavesdropping attacks, etc., are notable among the network-based attacks. Chapter nine presents all those network-based attacks, endpoint-based attacks, and sensor-based attacks on teleoperated surgical robots. After presenting the attacks, this chapter also presents mitigation techniques for each type of attack.

Brain-Computer Interface (BCI) technology is brought into existence to assist in treating serious neurological conditions. But researcher has a long-term goal with BCI, which is to enhance human capabilities by enabling human-machine symbiosis with artificial intelligence (Newitz et al., 2017). BCI systems consist of a lot of electrodes. These electrodes are used to read brain signals. The BCI device includes real-time temperature, accelerometer, and magnetometer sensors. These electrical systems can be exploited to attack the BCI system. Chapter ten discusses the attack model by providing insights into the attacker and the victim. The chapter then presented intentional EMI attacks and possible BLE stack to perform attacks on BCI systems.

Implantable Medical Devices (IMDs) are miniaturized computer devices that are implanted inside the patients. Some examples of IMDs are insulin pumps, pacemakers, neuro-stimulator, etc. When designing these devices, the main focus is the longevity of the devices because these devices are implanted by invasive surgeries. Most of the devices are implanted for decades in mind. IMDs automatically read the body parameters of the patients. Based on the received data, IMDs make some decisions to ensure the healthy functioning of the patient body. Since these devices play a direct role in the patient's well-being, it is vital to ensure the safety and security of these devices because an apparently gentle breach in the security of these devices will cause a life or death issue for the patient. Chapter eleven discusses the security of IMDs in detail. The chapter first discusses what IMDs are and the limitations and restrictions of IMDs. Then the chapter presented the types of attacks that can be mounted on this type of device and discussed the proposed solutions. The chapter also provides insights into attack detection and reaction. Finally, the chapter offers a case study by considering pacemakers as one of the most common implantable medical devices. This chapter also explains how pacemakers work, the attack vectors on pacemakers, network attacks, and countermeasures in the case study.

Xiali Hei
University of Louisiana at Lafayette, USA

REFERENCES

Kune. (2013). Ghost Talk: Mitigating EMI Signal Injection Attacks against Analog Sensors. *Proceedings - IEEE Symposium on Security and Privacy.*

Mardonova, M., & Choi, Y. (2018). Review of Wearable Device Technology and Its Applications to the Mining Industry. *Energies, 11*(3), 1–14. doi:10.3390/en11030547

Newitz. (2017). Elon musk is setting up a company that will link brains and computers. *Ars Technica.* doi:10.1145/3433210.3453097

Pennacchi, G. (2006). Deposit insurance, bank regulation, and financial system risks. *Journal of Monetary Economics, 53*(1), 1–30. doi:10.1016/j.jmoneco.2005.10.007

Roy, N. (2018). "naudible Voice Commands : The Long-Range Attack and Defense. *Proceedings of the 15th USENIX Symposium on Networked.*

Sugawara, T. (2020). Light Commands: Laser-Based Audio Injection Attacks on Voice-Controllable Systems. *Proceedings of the 29th USENIX Security Symposium.*

Tu, Y., Tida, V. S., Pan, Z., & Hei, X. (2021). Transduction Shield: A Low-Complexity Method to Detect and Correct the Effects of EMI Injection Attacks on Sensors. *Proceedings of the 2021 ACM Asia Conference on Computer and Communications Security.*

Wang, C., Daneshmand, M., Dohler, M., Mao, X., Hu, R. Q., & Wang, H. (2013). Guest Editorial-Special issue on internet of things (IoT): Architecture, protocols and services. *IEEE Sensors Journal, 13*(10), 3505–3510. doi:10.1109/JSEN.2013.2274906

Yan, Q. (2020). *SurfingAttack: Interactive Hidden Attack on Voice Assistants Using Ultrasonic Guided Waves.* Academic Press.

Zhang, G. (2017). DolphinAttack: Inaudible Voice Commands. *Proceedings of the ACM Conference on Computer and Communications Security.*

Chapter 1

Towards Named Data Networking for Internet of Things Search Engines

Hengshuo Liang
https://orcid.org/0000-0002-2366-5780
Towson University, USA

Weixian Liao
https://orcid.org/0000-0003-1444-8925
Towson University, USA

Lauren Burgess
Towson University, USA

Chao Lu
Towson University, USA

Wei Yu
Towson University, USA

ABSTRACT

The advance of internet of things (IoT) techniques enables a variety of smart-world systems in energy, transportation, home, and city infrastructure, among others. To provide cost-effective data-oriented service, internet of things search engines (IoTSE) have received growing attention as a platform to support efficient data analytics. There are a number of challenges in designing efficient and intelligent IoTSE. In this chapter, the authors focus on the efficiency issue of IoTSE and design the named data networking (NDN)-based approach for IoTSE. To be specific, they first design a simple simulation environment to compare the IP-based network's performance against named data networking (NDN). They then create four scenarios tailored to study the approach's resilience to address network issues and scalability with the growing number of queries in IoTSE. They implement the four scenarios using ns-3 and carry out extensive performance evaluation to determine the efficacy of the approach concerning network resilience and scalability. They also discuss some remaining issues that need further research.

DOI: 10.4018/978-1-7998-7323-5.ch001

INTRODUCTION

The Internet of Things (IoT) is a major part of our daily lives without many of us realizing it. These devices have re-defined how we improve healthcare (Philip et al., 1988), produce better energy (Xu et al., 2016), optimize industry processes (Xu et al., 2018; Da Xu et al., 2014), and so much more. Utilizing IoT devices has become more relevant and it is predicted there will be 41.6 billion devices connected and deployed worldwide by the year 2025 (Li et al., 2018). Not only do these devices enhance the connectivity of physical things/objects and cyber systems, but it also provides the ability for analytics and predictions to be made due to the massive amounts of data produced, supported by big computing and networking infrastructure, as well as big modeling techniques driven by artificial intelligence (Yu et al., 2017; Hatcher et al., 2018).

Although the amounts of data that these smart IoT devices produce can help assist the monitoring, control, and intelligence of IoT systems in general, it is also massive; thus, raising the issues of data management and sharing issues (Liang et al., 2018; Mohammadi et al., 2018). On the one hand, data management is a concern as each type of IoT system has its own defined data structure, data rate, as well as user and performance requirements, making it hard to manage all the data under one general method. On the other hand, data sharing (Cao et al., 2016; Liang et al., 2018; Gao et al., 2018} becomes an issue due to the different standards and defined settings, making it incompatible for sharing data among the devices, systems, and organizations.

One viable solution to address these issues is to utilize IoT Search Engine (IoTSE) (Liang et al., 2019; Lunardi et al., 2015; Tran et al., 2019) to efficiently manage and share the data, providing a viable platform to enable efficient data analytics and service. Nonetheless, a number of challenges need to be addressed, including performance, intelligence, and security, etc. (Hatcher et al., 2021). In this study, we focus on performance-related issues. The intuition of IoTSE comes from a typical Internet browser; all of IoT data can be treated as Uniform Resource Locator (URL) links, which can be resolved and displayed for users according to their queries. With regard to performance challenges in IoTSE, selecting communication networking architecture to support diverse data transmission and sharing protocols is the focus of this study. The main problem that we tend to address is whether Named Data Networking (NDN) can be a viable solution to address the performance issues of IoTSE.

In this study, we make the following two key contributions.

- **NDN-based Approach for IoTSE:** We design an NDN-based approach for IoTSE, which deals with the performance issues of IoTSE. We first develop a simulation environment to compare IP-based network and NDN performance, and then demonstrate the benefit of adopting NDN-based approach for IoTSE. We then design four scenarios tailored to study the resilience of NDN-based approach for IoTSE (e.g., dealing with prefix hijacking, congestion, and link failure) and the scalability to handle the growing number of queries in IoTSE.

- **Extensive Evaluation:** We have implemented the four scenarios mentioned above using ns-3, a known network simulator (Riley et al., 2010), to demonstrate the efficacy of our NDN-based approach with respect to packet successful ratio and average packet delay. Our extensive evaluation results confirm that NDN can maintain a resilient network infrastructure when the network suffers from prefix hijacking, congestion, and link failure, and is highly scalable to handle a growing number of queries.

The remainder of this paper is organized as follows: In Section PRELIMINARY, we briefly review IoTSE and NDN. In Section PERFORMANCE COMPARISON OF NDN AND TCP/IP, we setup a baseline environment and compare TCP/IP and NDN's performance. In Section NDN-BASED SOLUTION FOR IOT SEARCH, we design the scenarios for assessing the efficacy of NDN-based approach for IoTSE. In Section PERFORMANCE EVALUATION, we present the performance evaluation results. We study the Literature review of state-of-the-art in Section RELATED WORKS. In Section DISCUSSION, we discuss some remaining issues for future research. Finally, we conclude the paper in Section FINAL REMARKS.

PRELIMINARIES

In the following, we provide some background about IoTSE and NDN.

IoT Search Engine (IoTSE)

Due to the massive number of IoT devices, IoTSE aims to providing data-oriented service for IoT systems, dealing with IoT systems' search and management issues (e.g., devices and data), and others. Similar to the web-based search engine, IoTSE can provide the following functionalities (Liang et al., 2019: (i) Data Collection: The web-crawler-based scheme is one common way to crawling IoT data for IoTSE while crawling data is from IoT devices instead of from web servers. Some examples of IoTSE systems includes Shodan (Shodan Search Engine, 2021), Censys (Home - Censys, 2021), and (Thingful - a search engine for the Internet of Things, 2021). (ii) Indexing and organizing data: After crawling data, IoTSE will store the collected data in its storage facility (remote or local) and catalog the data into different sub-systems for future queries similar to the web-based search engine.

As for its searching process, IoTSE adopts a similar approach as web searching engine does, such as receiving a query, searching data based on query request, and then returning the data back to users. Generally speaking, IoTSE can support several typical queries. One is about searching IoT devices, which provides information about those discovered and connected. Another type is about searching and gathering information from IoT data. Examples include weather conditions, transportation traffic status, water usage in buildings, and others.

IoTSE brings several opportunities for a new alternative to search information (liang et al., 2019). Examples of opportunities include enabling efficient IoT data sharing and building intelligence in IoT systems. As more IoT data is generated with the growing number of IoT devices, big data analytics on IoT data is important (Cai et al., 2016; Mohammadi et al., 2018). Data analytics can gain insightful knowledge about IoT systems and the environment, and further improve IoT systems' operations using the acquired knowledge. Nonetheless, carrying out big data analytics suffers from inconsistent data standard format from heterogeneous IoT devices, operation domains, and systems. IoTSE can address this issue by regularizing different standard formats of IoT data into a universal format for users, which can accelerate the progress of data sharing in the various IoT devices and systems. With IoTSE, more data can be collected from IoT devices and IoT systems, and then shared across different entities (users, organizations, etc.); machine learning can be synergized in IoT systems, leading to artificial intelligence enabled IoT systems (Yu et al., 2018). For example, machine learning can be used to improve IoTSE searching efficiency by reducing workloads via reasoning several of queries are looking for the same data, and others (Hatcher et al., 2021).

Inevitably, IoTSE poses several challenges as well. One issue is related to the naming service (Hatcher et al., 2021). Using the web-crawler-based mechanism, IoTSE needs to assign a URL name for each IoT device or designated data. Each URL will be associated with an IP address. With the growing number of IoT devices and massive amounts of IoT data, more IP addresses will be used. Thus, how to design a scalable naming service for IoT systems is a challenging issue. Another issue is designing a cost-effective network infrastructure that can provide efficient data-oriented service for IoTSE. It is worth mentioning that the IP network itself is based on destination-oriented routing, not data itself. Also, if packets are lost during transmission, only the end host can tell the issue after the time out. Then, the end-user can resend the request again. Also, IoTSE supports critical infrastructure systems such as smart grid, smart transportation, and others. Networking infrastructure shall provide data transmission with high efficiency, low packet latency, and high packet reception ratio.

Naming Data Networking

Generally speaking, NDN is a new networking paradigm evolving the Internet's host-based packet delivery model (Zhang et al., 2014). Driven by the data-oriented design paradigm, NDN has two types of packets called Interest and Data packets. For example, a consumer node puts the name of the desired data into an Interest packet, which is then transmitted through the network. Routers then use the name and forward toward the correct data producer. When the Interest packet reaches the node that has the desired data, the Data packet is sent back with both the name and the content with a signature signed by the producer's key to secure the data to the sender, as shown in Fig. 1 (Zhang et al., 2014).

Figure 1. NDN data types
(Zhang et al., 2014)

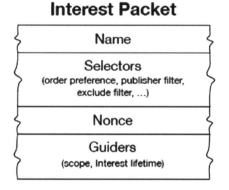
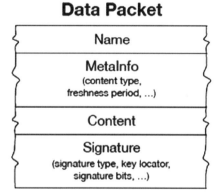

Based on its design, NDN has different forwarding modules than IP-based networks (Yi et al., 2013). The key components include: (i) Content Store – a temporary cache of Data packets that the router receives. (ii) Pending Interest Table (PIT) - records outgoing, incoming data interfaces, and Interest packets not completed. (iii) Forwarding Information Base (FIB) – has a name-prefix-based routing protocol and can have multiple output interfaces for each prefix. (iv) Forward Strategy – when and where to transfer the packets.

Fig. 2 (Zhang et al., 2014) shows the forwarding process within NDN. When an Interest packet arrives at the NDN node, it first checks whether Content Store has a matching entry. If an entry exists in the Content Store, the Data packet takes the reverse path to the source. If no entry is found, the NDN node uses the PIT to find a matching entry, and then forwards data to the listed downstream interfaces. Further,

5

the PIT entry is removed and the data is cached in the Content Store. The Data packet takes the reverse path of the Interest. One Interest Packet results in one Data Packet on each link. If there is no matching PIT entry, the NDN node will forward the Interest packet to the data producers using the information in the FIB and the forwarding rule. If more than one Interest packet from various downstream nodes arrives with the same name, only one is forwarded upstream to the data producers, for the sake of efficiency (Yi et al., 2013).

Figure 2. NDN forwarding plane
(Zhang et al., 2014)

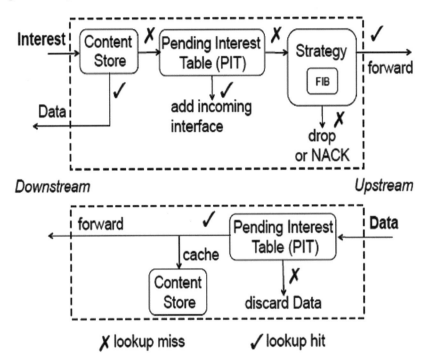

Although the NDN design provides numerous benefits, there are still a few issues that need to be considered. For example, even though it deals with IP-based attacks, such as distributed denial of service (DDoS) attacks, it can still be targeted by interest packet flooding (Compagno et al., 2013). Another issue is with large-scale deployments; NDN lacks a control plane in forwarding when high concurrency data are coming. Finally, NDN exits as an overlay of IP, which leads to the efficiency concern of data forwarding, compared to IP-based packet routing/forwarding.

PERFORMANCE COMPARISON OF NDN AND TCP/IP

After reviewing IoTSE and NDN, we now compare TCP/IP and NDN and introduce a baseline experimental scenario to compare their performance.

Performance Comparison of NDN and TCP/IP

To better understand NDN and TCP/IP, we first need to determine what makes them similar and what makes them different. Similarities include communication via the same hourglass shape structure, and both perform data-gram delivery. For the differences, NDN no longer carries source and destination IP addresses but named, secured data chunks: NDN network layer has no address, but an app-defined namespace and NDN consumer fetches data hop by hop, not by having senders send packets to their destinations. Further, the app-defined namespace in NDN simplifies the system: infinite of namespace, not like IP4/IPV6 as there are address limitations, NAT and DNS are not required, and no more IP address management (no local or global network concept).

We set up a simulation environment to conduct a simple experiment to better understand network performance between NDN and TCP/IP. We consider a basic client-server network with two paths, as shown in Fig. 3. From the figure, we let the lower link be the shortest path but is under DDoS attack; thus, only a few packets can be forwarded from attacked node to server node.

Figure 3. Baseline experimental topology

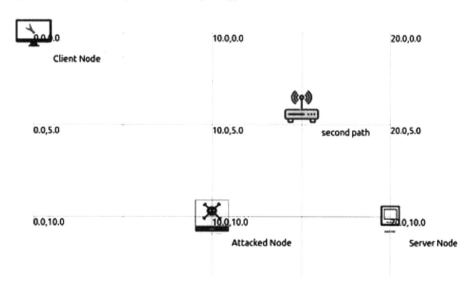

To complete this experiment, the following settings are used: (i) ns-3 as the simulation environment, (ii) Wired connection (10MB Bandwidth, 20ms delay), (iii) Total of 1200 TCP packets of consistent packet sizes of 1024B, and total of 1200 NDN interest-data packets of consistent packet sizes of 1024B, (iv) Simulation time of 20s, and (v) Open Shortest Path First (OSPF) routing protocol.

Based on the setting, we conduct experiment with comparing how TCP/IP and NDN respond to the network configuration. As shown in Fig. 4, we have the following observations. With TCP/IP, packets are sent to the attack node, and most of the packets are dropped due to DDoS attack. This is as expected; due to OSPF, most of the data will be dropped by the attacked node. In contrast, with NDN, the first path that is degraded after attempting to send a few packets can be identified so that packets can be re-routed to the second path. In the end, more packets are received using NDN.

Figure 4. Baseline experimental results

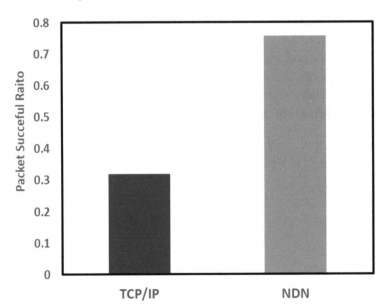

This ultimately shows that NDN can learn and adopt the current routing status while also doing multi-path routing. Whereas, TCP/IP does not perform well without any additional mechanism. The question now is whether NDN can still understand a dynamic network routing status and maintain a robust performance when some network issues occur.

NDN-BASED SOLUTION FOR IoT SEARCH

After introducing the initial performance assessment of NDN and TCP/IP, we first provide an overview of the NDN-based IoTSE architecture and then introduce several evaluation scenarios.

Architecture

Based on what we discussed about IoTSE issues in Section PRELIMINARIES and the benefits of NDN in Section PRELIMINARIES, we present an architecture of NDN-based IoTSE. IoTSE has three major components: Producers, IoTSE, and Users, as shown in Fig. 5. In this architecture, all the nodes are deployed with the NDN protocol; allowing the benefits of utilizing near cached forwarding and content-based design. Deployments can be publisher-subscriber to producer-user, depending on the user's behavior.

Figure 5. NDN based IoT search engine architecture

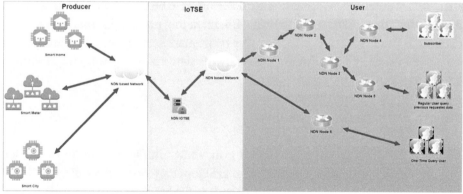

We consider several different types of users in the system: (i) A subscriber is a user who gets updated data on a regular basis. For instance, the producer is the node that produces the required data, and once that data is acquired, it will be sent to the search engine at regular intervals. The search engine will then store the data in its database and forward it to the subscribers. (ii) Regular users have to query IoTSE for previously requested data. For example, the second group user in Fig. 5tends to query data that the subscriber requested before. If the content in node 3 does not drop out due to the time-out, Node 3 will forward data to the user via Node 6. Otherwise, IoTSE will respond to the request and send data. (iii) In the case of the

9

one-time query users, users want to collect a different combination of data that has been requested before. In this case, the user would send an Interest packet to IoTSE, which is then forwarded to the producer. The producer with the required data will respond with a Data packet via following the same path back.

IoT Search Scenarios

With the basic idea of IoTSE and its structure, we now discuss how we design scenarios. To meet the requirements of IoTSE, we need to design the system from two aspects: (i) resilience of network status: The IoTSE should be adapted to the network status to self-maintain performance. There are three common network issues that IoTSE needs to handle, including prefix hijacking, congestion, and link failure. (ii) transmission performance in large scale: The IoTSE should also transmit as much data as possible in the face of a large number of data requests. To this end, we use data collection of a smart grid, as an example to validate whether the IoTSE can handle the massive number of queries and still keep an acceptable transmission performance.

In the following, we design four scenarios to evaluate the efficacy of NDN-based IoT search. Three of these scenarios are determined to be the most common network related issues that IoTSE needs to deal with, including prefix hijacking, congestion, and link failure. The last scenario is our benchmark testing scenario designed to investigate the system's scalability, i.e., network performance given a large number of queries in a short time.

Scenario 1: Prefix Hijacking

For scenario 1 design, we build a 3 x 3 grid, shown in Fig. 6 in order to provide various options for route forwarding. The grid topology offers the ability to follow different routes when the node is hijacked and unable to continue to forward the data.

For this scenario, Table 1 shows the settings that are used. For a quick reference though, the following settings are used, including the bandwidth of 1Mbps, link delay of 10ms, node 0 as data consumer, and node 8 as data producer. Three nodes are selected randomly throughout the experiment and become our hijacked nodes and drop all incoming packets. Ultimately, our goal is to determine whether the NDN network can continue forwarding the data.

Figure 6. Prefix hijacking topology

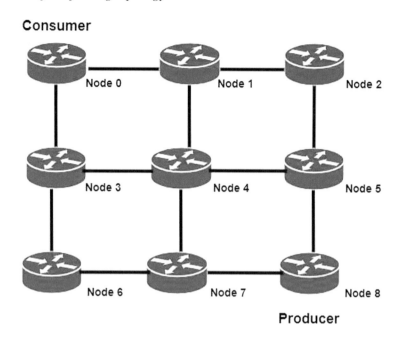

Table 1. Prefix hijacking link table

SrcNode	DstNode	Bandwidth	Metric	Delay	Queue
Node0	Node1	1Mbps	1	10ms	10
Node1	Node3	1Mbps	1	10ms	10
Node1	Node2	1Mbps	1	10ms	10
Node2	Node4	1Mbps	1	10ms	10
Node3	Node5	1Mbps	1	10ms	10
Node3	Node4	1Mbps	1	10ms	10
Node4	Node6	1Mbps	1	10ms	10
Node4	Node5	1Mbps	1	10ms	10
Node5	Node7	1Mbps	1	10ms	10
Node6	Node8	1Mbps	1	10ms	10
Node7	Node8	1Mbps	1	10ms	10

Scenario 2: Congestion

In order to simulate that the network is congested, scenario 2 is designed to use a bottleneck topology, as shown in Fig.7. There are only two paths between Routers 1, 2, and 12, shown as R1, R2 and R12 in the topology.

Figure 7. Congestion topology

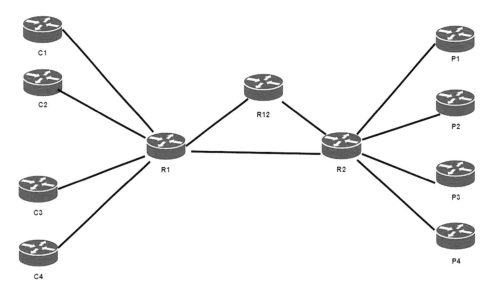

In order to create network congestion, the path from R1 to R2 is set with lower bandwidth but with a higher delay. The path that goes to all three routers R1 to R12 to R2 has lower latency and higher bandwidth. The experimental settings are shown in Table 2 for this experiment. In this table, C stands for consumer nodes and P stands for the producer nodes. The purpose of this scenario is to determine whether the NDN network can handle network congestion.

Table 2. Congestion link table

SrcNode	DstNode	Bandwidth	Metric	Delay	Queue
c1	r1	10Mbps	1	50ms	200
c2	r1	10Mbps	1	10ms	200
c3	r1	10Mbps	1	100ms	200
c4	r1	10Mbps	1	1ms	20
r1	r2	1Mbps	1176	20ms	20
r1	r12	1Mbps	587	1ms	20
r12	r2	1Mbps	846	1ms	20
r2	p1	10Mbps	260	1ms	200
r2	p2	10Mbps	700	1ms	200
r2	p3	10Mbps	1	1ms	200
r2	p4	10Mbps	1	1ms	200

Scenario 3: Link Failure

Going back to the grid topology designed for scenario 1, as shown in Fig. 6, scenario 3 is designed to select 3 links out of 12 to fail randomly. These failures are set anywhere from 0s to 5s. After time elapses, these links are brought back up, and 3 other links are randomly selected to go down; this time, between 15s to 20s. Overall, there are 10s link failures with 6 disconnected links in the 20s run-time of testing. This scenario also tests under two different link failure probability of 5% and 10%, giving us the opportunity to see how the network can deal with the dynamic changes. The purpose of this scenario is to determine NDN networks reaction to link failures.

Scenario 4: Data Collection of Smart Grid in Emergency Situation

Scenario 4 also follows the same grid network topology as scenario 1. In this scenario, 3 nodes are configured to be the smart meters, which transmit packets to the receiver nodes. To test the performance of this scenario, various bandwidth and query rates are configured. The purpose of this scenario is to determine whether NDN can handle massive queries with varying network resources (e.g., bandwidths).

Note that these scenario-based experiments that are designed and tested would be considered a feasibility study. The feasibility study provides greater insight into the various configurations and potential problems in the network environment. In the end, by completing this feasibility study, we can determine whether this is a path worth going down further and expanding upon.

PERFORMANCE EVALUATION

In this section, we show the performance evaluation results to validate the efficacy of our approach.

Methodology

We use ns-3 as the simulation platform to carry out our experiments as it is a known open-source network simulator. We implemented the four scenarios and tested the network performance of an NDN-based IoTSE by using a model called NDNsim (Afanasyev et al., 2012), which was developed to simulate the NDN protocol.

While experimenting with the scenarios above, we need a way to determine and evaluate the efficacy of utilizing NDN with IoTSE. For the first three scenarios, the settings are shown in

Table 1 and Table 2, which provide in the description of the scenarios. There are also 6 different queries used in these scenarios shown in Table 3.

Table 3. Query rate table

Queries Types	Payload (Byte)	Query Rate (/s)
1st	1024	10
2nd	512	15
3rd	256	20
4th	128	25
5th	64	30
6th	200	50

In the evaluation, we define the following queries: (i) Baseline Query Set: One query running; uses 1st setting only in the table. (ii) Lite Query Set: Three queries running; uses 1st, 2nd, and 3rd settings in the table. (iii) Heavy Query Set: Five queries running; uses 1-5 settings in the table. (iv) Load Query Set: Increases network traffic by loading two sets of the 6th setting as well as running all other query settings.

In order to complete the last scenario, data collection in an emergency to support critical infrastructure systems, there are four different bandwidth settings: 5Mbps, 10Mbps, 15Mbps, and 20Mbps. The phasor measurement unit (PMU) is able to generate about 5,000-15,000 samples per second. In order to simulate an emergency, a reporting rate of 7000 samples per second is set. For instance, one PMU sample packet is set to be 38bytes, so that the total sampling data rate of the emergency for this scenario ends ups being: 7000 (sample)*38bytes=2.128Mbps. Again, the purpose for this scenario determines how NDN handles large queries and varying bandwidths in emergencies.

To evaluate the performance of four defined scenarios, we consider the following two metrics: (i) packet successful ratio, and (ii) average packet delay. Packet successful ratio is determined by calculating the number of packets received compared to the total number of packets sent. The average packet delay is the average transmission time the packets take to transmit from the sender to the receiver.

Results

We now analyze and demonstrate understanding of the network performance of various scenarios using NDN protocol in IoTSE with respect to packet success ratio and average packet delay. These results will discuss the key performance indicators of packet success ratio and the average packet delay.

Scenario 1: Prefix Hijacking

For the first scenario, Table 4 shows the experimental results. As shown in the figure, we can see that a large percent of the data is received successfully at the different query rates, shown in the reception ratio column. Recall that the reception ratio means the ratio of successfully received packets from a tagged node among the receivers. Nonetheless, once the settings for Load 4 begins, the network starts to reach its capacity as the number of packets sent increases. Surprisingly, even though Load 5 has a less successful ratio, it still delivers more packets than Load 4. From this result, NDN tries to optimize the max number of delivered packets, although the bandwidth limitation per link is reached.

Table 4. Packet successful ratio for prefix hijacking

	Received Packet	Requested Packet	Reception Successful ratio
Baseline	188	189	99.47%
Lite	848	853	99.41%
Heavy	1887	1897	99.47%
Load 1	3775	3795	99.47%
Load 2	5663	5693	99.47%
Load 3	7551	7591	99.47%
Load 4	8881	8993	98.75%
Load 5	8928	10163	87.84%

In addition to the table, Fig. 8 shows the average packet delay during the experiments for the scenario tested. Here, we can see that after the Heavy Query Set load, the delay is increasing. This indicates that the network reaches its limits during the third test (Heavy Set). By the seventh test (Load 4), the same ratio is seen even with the large delays.

Figure 8. Average packet delay for prefix hijacking

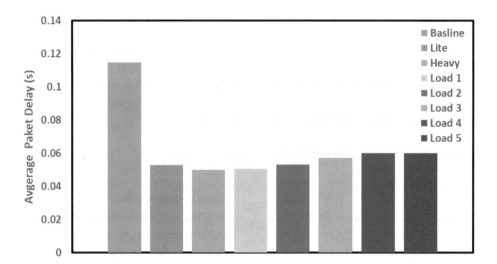

To summarize, our experimental results in scenario 1 show that NDN is a robust one. From these results, it appears that NDN tries to continue to forward data by re-routing to a different path to improve performance even when prefix hijacking is launched.

Scenario 2: Congestion

Throughout the congestion scenario, Fig. 9 shows the ratio of data received successfully based on the different query rates. As shown in the figure, we can see that when the density and quantity of queries increased, the ratio significantly increased as well.

Figure 9. Packet successful ratio for congestion

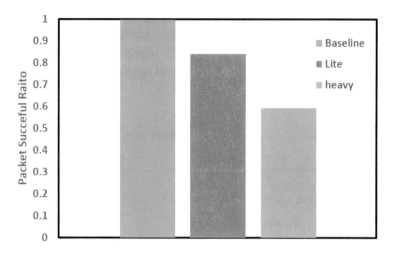

Via the experiments on this scenario, we collect results to measure the average packet latency shown in Fig. 10. From the figure, we can see even as the network traffic increases, and the network delay is also increased. This shows that NDN does not reach out its limit.

Figure 10. Average packet delay for congestion

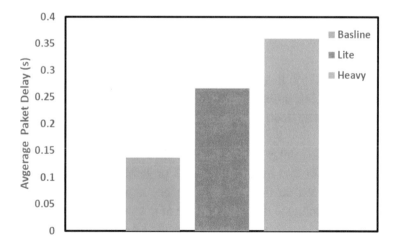

Scenario 3: Link Failure

Recall that the third scenario is with link failure. During this experiment, links are taken down and brought back up to determine how NDN would handle the route forwarding. Fig. 11 shows the packet successful ratio based on the different query rate at a 5% link failure probability.

Figure 11. Packet successful ratio for link failure with 5% probability

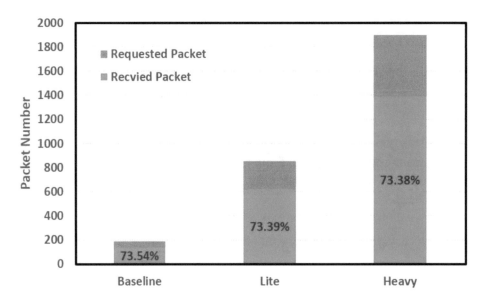

In addition to the 5% link failure probability, Fig. 12 shows the results of the system with a 10% link failure probability. From both figures, we can see that as query frequency and payload size increase, it still maintains the same ratio of data successful receipt.

The average packet delay during this scenario is shown in Fig. 13 for the 5% probability link failure and in Fig. 14 for 10% probability link failure. When more network traffic is loaded into the network, NDN begins to reach limitations to transmit data. These figures indicate that with the rise of network traffic, the network delay is also decreased and optimized. Due to changes in available routes, a new path is selected to optimize network delay. This scenario again shows that NDN is a resilient system and continuously tries to optimize network performance.

Figure 12. Packet successful ratio for link failure with 10% probability

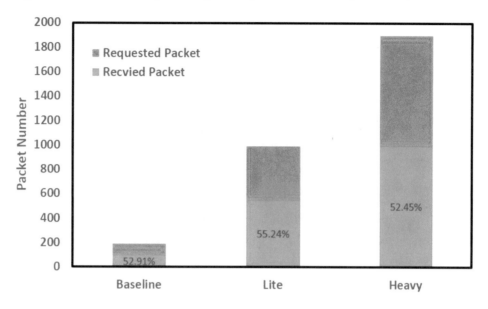

Figure 13. Average packet delay for link failure with 5% probability

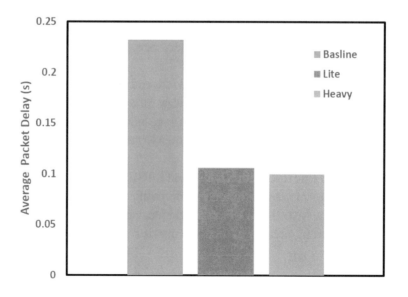

Figure 14. Average packet delay for link failure with 10% probability

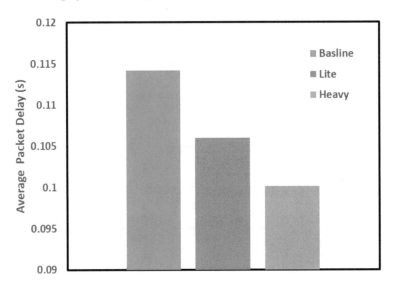

Scenario 4: Data Collection of Smart Grid in Emergency Situation

In emergencies, one can expect that the amount of network traffic can easily overwhelm the systems. The packet successful ratio with the varying bandwidth and query rates is shown in Fig. 15. From the figure, we can observe that when the bandwidth is at a fixed rate, the performance decreases while the queries are increasing. Nonetheless, when we fix the query rate, the network performance is improved when a larger bandwidth is given.

The average delay, with the varying bandwidth and query rates, is shown in Fig. 16. Similarly, like the successful packet delivery ratio, this figure also shows that when we fix the network bandwidth, the average network delay increases when the query rate grows. Then, when we fix the query rate, the average network delay decreases given a larger network bandwidth.

Overall, these varying tests with NDN-based IoTSE together show that the NDN is resilient and is capable of continuously improving network performance when facing network issues. Also, the NDN can provide scalable networking infrastructure to support the increasing number of received queries.

Figure 15. Packet successful ratio for smart grid in emergency situation

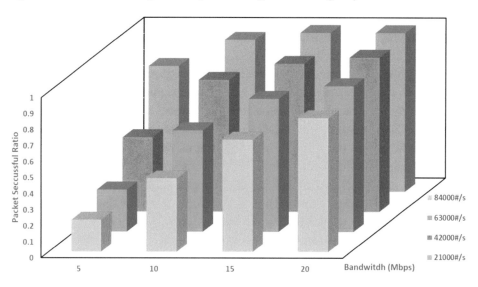

Figure 16. Average packet delay for smart grid in emergency situation

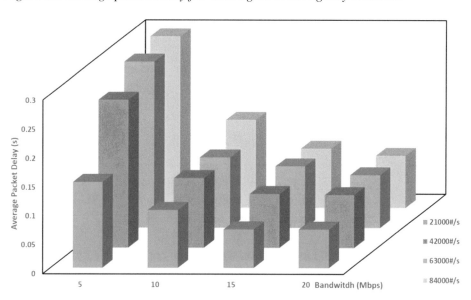

RELATED WORKS

In the following, we review research efforts that are most relevant to our study in this paper.

Existing research efforts on NDN have been explored to enhance supported features and services, improve performance and security, and support more applications. For example, Afanasyev et al. proposed a routing protocol to support Domain Name System (DNS) functionality for NDN so that NDN transmission efficiency can be improved (Afanasyev et al. 2012). Mastorakis et al. developed a peer-to-peer file-sharing system by utilizing the benefit of NDN's nearest location forward strategy (Mastorakis et al. 2017). Likewise, Li et al. proposed a secure sign-on protocol for NDN-based smart home devices (Li et al. 2019). When a new device is connected to the smart home, it will be verified by the designed sign-on protocol within the NDN network instead of outside network server verification. By doing this, the smart home can avoid unauthorized connection.

There are some existing efforts on leveraging NDN to support IoT systems. For example, Mick et al. proposed a secured routing protocol for NDN-IoT devices in smart cities with lightweight authentication (Mick et al. 2017). Likewise, Baccelli et al. built and tested a real NDN-based IoTs network, and confirmed that the NDN-based network could achieve low energy consummation like 6LoWPAN (Baccelli et al. 2014).

There are some research efforts on IoTSE. For example, Hatcher et al. applied Long Short-Term Memory (LSTM) machine learning scheme in IoTSE to predict incoming query volume, leading to query efficiency (Hatcher et al. 2021). Cheng et al. designed an IoTSE platform based on Constrained Application Protocol (COAP) and conducted experiments on query optimization algorithms (Cheng et al. 2020).

DISCUSSION

We now discuss some potential future research directions for NND-based IoTSE concerning performance, intelligence, and security.

- **Performance Issue:** One direction would be to continue this line of research and determine whether NDN can further enhance network performance for IoTSE via conducting more investigation on other smart-world systems such as smart cities, smart manufacturing, etc. New algorithms and protocols need to be developed to deal with the deployment of large complex IoTSE systems to support smart-world systems (smart cities, etc). On the one hand, we shall design IoT query and data aggregation techniques to reduce the overhead to the network. On the other hand, we shall find ways to embrace the limitations seen in some evaluations to determine whether there is a way to improve forwarding strategies to support real-world applications at a large scale. For example, to support massive number of complex queries and data delivery, prioritizing limited resources on NDN with the consideration of IoT applications' performance requirements is an interesting issue.

- **Intelligence Issue:** To embed intelligence in NDN-based IoTSE, we shall investigate how to integrate machine learning techniques into the system such as managing queries, data, and network resources. We can leverage machine learning algorithms to constantly analyze the data provided to determine and learn appropriate actions while handling queries and data. For example, we can leverage recurrent neural networks (RNN) to predict the types and volume of queries and data so that NDN-based IoTSE can be schedule resources in an efficient manner. We shall also leverage machine learning to improve automation, which allows for IoT systems to self-understand issues and correct them with little human interaction.

- **Security Issue:** As NDN-based IoTSE is critical infrastructure, it can be compromised by cyber-attacks. The adversary can launch a variety of attacks against availability (e.g., flooding Interest packets), confidentiality (e.g., stealing and forging signature in Data packet), and integrity (e.g., manipulating the packet name in Interest). The adversary could compromise key components (gateway, nodes, and sensors, etc.). To make NDN-based IoTSE system secure and reliable, we shall first investigate the security risks of different attacks, understand their impact on the system, and then develop countermeasures (e.g., protection, detection, and reaction) to deal with such attacks.

FINAL REMARKS

In this paper, we addressed the performance issue of Internet of Things Search Engines (IoTSE) and proposed the NDN-based approach for IoTSE. To validate the feasibility of our approach, we first designed a simple simulation environment to compare the performance of NDN and TCP/IP. We then proposed four scenarios and settings developed in ns-3 to demonstrate the feasibility of NDN improving network performance. Our experimental results confirmed that NDN was not only able to adapt in a degraded network in these scenarios, but was also able to be scalable to handle a large number of queries. Further, we discuss future directions that researchers could pursue to improve upon NDN-based IoTSE.

ACKNOWLEDGMENT

This material is based upon work supported by the Air Force Office of Scientific Research under award number FA9550-20-1-0418. Any opinions, findings, and conclusions or recommendations expressed in this material are those of the author(s) and do not necessarily reflect the views of the United States Air Force.

REFERENCES

Afanasyev, A., Moiseenko, I., & Zhang, L. (2012). ndnSIM: NDN simulator for NS-3. University of California, Los Angeles, Tech. Rep, 4, 1-7.

Baccelli, E., Mehlis, C., Hahm, O., Schmidt, T. C., & Wählisch, M. (2014, September). Information centric networking in the IoT: Experiments with NDN in the wild. In *Proceedings of the 1st ACM Conference on Information-Centric Networking* (pp. 77-86). ACM.

Cai, H., Xu, B., Jiang, L., & Vasilakos, A. V. (2016). IoT-based big data storage systems in cloud computing: Perspectives and challenges. *IEEE Internet of Things Journal*, 4(1), 75–87.

Cao, Q. H., Khan, I., Farahbakhsh, R., Madhusudan, G., Lee, G. M., & Crespi, N. (2016, May). A trust model for data sharing in smart cities. In *2016 IEEE International Conference on Communications (ICC)* (pp. 1-7). IEEE.

Censys. (2021). *Home*. Available at: https://censys.io/

Compagno, A., Conti, M., Gasti, P., & Tsudik, G. (2013, October). Poseidon: Mitigating interest flooding DDoS attacks in named data networking. In *38th annual IEEE conference on local computer networks* (pp. 630-638). IEEE.

Da Xu, L., He, W., & Li, S. (2014). Internet of things in industries: A survey. *IEEE Transactions on Industrial Informatics*, 10(4), 2233–2243. doi:10.1109/TII.2014.2300753

Gao, W., Yu, W., Liang, F., Hatcher, W. G., & Lu, C. (2018). Privacy-preserving auction for big data trading using homomorphic encryption. *IEEE Transactions on Network Science and Engineering*, 7(2), 776–791.

Hatcher, W. G., Qian, C., Gao, W., Liang, F., Hua, K., & Yu, W. (2021). Towards Efficient and Intelligent Internet of Things Search Engine. *IEEE Access: Practical Innovations, Open Solutions*, 9, 15778–15795.

Hatcher, W. G., & Yu, W. (2018). A survey of deep learning: Platforms, applications and emerging research trends. *IEEE Access: Practical Innovations, Open Solutions*, *6*, 24411–24432. doi:10.1109/ACCESS.2018.2830661

Li, S., Da Xu, L., & Zhao, S. (2018). 5G Internet of Things: A survey. *Journal of Industrial Information Integration*, *10*, 1–9. doi:10.1016/j.jii.2018.01.005

Li, Y., Zhang, Z., Wang, X., Lu, E., Zhang, D., & Zhang, L. (2019). A secure sign-on protocol for smart homes over named data networking. *IEEE Communications Magazine*, *57*(7), 62–68.

Liang, F., Qian, C., Hatcher, W. G., & Yu, W. (2019). Search engine for the internet of things: Lessons from web search, vision, and opportunities. *IEEE Access: Practical Innovations, Open Solutions*, *7*, 104673–104691.

Liang, F., Yu, W., An, D., Yang, Q., Fu, X., & Zhao, W. (2018). A survey on big data market: Pricing, trading and protection. *IEEE Access: Practical Innovations, Open Solutions*, *6*, 15132–15154. doi:10.1109/ACCESS.2018.2806881

Liang, F., Yu, W., An, D., Yang, Q., Fu, X., & Zhao, W. (2018). A survey on big data market: Pricing, trading and protection. *IEEE Access: Practical Innovations, Open Solutions*, *6*, 15132–15154.

Lunardi, W. T., de Matos, E., Tiburski, R., Amaral, L. A., Marczak, S., & Hessel, F. (2015, September). Context-based search engine for industrial IoT: Discovery, search, selection, and usage of devices. In *2015 IEEE 20th Conference on Emerging Technologies & Factory Automation (ETFA)* (pp. 1-8). IEEE.

Mastorakis, S., Afanasyev, A., Yu, Y., & Zhang, L. (2017, July). ntorrent: Peer-to-peer file sharing in named data networking. In *2017 26th International Conference on Computer Communication and Networks (ICCCN)* (pp. 1-10). IEEE.

Mick, T., Tourani, R., & Misra, S. (2017). LASeR: Lightweight authentication and secured routing for NDN IoT in smart cities. *IEEE Internet of Things Journal*, *5*(2), 755–764.

Mohammadi, M., Al-Fuqaha, A., Sorour, S., & Guizani, M. (2018). Deep learning for IoT big data and streaming analytics: A survey. *IEEE Communications Surveys and Tutorials*, *20*(4), 2923–2960. doi:10.1109/COMST.2018.2844341

Philip, N. Y., Rodrigues, J. J., Wang, H., Fong, S. J., & Chen, J. (2021). Internet of Things for in-home health monitoring systems: Current advances, challenges and future directions. *IEEE Journal on Selected Areas in Communications*, *39*(2), 300–310. doi:10.1109/JSAC.2020.3042421

Qian, C., Gao, W., Hatcher, W. G., Liao, W., Lu, C., & Yu, W. (2020, August). Search Engine for Heterogeneous Internet of Things Systems and Optimization. In *2020 IEEE Intl Conf on Dependable, Autonomic and Secure Computing, Intl Conf on Pervasive Intelligence and Computing, Intl Conf on Cloud and Big Data Computing, Intl Conf on Cyber Science and Technology Congress (DASC/PiCom/ CBDCom/CyberSciTech)* (pp. 475-482). IEEE.

Riley, G. F., & Henderson, T. R. (2010). The ns-3 network simulator. In *Modeling and tools for network simulation* (pp. 15–34). Springer.

Shodan.io. (2021). *Shodan Search Engine*. Available at: https://www.shodan.io

Thingful. (2021). *Thingful - a search engine for the Internet of Things*. Available at: http://www.thingful.net/

Tran, N. K., Sheng, Q. Z., Babar, M. A., Yao, L., Zhang, W. E., & Dustdar, S. (2019). Internet of Things search engine. *Communications of the ACM*, *62*(7), 66–73.

Xu, G., Yu, W., Griffith, D., Golmie, N., & Moulema, P. (2016). Toward integrating distributed energy resources and storage devices in smart grid. *IEEE Internet of Things Journal*, *4*(1), 192–204. doi:10.1109/JIOT.2016.2640563 PMID:29354654

Xu, H., Yu, W., Griffith, D., & Golmie, N. (2018). A survey on industrial Internet of Things: A cyber-physical systems perspective. *IEEE Access: Practical Innovations, Open Solutions*, *6*, 78238–78259. doi:10.1109/ACCESS.2018.2884906

Yi, C., Afanasyev, A., Moiseenko, I., Wang, L., Zhang, B., & Zhang, L. (2013). A case for stateful forwarding plane. *Computer Communications*, *36*(7), 779–791.

Yu, W., Liang, F., He, X., Hatcher, W. G., Lu, C., Lin, J., & Yang, X. (2017). A survey on the edge computing for the Internet of Things. *IEEE Access: Practical Innovations, Open Solutions*, *6*, 6900–6919. doi:10.1109/ACCESS.2017.2778504

Yu, W., Zhao, W., Schmeink, A., Song, H., & Dartmann, G. (2021). Guest Editorial: Special Issue on AI-Enabled Internet of Dependable and Controllable Things. *IEEE Internet of Things Journal*, *8*(5), 3053–3056.

Zhang, L., Afanasyev, A., Burke, J., Jacobson, V., Claffy, K. C., Crowley, P., ... Zhang, B. (2014). Named data networking. *Computer Communication Review*, *44*(3), 66–73.

Chapter 2
The Internet of Things From a Legal Perspective:
The Concern About Personal Data

Sidi Mohamed Sidi Ahmed
Independent Researcher, Mauritania

ABSTRACT

The internet of things (IoT) is one of successive technological waves that could have great impact on different aspects of modern life. It is being used in transport, smart grids, healthcare, environmental monitoring, logistics, as well as for processing pure personal data through a fitness tracker, wearable medical device, smartwatch, smart clothing, wearable camera, and so forth. From a legal viewpoint, processing personal data has to be done in accordance with rules of data protection law. This law aims to protect data from collection to retention. It usually applies to the processing of personal data that identifies or can identify a specific natural person. Strict adherence to this law is necessary for protecting personal data from being misused and also for promoting the IoT industry. This chapter discusses the applicability of the data protection law to IoT and the consequences of non-compliance with this law. It also provides recommendations on how to effectively comply with the data protection law in the IoT environment.

INTRODUCTION

Collecting information about surrounding environments is natural part of life of every living human or even animal as such information enables that human and animal to properly interact with the environments and their inhabitants. Accordingly,

DOI: 10.4018/978-1-7998-7323-5.ch002

collecting information about people is an old habit or practice that is extended in the computer era (Rowland et al., 2012), where data or information is of the essence. Without doubt, the Internet of Things (IoT) is one of the waves of technology that expand collection of data through interconnecting countless objects and enabling them to process information about things that they are attached to and about their surrounding environments. This particular technology has penetrated in almost all sectors of modern life such as transport, smart grids, e-health, environmental monitoring, logistics (River Publishers Series in Communication, 2014). Not only that, IoT devices and applications become part of everyday lives of ordinary people. Moreover, IoT is capable of collecting pure personal data through a fitness tracker, wearable medical device, smartwatch, smart clothing, wearable camera (Mardonova & Choi, 2018) and so on. In this regard, Gartner (2017) proclaimed that consumer applications represented 63% of IoT applications (5.2 billion units) used in 2017. This means that the bulk of IoT data is likely to be data related to human beings. Protecting personal data in the IoT environment is a major worry for many data protection stakeholders because the nature of IoT as ever-connected objects is not in line with data protection principles which, inter alia, seek to minimise the process of personal data and process it for specific known purposes.

The existence of countless data flowing and residing in smart objects (Singh & Gandhi, 2014) necessitates ensuring security and protection of this data, especially data related to individuals. Securing and protecting data in the technological age are not an easy task. On one hand, technology is susceptible to security breach or vulnerabilities: "weaknesses in a system or its design that allow an intruder to execute commands, access unauthorized data, and/or conduct denial-of-service attacks" (Abomhara & Køien, 2015, p. 71). These general weaknesses are expected to sharply increase in the IoT era as statistics showed that attacks against IoT devices increased by 600% from 2016 to 2017 (Symantec, 2018). On the other one, data of all types has economic, (Ahmed & Mohamed, 2020) social and other values. Accordingly, it will always be targeted by criminals and other intruders. Needless to say, that personal data could be used by criminals and malicious people to harm the data subjects (Ahmed, 2019). As a result, protection of personal data in the IoT environment is necessary, not only for safeguarding interests related to this data, but also for development of the IoT industry.

As in the real world, security in cyberspace is a challenging matter. As an illustration, security of data in the IoT environment requires ensuring authenticity (to confirm that access only given to legitimate users), authorisation (to enable IoT device components or applications to only access to specific resources), as well as confidentiality, integrity and availability (Leloglu, 2017) and these requirements are not easy to be achieved in ever-connected systems and devices that have limited "computational capabilities, memory and battery power" (Abomhara & Køien, 2015,

p. 65) Vulnerability of IoT devices and systems, the cause of such vulnerability and the challenges of IoT to privacy and data protection law have been pointed out and discussed by various researchers (Roman et al., 2013; Peppet, 2014; Wachter, 2018; Ahmed & Zulhuda, 2015). This chapter will discuss this matter in more details in the coming subsections.

Legally speaking, data protection law is considered as a branch of privacy and the digital revolution affects privacy in three dimensions namely, it Recommendation (1) eases the collection of data which in turn leads to accumulation of massive personal data, (2) flourishes the data market and (3) endangers data in that there is no sufficient means that can be relied on to surely protect data (DeVries, 2003). In response to the technological challenges, data protection law emerged as a new field of cyber or computer law. This law has been around for more than four decades and it aims to protect personal data and smooth its flow. To do so, this law came with several principles to be implemented in processing personal data and imposed heavy fines or even imprisonment on individuals or entities who contravene those principles. More details about data protection law in national, regional and international levels and about its principles will be provided in the coming sections of this chapter.

This chapter discusses the protection offered by data protection law to personal data and the applicability of this law to personal data in the IoT environment. The concentration of the chapter is on protection of personal data from a legal viewpoint and what IoT stakeholders could do to meet the legal requirements. To achieve this objective, Part 2 of the chapter provides a brief discussion of data protection development and its relevance to the information age. This will be done by analysing the efforts of regional and international organisations pertinent to data protection, as well as that efforts in the national level. The aim of such analysis is to fully understand data protection law and the global efforts thereof. This is an important preamble to the discussion of the relation between IoT and data protection law which is the main focus of this chapter. In Part 3, data protection law will be discussed and analysed in order to know its relevance to the IoT industry. This Part is the most important part of the chapter as it is going to point out the applicability or inapplicability of data protection law to personal data flow in the IoT environment and also discuss the so-called data protection principles which are at the heart of data protection law. The aim of this Part is to emphasise the importance of adherence to rules of data protection law especially in the IoT industry where IoT devices are inherently vulnerable to security breach and "often manufactured by traditional consumer-goods makers rather than computer hardware or software firms" (Peppet, 2014, p. 135). In this regard, explaining data protection principles in plain language could benefit IoT stakeholders, whom the authors of this book, "Security, Data Analytics, and Energy-Aware Solutions in the IoT" are targeting. Part 4 focuses on the importance of compliance with data protection law in the IoT sphere and consequences of overlooking such matter from the legal perspective. Especial attention will be paid to such consequences on data subjects and data controllers. Part 5 suggests solutions and make recommendations in light of data protection principles. This Part aims to shortly explain data protection principles, point out the challenges brought by IoT to these principles and guide IoT stakeholders through the process of compliance with data protection law. Finally, Part 6 gives a summary of the main points discussed in the chapter and provides concluding remarks.

Methodology

The method used in this chapter is a doctrinal search method. The sources include primary sources of data protection law such as national legislation, regional and international instruments, as well as secondary sources such as books, journal articles and so on. The chapter also does not restrict itself to specific jurisdictions, rather it may include examples taken from different international and regional instruments, as well as from different national legislation. This is because on one hand, data protection principles are almost the same in all global legislation and on the other, the chapter aims to give a general idea about data protection law to global readers. This method is believed to suit the nature of IoT as global technology that promotes the banner of connectivity 'anytime anywhere.

DEVELOPMENT OF DATA PROTECTION LAW

Modern technology has great impact on all aspects of people lives. In terms of data collection and dissemination, this technology eases aggregation of countless of data about things and particularly expands the traditional and usual habit of collecting data related to people (Rowland et al., 2012). The important of data as the engine or the oil of the information age necessitated looking for a mechanism that ensures the availability of data to authorised users and safeguards it from being misused by those users or being in hands of intruders. Achieving these dual purposes requires technical standards to ensure confidentiality, authenticity and availability of data to lawful users and also law to regulate the process and specifies duties and rights of all parties. Needless to say, that data protection law has a close relation with technology in that every new development of technology could have an impact on this law. Being one of the emerging waves of technology, IoT, which is basically understood as "things or objects that connect to the Internet and each other" (Greengard, 2015, p. 15), challenges data protection law and makes its implications difficult. The nature of the challenges and its extent will be pointed out in the following subsections.

In 1970s of the twentieth century, the first waves of data protection legislation were enacted (Poullet, 2010) with the aim of safeguarding personal data and smoothing its movement. For example, the first known local data protection legislation was 'the Hesse Data Protection Act' of the State of Hesse in Germany in 1970, followed by the first national data protection law in Sweden in 1973 and thereafter other Scandinavian countries such Norway and Denmark enacted laws in 1978 (Burkert, 2000). From 1980s onwards, data protection legislation began to flourish in different countries and regions of the world. According to the United Nations Conference on Trade and Development [UNCTAD] (2016), data protection legislation can now be found in more than 100 different countries of the world.

Like the situation in the national level, data protection also started to flourish in the international and regional levels from 1980s and thereafter. For example, the earliest and most important instruments in the international level (Privacy International, 2018) that played a major part in shaping data protection law are Recommendation of the Organisation for Economic Co-operation and Development [OECD] (2013) which was firstly adopted in 1980 and revised in 2013, the Council of Europe Convention for the Protection of Individual with regard to Automated Processing of Personal Data' in (1981) and the United Nations [UN] 'Guidelines for Regulation of Computerized Personal Data Files (1990). Other than these three important instruments, there are also other documents related to data protection such as the Asia-Pacific Economic Cooperation [APEC] Privacy Framework (2017), the African Union Convention on Cyber Security and Personal Data Protection (2014), the Commonwealth Model Bill on the Protection of Personal Information (2017) and, of course, the GDPR (2016) which is considered as "an evolution in data protection" (Smith, 2018).

Through the existence of data protection in the national, regional and international levels, the method of protecting personal data may practically differ from a place to another. Some countries have a "comprehensive data protection framework" and others protect data "through sectorial laws" (Privacy International, 2018, p. 17). The most obvious example of these different approaches could be seen in the approaches taken by the EU and the United States (US) towards data. While the EU adopts a one-size-fits-all approach to data, the US follows the sectoral approach. In the EU side, protection of personal data is considered as a fundamental right by virtue of Art. 8 (1) of Charter of Fundamental Rights of the European Union which states that "everyone has the right to the protection of personal data concerning him or her" and it is also protected by one of the most comprehensive regulation (GDPR). By contrast, US does not have one legislation applicable to all types of data. Instead, it "relies on a "patchwork" approach-combined with industry self-regulation" (Gady, 2014, p. 12) and "federal and state statutes" (Weiss & Archick, 2016, p. 3).

These different approaches could create a problem for a global technology such as IoT and make compliance with these different regulations a challenging task. It could also impede the effectiveness of those laws and regulations in dealing with new technology such as IoT. In countries where sectoral approaches are followed, IoT wearable devices, etc., that collect health information from users may not be covered by law applicable to medical data and connected cars that collect information from passengers may not be covered by law applies to transportation vehicles (Internet Society, 2019). As an illustration, the Malaysian PDPA (2010), which only applies to personal data processed in commercial transactions (s 2), may not protect personal data processed in non-commercial transactions. In addition to the sectoral impediment, Peppet (2014) who examined IoT from various aspects including privacy, asserted the current law of privacy (in the US) is incapable of protecting privacy in the IoT sphere because that law depends on anonymisation which is unlikely to properly suit the inherent sparsity of IoT data.

In the EU side where there is one law for all personal data, Article 29 Data Protection Working Party [WP29] (2013) opined that the EU law "applies in any case where the use of apps on smart devices involves processing personal data of individuals" (p. 7). In the IoT particularly, the WP29 opined that IoT manufacturers, social platforms, IoT device users (e.g., health-insurances) and IoT application developers are all qualified as data controllers (2014) under the EU data protection law.

It is clear from the above that while the discussion in countries relay on the sectoral approach to regulate data protection such as the US is about the ability or inability of the legal framework to cope with the new technology (IoT), the discussion in the countries applies one-size-fits-all approach such as the EU region is on the challenges of compliance with data protection law in the IoT environment. These differences and challenges should encourage all stakeholders to comply with data protection laws. After discussing the nature and development of data protection law, the next step is to point out challenges of IoT to this law. The coming subsection is endeavouring to achieve this task.

DATA PROTECTION AND THE IOT INDUSTRY

The previous sections tried to summarise the history of data protection law and highlight its importance in saving interests of parties involved in the processing of personal data and then the society as a whole. After coming across the above, the readers are expected to be longed to know whether data protection law applies to the IoT industry or not and also to know the so-called data protection principles. All these matters will be discussed here in order to demonstrate the legal concern about IoT. This chapter deals with IoT as a "term used to describe the numerous objects and devices that are connected to the Internet and that send and receive data" (UNCTAD, 2016, p. 12). The effect of these connected objects on the law was anticipated by some to " be a legal tsunami, the intensity and magnitude of which are unknown to date" (Barbry, 2012, p. 83). The first important step could be to demonstrate relevancy or applicability of data protection law to the IoT industry and this will be done in the following subsection.

Does Data Protection Law Apply to IoT?

As every law has limitations in its material and territorial scope, it is important to determine whether data protection law applies to data flow in the IoT environment or not. This can be done by overviewing the subject matter of this law and its jurisdiction or in other words, the material and territorial scope of this law.

The Material Scope of Data Protection Law

In term of material scope, data protection law usually deals with one type of data namely, data or information related to natural persons. In this regard, data related to organisations or other entities is outside the scope of this law. For example, GDPR (2016) mentions that it "lays down rules relating to the protection of natural persons with regard to the processing of personal data" and defines its material scope by stating that it "applies to the processing of personal data wholly or partly by automated means and to the processing other than by automated means of personal data which form part of a filing system or are intended to form part of a filing system." Based on the above, there are two important terms that are considered as a key to understand the subject matter and the material scope of data protection law: processing and personal data.

Processing

The term processing is a term used to include almost all dealing with data such as collecting, recording, sending of such data. For illustration, GDPR (2016) defines processing as "any operation or set of operations which is performed on personal data or on sets of personal data." As some noted, the term processing can include "almost anything that might be done to or with personal data" (Munir & Yasin, 2010, p. 76). This means that processing data can include collecting, sending, storing, etc., personal data in the IoT sphere. Does IoT include personal data in the meaning of data protection law? Before answering this question, it is vital to know the exact meaning of personal data or personal information from a data protection law perspective. This is important because the notion of personal information in the context of privacy is wider than the notion of this term in data protection law. As an illustration, while personal information or data in the data protection law includes only information that identifies or could identify a specific natural person, personal information in the privacy sphere could include information related to property of a person (a car, house, etc.,) and people related to him such his wife and children (Gavison, 1980).

Personal Data

The term 'personal data' centres around personally identifiable information (PII) or in other words, information or data related to an identified or identifiable person. To determine whether data is considered as personal data or not, a distinction has been made between approaches taken in the US and EU towards the matter. While the US follows the reductionist approach which considers data as personal or PII when it clearly links to a specific person, the EU follows the expansionist approach which defines personal data as data that identifies or can identify a specific person (Li, 2018; Schwartz & Solove, 2011). The expansionist approach seems to be followed by most legislation related to personal data, as well as by international instruments. For example, the OECD Recommendation (2013) defines personal data as "any information relating to an identified or identifiable individual." Additionally, GDPR (2016) comes with a similar definition as it refers to personal data as "any information relating to an identified or identifiable natural person." According to this, any information or data that leads or can lead to identification of a specific natural person can be considered as personal data under data protection law.

As technology used in various sectors such as transport, healthcare, security and smart home which all use "diverse and vast amounts of personal information" (Seo et al., 2018, p. 1), the IoT industry is surely comes under the material scope of data protection law. Not only that, IoT also has an effect on the notion of personal data in that the aggregation of countless data makes it is easy to link anonymised data to a specific person. According to Peppet (2014), associating anonymised data of IoT devices such as Fitbit with a specific user is easy because every person "has a unique gait… or style of walking" that could be used by those who know that data to link the anonymous data to the specific user or users (p. 129). Moreover, IoT has been counted among new waves of technology that represent "new challenges to data protection, particularly in the areas of the definition of 'personal data' and the management of cross-border data transfers" (UNCTAD, 2016, p. 10). From the perspective of material scope of data protection law, IoT device users (e.g., health-insurances), application developers manufacturers, etc., have been considered as data controllers under the EU law (WP29, 2014) because they all process personal data.

Based on the above discussion of the usual material scope of data protection law, IoT devices or systems that processed personal data of natural persons come under the scope of this law in the EU region and also elsewhere because the same criteria are shared by data protection laws of the world. However, the material scope is not enough to determine the applicability of data protection law to IoT because the territorial scope of this law also plays an important role in applicability of this law. The next paragraph is going to discuss the territorial scope of data protection law.

Territoriality of Data Protection Law

Knowing the exact territoriality or jurisdiction of data protection law is important for determining its relationship with a global technological industry such as IoT which is likely to be operated in multiple jurisdictions. Generally speaking, international law gives states the right to exercise their jurisdiction over their territory (including ships and aeroplanes) and excludes them from exercising such jurisdiction outside that territory (Martin, 2003). Data protection law has a close relation with technology in that any new advance in technology can bring new challenges to this law. Accordingly, the territorial scope of national data protection legislation usually includes processing personal data that takes place in jurisdiction of the respective country. For example, the territorial scope of Malaysia PDPA (2010) and the Mauritanian Personal Data Protection Law [PDPL] (2017) includes data processed by someone who establishes in these countries or uses equipment in them for purposes other than transiting such data through these countries. Additionally, GDPR (2016), which could be considered as an ideal data protection law, states that it "applies to the processing of personal data in the context of the activities of an establishment of a data controller or a processor in the Union,…" and also "to the processing of personal data of data subjects who are in the Union by a controller or a processor not establish in the Union" in case of (1) "offering goods or services" to a person in the Union or (2) "the monitoring of their behaviour as far as their behaviour takes place within the Union" (Art, 3). According to the European Data Protection Board [EDPB] (2018), the territorial scope of GDPR can be determined by two criteria namely, the 'establishment' and the 'targeting', adding that the Regulation will apply to those who process personal data when these criteria or one of them are met.

As can be seen, these criteria lay down by GDPR enable this Regulation to apply to the processing of personal data, not only by domestic entities, but also by foreign entities that target the EU residents. From a data protection perspective, this approach seems to be good as it offers protection to the inhabitants of the Union from outsider-threats. It could also suit the nature of IoT as a global service. From the IoT industry perspective, however, this could be bad news as GDPR protection measurements could be harder, in comparison with its counterparts in other jurisdictions. For example, some researchers who compared a data breach fine of $ 2.2 million with the fine that could be imposed by GDPR on the same breach found that "if the GDPR is applied, the fine would have been $ 292 million, more than 100 times larger than the previous judgment" (Seo et al., p. 3). This and like news should persuade the IoT industry to take a proactive approach towards personal data protection law.

As a conclusion to this discussion, it can be said that there are two criteria that determine the applicability or inapplicability of data protection law to specific activities or sectors. They are the material and the territorial scope. applying these criteria to data processed in the IoT industry provides that IoT is subject to data protection law, at least in various jurisdictions of the world. In light of this finding, it is necessary to discuss data protection principles in order to properly comply with them in the IoT industry. Knowing these principles could be a prerequisite for IoT stakeholders to prepare for their implementation. Therefore, it important to talk about these principles and the rules established by them.

Principles of Data Protection

Data protection principles are at the heart of personal data protection law. Accordingly, they can be found in all national, regional and international instruments related to data protection. For example, the OECD Recommendation (2013) which is considered as the oldest regional instrument established 'minimum standards' to be followed in processing personal data. The OECD Recommendation consist of 8 principles namely, (1) 'collection limitation'; (2) 'data quality'; (3) 'purpose specification'; (4) 'use limitation'; (5) 'security safeguards'; (6) 'openness'; (7) 'individual participation'; and (8) 'accountability'. These principles can fully or partly be found in national legislation around the world. For example, similar principles can be seen in Data Protection Act (2018) of the United Kingdom (UK), Protection of Personal Information Act (2013) of South Africa, Data Protection Act (2012) of Ghana and Personal Data Protection Act (2012) of Singapore. Moreover, the EU GDPR (2016), which is considered as the latest comprehensive regional regulation in the data protection field, comes with the same principles. For example, it stipulated 7 principles namely, (1) 'lawfulness, fairness and transparency'; (2) 'purpose limitation'; (3) 'data minimisation'; (4) 'accuracy'; (5) 'storage limitation'; (6) 'integrity and confidentiality'; and (7) 'accountability' (art, 5).

Regardless of the words and the numbers of the above two regional instruments and the domestic legislation mentioned thereof, the same principles are almost shared by data protection law around the world. Therefore, all IoT stakeholders are strongly advised to be ready to comply with these principles regardless of the current jurisdictions or geographical operations of those stakeholders. Such preparedness will enable the IoT industry to expend worldwide and easily comply with data protection law therein. Though compliance with data protection principles in a vulnerable connected environment such as the IoT one is not an easy task, it is not impossible, too. IoT stakeholders should consider data protection law as necessary obstacles aimed to protect legitimate rights of the data subjects and at the same time to facilitate the free flow of data between legitimate parties.

To emphasise the importance of compliance with these principles, the next subsection discusses the necessity of adherence to data protection law and regulations in the IoT industry and the consequences of overlooking that adherence on parties involved in the process.

THE IMPORTANCE OF COMPLIANCE WITH DATA PROTECTION LAW IN IOT

As mentioned above, data protection law has an important aim to achieve, that is to smooth the flow of personal data and ensure its protection from collection to deletion. For example, GDPR (2016), which is considered as the most updated law in this field, states in its first Art 1 (1) that it "lays down rules relating to the protection of natural persons with regard to the processing of personal data and rules relating to the free movement of personal data." Data protection principles serve these two purposes through giving clear guidelines to be followed by those who involve in the process. As an illustration, processing personal data assumes participation of various parties including two main parties namely, a data subject: the one whom personal data is taken and a data controller or user: the one who collects and processes the collected data. Data protection law gives data subjects various rights related to their data and imposes some responsibilities on data controllers.

In the digital era, data of all types is considered as an asset or currency (Schwart, 2004) and thus it needs to be protected. Moreover, personal information is an aspect of privacy and protecting privacy is seen as protection of human integrity and dignity and as fundamental for the modern notion of an individual's freedom and autonomy (Nowak et al., 2012). Accordingly, strict adherence to data protection law is necessary because non-compliance with this law does not serve interests of data subjects and data controllers. In the IoT era particularly, misusing personal data could negatively affect people in many ways including safety risks. Such scenario could happen when automated cars or IoT health devices are remotely controlled and reprogrammed by malicious hackers (The Federal Trade Commission Staff Report, 2015). Examples of IoT medical devices that malicious hackers could misuse to endanger safety of people could be the Implantable Medical Devices (IMDs) which can be defined as "electronic devices implanted within the body to treat a medical condition, monitor the state or improve the functioning of some body part,..." (Camara et al., 2015, p. 272). Hacking and an unauthorised manipulation of information of these devices may not only invade privacy of its users, but it could also threaten their safety (Camara et al., 2015; Abdur-Razzaq et al., 2017). As for privacy concern, researchers in this field point out various privacy threats associated with IoT technology including, for instance, expanding collection of personal data, easing finding users of the devices, profiling, revealing location and private life and activities (Peppet, 2014; Greengard, 2015; Wachter, 2018; Ahmed & Zulhuda, 2019).

Compliance with data protection law is also important for the IoT industry as from the economical view, compliance with this law could help the IoT industry to win trust of consumers which is considered as "one of the important issues in modern business" (Li et al., 2019, p. 1). Moreover, data protection law also imposes heavy penalties on data controllers who contravene its rules. These penalties can be in the form of a fine or imprisonment or both. For example, under GDPR (2016), which applies to personal data linked to the EU region, a fine for non-compliance with data protection rules could reach twenty million EUR or "4% of the total worldwide annual turnover of the preceding financial years" in some cases. This amount is considered as administrative fees and there could be another fee imposed by this Regulation under the umbrella of compensation and liability (Art. 82). Some data protection laws such as the Malaysian PDPA (2010) punishes data users who contravene its rules by a fine (up to RM 300 000) or imprisonment (up to 2 years) or by both (s 5). In the US, the FTC (2019) warned that "manufacturers and sellers of connected devices should be aware that the FTC will hold them to account for failures that expose user data to risk of compromise."

The above consequences should lead the IoT stakeholders to look for a way that enable them to strictly comply with data protection law to avoid the unwanted consequences and also to promote and expand the IoT industry. The coming subsection will be devoted to solutions and recommendations that the author of this chapter believes to be useful for compliance with data protection in the IoT environment.

SOLUTIONS AND RECOMMENDATIONS

From the above discussion, it becomes obvious that data protection law applies to the processing of personal data in the IoT sphere and therefore, the IoT industry is obliged to comply with all data protection rules including the principles which are of the essence. As the most updated law that has been described "as the gold standard in the protection of privacy of information" (Mark Heyink, 2018, p. 7), the ability to comply with GDPR could arguably be taken as a benchmark for ability of compliance with data protection law throughout the world. Here the chapter will provide solutions and recommendations that will hopefully help the IoT industry to easily understand data protection principles and then implement them in the processing of personal data of a natural person. This will be done by providing a brief overview of the seven principles set by the GDPR, explaining them in light of some other relevant national legislation and regional instruments of the world and pointing out what IoT stakeholders, who process personal data of natural person, should do or not do to keep their fingers on the pulse. Some recorded incidents or practices seemed to contradict or challenge data protection principles in the IoT environment will also be highlighted.

First Principle: Lawfulness, Fairness and Transparency

This is an important principle that obliges those who process personal data to have a legitimate reason for the processing and do it in a transparent manner. The state of lawfulness occurs, inter alia, when the data subject gives his consent to the processing of his data or the processing is necessary for protecting interests of the parties or one of them or in compliance with law. Moreover, the concept of transparency requires, among others, the data controller to use a suitable means to inform the data subject about this identity (the identity of the data controller), his contact and the purposes of the collection of the personal data. The OECD Recommendation (2013) referred to transparency as openness and pointed out that it includes finding means to establish "the existence and nature of personal data, and the main purposes of their use, as well as the identity and usual residence of the data controller."

To comply with this principle, IoT stakeholders should take the consent of the data subject, or rely on other legal grounds and also provide all required information to the data subject in the time and manner stipulated in data protection law that applies to their activities. Unfortunately, the ability of IoT devices to automatically interact and communicate with other connected things such as cars or surveillance cameras without awareness of the one who uses such devices (Kamrani et al., 2016) is a real example of the challenges brought by IoT to this principle. In fact, some IoT devices such as smart TVs were found to be used as a means to secretly collect information of their users and send it to manufacturers (Vrabec, 2019). An activity such as this surely contravenes the spirit and letter of data protection law, specifically the principle of lawfulness, fairness and transparency. For so, a fine of $ 2.2 million was already imposed on a "company sold 11 million IoT TVs with a software program installed intentionally to track customers' detailed viewing habits (Seo et al., 2018, p. 3).

Second Principle: Purpose Limitation

Generally, this principle provides that personal data should be collected for specific, explicit and legitimate purposes and used only for those purposes. To comply with this principle, the IoT industry should have a clear policy about the purposes of the collection of personal data and stick to that purposes. Practically speaking, IoT devices such as those used for the purposes of collecting biological data (heart rate, blood pressure, etc.) are capable of collecting information about nearby activities and environment like changing indoor temperature and locations (Zhou et al., 2019). If the controllers of these devices do not inform the data subject about the extra data that could be collected by these devices, they are supposedly breaching the principle of Purpose Limitation because the extra data is data collected without consent or specifying legitimate purposes. Additionally, this collection could also violate the principle of Lawfulness, Fairness and Transparency.

Is there a thing that the IoT industry can do to comply with data protection principles in a connected environment such as in the above example? Indeed, the answer is yes. Data protection wants the controllers to deal honestly and fairly with the users of their products and informs them about the function of the devices and all types of information that they are capable of collecting. By doing so, the data controllers are deemed to comply with the law because consent of the users can be considered as a means to reconcile the competition between the users desire to utilise IoT devices and the reality that these devices could harm those users (Peppet, 2014).

Third Principle: Data Minimisation

This principle sometimes refers to as the principle of data integrity or quality and it requires data controllers to minimise the collection and process of personal data through sticking to data relevant to the intended purposes, but also accurate, complete and up-to-date for that purposes. To comply with the Minimisation Principle, the IoT industry should ensure that their devices or systems collect only relevant and accurate data and not go beyond that. Unfortunately, the nature of IoT as ever-connected devices and systems makes minimising collection of data a difficult job, if not impossible. It has been said that some important concepts such data minimisation and notice and choice will be less useful (Cerf et al., 2016) in a connected environment such as the IoT one. This is right and the fact that some IoT devices are found to be collecting information about the environment surrounding them (Zhou et al., 2019) is a clear example on that challenges.

Fourth Principle: Accuracy

The Accuracy Principle is related to the nature and types of personal data in that this principle obliges the data controller to take reasonable steps to ensure the accuracy of the data and keep it up to date to enable it to be used in the purposes of its collection. To comply with this principle, the IoT industry has to find suitable tools to communicate with the users of IoT devices and systems in order to enable such users to update and correct their personal information. From a data protection perspective, communications between the data subjects and data controllers are necessary for the former to execute their rights and also for the latter to do their obligations.

Regrettably, some IoT devices do not facilitate communications between data subjects and data collectors because these "devices are often small, screenless and lacking an input mechanism such as a keyboard or touch screen" (Peppet, 2014, p. 140). This fact led some to argue that the principle of notice and choice which facilitates communications between data subjects and data collectors cannot practically be executed in the IoT wearable devices because in most cases the notice is absented from the design of those devices (Edwards, 2016). Though the argument of those authors is somewhat true, the author of the present chapter argues that IoT stakeholders can find a practical means to overcome these obstacles because IoT which aims to communicate everything will surely facilitate communications between its parties. Therefore, IoT stakeholders are advised to repair the design faults diagnosed in the IoT devices and have suitable tools to communicate with users of their products.

Fifth Principle: Storage Limitation

The Storage or Retention Principle talks about the necessity of deleting and destroying data after the purposes of its collection has been fulfilled. It is the responsibility of the data controllers to take reasonable steps to permanently delate and destroy the personal data after the fulfilment of its collection purposes. To comply with this principle, IoT stakeholders should take reasonable steps to delate and destroy that personal data unless there is another legal ground for continuing its storage. It is worth to mention here that data protection law and particularly, GDPR (2016), allows storing personal data for longer period if such data is intended to be processed for purposes like public interest, historical or scientific research, etc., under certain conditions (art., 5).

Sixth Principle: Integrity and Confidentiality

This principle also called the security principle and it aims to secure personal data during its lifetime. Accordingly, it obliges the data controllers to take practical steps (technical, organisational measures, etc.,) to secure data, inter alia, from any misuse, unlawful or unauthorised processing. Compliance with this particular principle could be a challenging task in a connected environment such as the IoT one because technology is vulnerable to security breach (Abomhara & Køien, 2015) and the IoT is characterised as "a cyber-physical system that integrates billions of heterogeneous devices and smart objects" (Abdul-Qawy et al., 2015, p. 70). In this regard, it eases identifying, tracking and profiling individuals (Internet Society, 2019).

Regardless of these difficulties, IoT stakeholders could and should comply with Security Principle by implementing appropriate measures required by data protection law they are subject to. To do so, they need to take reasonable steps including, inter alia, technical, organisational, informational and physical measures (Privacy International, 2018) to protect data from all types of threats or misuse. Such measures should consider the location of the data, its nature and the harm that could be caused by misusing, losing, modification, etc., of the data. Based on the fact that IoT could include various types of data including very sensitive data, IoT stakeholders should consider that and provide appropriate protection thereof. As an illustration, IoT used in healthcare or transport, etc., should be given high measures of protection because malicious attack against smart healthcare or smart transport systems could endanger the life of patients and passengers (The FTC, 2015; Ali et al., 2016).

Seventh Principle: Accountability

This principle obliges data controllers to comply with data protection law, especially with data protection principles. The OECD Recommendation (2013) affirmed this meaning by stating that "a data controller should be accountable for complying with measures which give effect to the principles stated above." The principle of accountability seems to implicitly or explicitly be found in all data protection law because all data protection laws oblige data controllers to comply with data protection principles otherwise they will be liable for a fine or imprisonment as the case may be. For the IoT industry particularly, compliance with the Accountability requires IoT stakeholders who process personal data "to adopt technical and organisational measures" that enable them to comply with data protection law and prove such capability (Eskens, 2016).

CONCLUSION

The chapter purported to shed light on the concern about personal data protection in the IoT sphere in order to help the IoT stakeholders to properly comply with data protection law. To achieve this objective, Part 2 of the chapter discussed the development of personal data protection law in national, regional and international levels. It also made a distinction between different approaches taken in different jurisdictions toward data protection law and the effect of these approaches on a global industry such as the IoT. Part 3 of the chapter was devoted to data protection and the IoT industry in terms of applicability of this law to personal data processed in the IoT environment and the principles established by that law. This required the chapter to analyse the material and territorial scope of data protection law. Such analysis proved the applicability of data protection law to the processing of personal data in the IoT sphere. This Part also counted data protection principles and discovered similarities between them in all data protection of the world. After that, the discussion in Part 4 focussed on the necessity of compliance with data protection principles to protect interests of both the data subjects and data controllers, as well as to promote the IoT industry and enable it to globally expend. Additionally, Part 5 of the chapter provided solutions to problems related to processing personal data in the IoT environment and advised IoT stakeholders by providing some recommendations that could help them keep their fingers on the pulse.

REFERENCES

Abdul-Qawy, A. S., J., P. P., Magesh, E., & Srinivasulu, T. (2015). The Internet of Things (IoT): An Overview. *Journal of Engineering Research and Applications*, 5(12), 71–82.

Abdur-Razzaq, M., Gill, S. H., Qureshi, M. A., & Ullah, S. (2017). Security Issues in the Internet of Things (IoT): A Comprehensive Study. *International Journal of Advanced Computer Science and Applications*, 8(6), 383–388.

Abomhara, M., & Køien, G. M. (2015). Cyber Security and the Internet of Things: Vulnerabilities, Threats, Intruders and Attacks. *Journal of Cyber Security*, *4*, 65–88. doi:10.13052/jcsm2245-1439.414

African Union. (2014, June 27). *African Union Convention on Cyber Security and Personal Data Protection*. African Union. https://au.int/en/treaties/african-union-convention-cyber-security-and-personal-data-protection

Ahmed, S. M. (2019). Identity Crime in the Digital Age: Malaysian and Mauritanian Legal Framework. *International Journal of Law, Government, and Communication*, *4*(15), 154–165. doi:10.35631/ijlgc.4150016

Ahmed, S. M., & Mohamed, D. (2020). Data in the Internet of Things Era: The Propertization of Data In Light of Contemporary Business Practices. *International Journal of Business and Society*, *21*(1), 81–94.

Ahmed, S. M., & Zulhuda, S. (2015). The Concept of Internet of Things and Its Challenges to Privacy. *South East Asia Journal of Contemporary Business, Economics and Law*, *8*(4), 1–6.

Ahmed, S. M., & Zulhuda, S. (2019). Data Protection Challenges in the Internet of Things Era: An Assessment of Protection Offered by PDPA 2010. *International Journal of Law, Government and Communication, 4*(17), 1-12. doi:10.35631/ijlgc.417001

Ali, I., Sabir, S., & Ullah, Z. (2016). Internet of Things Security, Device Authentication and Access Control: A Review. *International Journal of Computer Science and Information Security*, *14*(8), 1–11.

Article 29 Data Protection Working Party. (2013, February 27). *Opinion 02/2013 on Apps on Smart Devices*. Pdpjournals. https://www.pdpjournals.com/docs/88097.pdf

Article 29 Data Protection Working Party. (2014, September 16). *Opinion 8/2014 on the on Recent Developments on the Internet of Things*. Pdp. https://www.pdpjournals.com/docs/88440.pdf

Asia-Pacific Economic Cooperation. (2017, August). *APEC Privacy Framework [2015]*. APEC Secretariat.

Barbry, E. (2012). The Internet of Things, Legal Aspects: What Will Change (Everything). *Communications & Stratégies*, *1*(87), 83–100.

Burkert, H. (2000). Privacy-Data Protection: A German/ European Perspective. In E. Christoph & H. K. Kenneth (Eds.), *Governance of Global Networks in the Light of Differing Local Values* (pp. 44–48). Nomos Verlagsgesellschaft.

Camara, C., Peris-Lopez, P., & Tapiador, J. E. (2015). Security and privacy issues in Implantable medical devices: A comprehensive survey. *Journal of Biomedical Informatics*, *55*, 272–289. doi:10.1016/j.jbi.2015.04.007 PMID:25917056

Cerf, V. G., Ryan, P. S., Senges, M., & Whitt, R. S. (2016). IoT Safety and Security as Shared Responsibility. *Business Info*, *1*(35), 7–19. doi:10.17323/1998-0663.2016.1.7.19

Convention for the Protection of Individuals with regard to Automatic Processing of Personal Data, ETS No.108 (The Council of Europe 01 28, 1981) .

Data Protection Act (Ghana 2012).

Data Protection Act, Chapter 12 (UK 2018).

DeVries, W. T. (2003). Protecting Privacy in the Digital Age. *Berkeley Technology Law Journal, 18*(19), 283–311.

Edwards, L. (2016). Privacy, Security and Data Protection in Smart Cities: A Critical EU Law Perspective. *European Data Protection Law Review, 2*(1), 28–58. doi:10.21552/EDPL/2016/1/6

EskensS. J. (2016, February 29). *Profiling the European Citizen in the Internet of Things: How Will the General Data Protection Regulation Apply to this Form of Personal Data Processing, and How Should It?* https://papers.ssrn.com/sol3/papers.cfm?abstract_id=2752010 doi:10.2139/ssrn.2752010

Gady, F.-S. (2014). EU/U.S. Approaches to Data Privacy and the "Brussels Effect": A Comparative Analysis. *Georgetown Journal of International Affairs,* 12-23.

Gartner. (2017, February 7). *Gartner Says 8.4 Billion Connected "Things" Will Be in Use in 2017, Up 31 Percent From 2016.* Gartner-Newsroom. https://www.gartner.com/en/newsroom/press-releases/2017-02-07-gartner-says-8-billion-connected-things-will-be-in-use-in-2017-up-31-percent-from-2016

Gavison, R. (1980). Privacy and the Limits of Law. *The Yale Law Journal, 89*(3), 421–471. doi:10.2307/795891

Greengard, S. (2015). *The Internet of Things.* Massachusetts Institute of Technology. doi:10.7551/mitpress/10277.001.0001

Guidelines for the Regulation of Computerized Personal Data Files, Resolution 45/95 (United Nations December 14, 1990).

Internet Society. (2019, September). *Policy Brief: IoT Privacy for Policymakers. Internet Society.* https://www.internetsociety.org/wp-content/uploads/2019/09/IoT-Privacy-Brief_20190912_Final-EN.pdf

Kamrani, F., Wedlin, M., & Rodhe, I. (2016*). Internet of Things: Security and Privacy Issues.* Docplayer. http://docplayer.net/50469759-Internet-of-things-security-and-privacy-issues.html

Leloglu, E. (2017). A Review of Security Concerns in Internet of Things. *Journal of Computer and Communications, 5*(1), 121–136. doi:10.4236/jcc.2017.51010

Li, H., Yu, L., & He, W. (2019). The Impact of GDPR on Global Technology Development. *Journal of Global Information Technology Management, 22*(1), 1–6. doi:10.1080/1097198X.2019.1569186

Li, W. (2018). A tale of two rights: Exploring the potential conflict between right to data portability and right to be forgotten under the General Data Protection Regulation. *International Data Privacy Law, 8*(4), 309–317. doi:10.1093/idpl/ipy007

Malaysian Personal Data Protection Act [PDPA], 709 (2010).

Mardonova, M., & Choi, Y. (2018). Review of Wearable Device Technology and Its Applications to the Mining Industry. *Energies, 11*(3), 1–14. doi:10.3390/en11030547

Mark Heyink. (2018). *Protection of Personal Information for South African Law Firms*. Mark Heyink.

Martin, E. A. (Ed.). (2003). *Oxford Dictionary of Law*. Oxford University Press.

Mauritanian Personal Data Protection Law, 020 (2017).

Munir, A. B., & Yasin, S. H. (2010). *Personal Data Protection in Malaysia: Law and Practice*. Sweet & Maxwell Asia.

Nowak, M., Januszewski, K. M., & Hofstätter, T. (Eds.). (2012). *All Human Rights for All – Vienna Manual on Human Rights*. NWV Neuer Wissenschftlicher Verlag.

Peppet, S. R. (2014). Regulation of the Internet of Things: First Steps Toward Managing Discrimination, Privacy, Security, and Consent. *Texas Law Review, 93*, 85–166.

Personal Data Protection Act, 26 (Singapore 2012).

Poullet, Y. (2010). About the E-Privacy Directive: Towards a Third Generation of Data Protection Legislation? In G. Serge, P. Yves, & D. Paul (Eds.), Data Protection in a Profiled World (pp. 3-30). SpringerScience+Business Media B.V.

Privacy International. (2018). *The Keys to Data Protection*. Privacy International.

Protection of Personal Information Act, Act No. 4 (South Africa 2013).

Regulation (EU) 2016/679 on the protection of natural persons with regard to the processing of personal data and on the free movement of such data, and repealing Directive 95/46/EC (General Data Protection Regulation), 2016/679 (The European Parliament and of the Council April 27, 2016).

River Publishers Series in Communication. (2014). *Internet of Things- From Research and Innovation to Market Development* (V. Ovidiu & F. Peter, Eds.). River Publisher.

Roman, R., Zhou, J., & Lopez, J. (2013). On the Features and Challenges of Security and Privacy in Distributed Internet of Things. *Computer Networks*, *57*(10), 2266–2279. doi:10.1016/j.comnet.2012.12.018

Rowland, D., Kohl, U., & Charlesworth, A. (2012). Information Technology Law (4th ed.). Routledge.

Schwart, P. M. (2004). Property, Privacy and Personal Data. *Harvard Law Review*, *117*(7), 2056–2128. doi:10.2307/4093335

Schwartz, P. M., & Solove, D. J. (2011). The PII Problem: Privacy and a New Concept of Personally Identifiable Information. *New York University Law Review*, *86*, 1814–2011.

Seo, J., Kim, K., Park, M., Park, M., & Lee, K. (2018). An Analysis of Economic Impact on IoT Industry under GDPR. *Mobile Information Systems*, 1-6. doi:10.1155/2018/6792028

Singh, P. M., & Gandhi, K. (2014). Interconnected Smart Objects: Era of Internet of Things. *IJARCET*, *3*(6), 2041–2046.

Smith, D. (2018). *Forwards for "Preparing for General Data Protection Regulation"*. Allenovery. https://www.allenovery.com/SiteCollectionDocuments/Radical%20 changes%20to%20European%20data%20protection%20legislation.pdf

Symantec. (2018, Murch). *Internet Security Threat Report. Symantec*. https://www. symantec.com/content/dam/symantec/docs/reports/istr-23-2018-en.pdf

The Commonwealth. (2017). *Model Bill on the Protection of Personal Information*. The Commonwealth. https://thecommonwealth.org/sites/default/files/key_reform_ pdfs/P15370_9_ROL_Model_Privacy_Bill_0.pdf

The European Data Protection Board. (2018, November 16). G*uidelines 3/2018 on the territorial scope of the GDPR (Article 3)*. Edpb. https://edpb.europa.eu/sites/ edpb/files/files/file1/edpb_guidelines_3_2018_territorial_scope_after_public_ consultation_en_1.pdf

The European Union (EU) General Data Protection Regulation [GDPR], 679 (2016).

The Federal Trade Commission. (2019, July 2). D-*Link Agrees to Make Security Enhancements to Settle FTC Litigation*. FTC Gov. https://www.ftc.gov/news-events/ press-releases/2019/07/d-link-agrees-make-security-enhancements-settle-ftc- litigation

The Federal Trade Commission Staff Report. (2015, January). *Internet of Things Privacy & Security in a Connected World*. ftc.gov.https://www.ftc.gov/system/files/documents/reports/federal-trade-commission-staff-report-november-2013-workshop-entitled-internet-things-privacy/150127iotrpt.pdf

The Organisation for Economic Co-operation and Development. (2013, July 11). *Recommendation of the Council concerning Guidelines governing the Protection of Privacy and Transborder Flows of Personal Data*. oecd.org. https://www.oecd.org/sti/ieconomy/2013-oecd-privacy-guidelines.pdf

United Nations Conference on Trade and Development. (2016). *Data Protection Regulations and International Data Flows: Implications for Trade and Development*. United Nations Publication.

Vrabec, H. U. (2019). *Uncontrollable: Data Subject Rights and the Data-driven Economy*. Universiteit Leiden.

Wachter, S. (2018). The GDPR and the Internet of Things: A Three-Step Transparency Model. *Law, Innovation and Technology*, *10*(2), 266–294. doi:10.1080/17579961.2018.1527479

Weiss, M. A., & Archick, K. (2016). *U.S.-EU Data Privacy: From Safe Harbor to Privacy Shield*. FAS. https://fas.org/sgp/crs/misc/R44257.pdf

Zhou, W., Jia, Y., Peng, A., Zhang, Y., & Liu, P. (2019). The Effect of IoT New Features on Security and Privacy: New Threats, Existing Solutions, and Challenges Yet to Be Solved. *IEEE Internet of Things Journal*, *6*(2), 1606–1616. doi:10.1109/JIOT.2018.2847733

KEY TERMS AND DEFINITIONS

Data: Information about human beings.

Data Controller: A natural or legal person who processes data of natural persons.

Data Protection Law: All statutes and regulations related to the processing of personal data.

Data Subject: A natural person whom data is processed by the data controller.

Internet of Things: A term used to describe objects/things (devices, cars, trees,) that can connect to a network.

IoT Stakeholders: Data controllers.

Natural Person: A human being as opposed to a legal person or entity.

Personal Data: Information that identifies or can identify a specific natural person.

Principles of Data Protection: Common standards and rules established by data protection law to be followed in dealing with personal data.

Chapter 3
Analysis of Cell Phone Biometric Sensors and Security Risk of the Sensors

D'Tron James
University of Louisiana at Lafayette, USA

Md Abdullah Al Momin
University of Louisiana at Lafayette, USA

ABSTRACT

Biometric sensors are becoming more commonplace in today's world. These biometric sensors are especially common in today's smartphones. Billions of smartphones use these sensors for security purposes, and these are slowly but surely replacing traditional forms of password authentication. Biometrics are commonly used to unlock devices and also for purchases. In this chapter, the focus will be on the most common types of biometrics featured in phones along with the sensors associated with them. Next, an analysis of the security risk of these sensors along with common attacks to exploit these risks are discussed. Lastly, various ways to patch and combat these various risks will be discussed.

INTRODUCTION

Biometrics are common in many devices used for device security. The logic behind biometrics is that humans have certain features that are unique to each individual. These features are used to create a digital signature that is stored and is used to be later matched by the person the signature belongs to. These unique features include

DOI: 10.4018/978-1-7998-7323-5.ch003

fingerprints, facial features, voice, iris, and retina of the eye, keystroke, and lastly, the signature. Fingerprint recognition is one of the most common biometric techniques. Fingerprint recognition sensors can detect a person's unique fingerprint, usually through touch, and create a unique signature as a form of authentication. Facial recognition captures an image of an individual's facial features, and an algorithm creates a signature based on the geometry of those features. Voice recognition is used by analyzing a person's voice, accent, tone, pace, and overall speech patterns. Iris recognition focuses on the colored ring-shaped portion of an individual's eye. In the iris there are threadlike structures that are unique to each individual, which is used to create a signature. Retina scanning uses the capillaries found in the retina by infrared cameras to create a digital signature. Keystroke Dynamics focuses on the pattern in which someone types on the touch screen and keypad. And lastly, signature recognition uses a person's unique signature for authentication.

Even though all the biometric techniques are discussed in this chapter, the main focus will be on two of the most common ones used in smartphones fingerprint recognition and facial recognition. First, the hardware associated with these sensors will be discussed. Then the various attacks of each type of sensor will be considered. For voice recognition, the focus will be on voice impersonation attacks. For fingerprint recognition, the focus will be on fingerprint fabrication. And lastly, for facial recognition, the focus will be on presentation vs. indirect and photo/video attacks, 3D mask attacks, and makeup and surgery.

FINGERPRINT RECOGNITION

Figure 1. Shows a front fingerprint sensor along with a back fingerprint sensor (Patrick, 2017).

Fingerprint recognition sensors are able to detect a person's unique fingerprint usually through touch and creates a unique signature as a form of authentication based on a user's fingerprint.

Hardware and Algorithm

Figure 2.

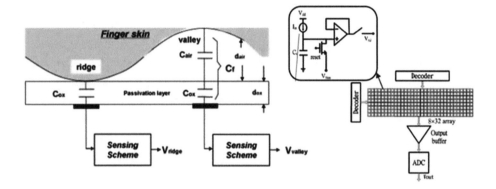

There are various types of hardware ways in which fingerprints are acquired and various locations in which these sensors are placed. Some are placed on the back of a device, while others, including in-screen sensors, are usually placed in the front of the device at the bottom, as shown in figure 1. The type of scanners used are usually optical, capacitive scanners, ultrasonic scanners, and optical capacitive scanners. Optical scanners use an image or photo to record an image and then use an algorithm that uses design and shape to create a digital signature. This is the oldest technique for fingerprint recognition. This technique isn't as frequently used since it isn't very secure. Prosthetics and even high-quality photos can fool these sensors. Next are capacitive scanners, which are the most common and arguably the most secure. These sensors use tiny capacitors to collect information on the fingerprint. "As capacitors can store electrical charge, connecting them up to conductive plates on the surface of the scanner allows them to be used to track the details of a fingerprint. The charge stored in the capacitor will be changed slightly when a finger's ridge is placed over the conductive plates, while an air gap will leave the charge at the capacitor relatively unchanged. An op-amp integrator circuit is used to track these changes, which can then be recorded by an analog-to-digital converter." (See figure 2) This information, once gathered, is stored and used for later. This is considered one of the most secured since it cannot be done by an image alone.

Moreover, prosthetics have a hard time duplicating since different materials cause a different charge by the capacitors. These can be bypassed through hardware and software hacking. The following technique that is used is ultrasonic scanners. These consist of a transmitter and receiver. This technique works by having the user place a finger on the sensor, which produces the ultrasonic pulse that sends feedback to the sensor and some of which is absorbed. This creates a unique input that is used to create the signature. This technique is highly secure and commonly used for in-screen sensors. This technique has its drawbacks, though, as some screen protectors can affect its ability to read the fingerprint. Lastly, optical capacitive sensors are also used for in-screen sensors. It only works on OLED displays and shines a light on your finger similar to regular optical scanners but is better able to sense if it's a real finger or not.

The algorithms and software play a significant role in these sensors as well. For all of these sensors to work, there must be software to interpret the information and algorithms to create the keys. Different manufactures use different algorithms, and these algorithms differ in speed and accuracy. For example, some algorithms examine the whole finger while others examine just crucial features which can help increase the speed and efficiency of the algorithm. These algorithms differ because the basic concept is illustrated in figure 3. Moreover, there must be a way to keep these signatures secure. This is usually done through cryptography. In figure 4, we will see an example of the ARM Trust-zone system, which uses apps and cryptography to keep the biometrics safe.

Figure 3. Basic concept graph fingerprint recognition algorithm.

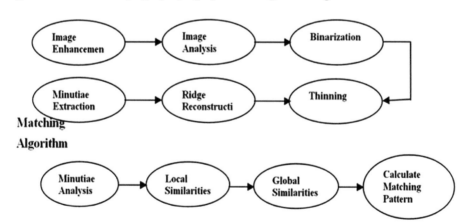

Figure 4. Cryptography for biometric signature storage.

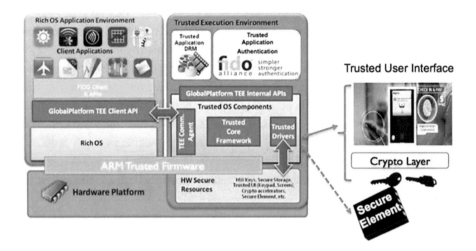

Fingerprint Recognition Attacks

Figure 5.

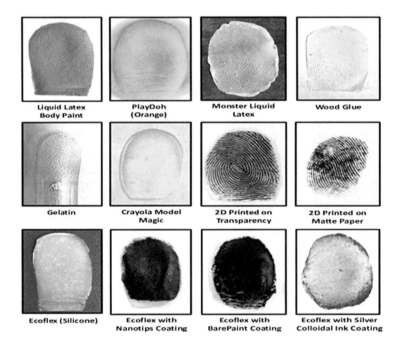

The most popular way to attack the fingerprint sensor is through fingerprint fabrication. This is done by first acquiring the fingerprint of the owner or user of the device. Acquiring these prints can be done relatively easily through lifting prints. Prints can be lifted as easily as taking the clear tape and pressing it on the device where the print is present. Then the fingerprint is then printed on various materials such as play dough, wood glue, and gelatin. Some of these materials are relatively inexpensive. In figure 5, there is a chart of some of the materials used ("Facial recognition technology explained," 2019). These attacks effectively have a 70% success rate, depending on factors such as type of sensor, material, and 3d printing technique.

Attack Prevention

One of the best ways to stop these types of attacks is Presentation Attack Detection (PAD). A presentation attack is a "presentation to the biometric data capture subsystem to interfere with the operation of the biometric system" ("Facial recognition technology explained," 2019) PAD technique usually falls into two categories software-based techniques and hardware-based techniques. Software techniques use software to gather more information on the print, while hardware adds more sensors to try to gain more critical information. An example of what software may be used to detect in the print sample would be the presence of sweat pores. Sweat pores are tough to replicate because of their small size, which is a good way to tell if the sample is legitimate. One example of what hardware is used would be the utilization of "different illumination techniques or capture the pulse frequencies." ("Facial recognition technology explained," 2019) These sensors can focus on certain things such as how blood in the finger is affected when a finger is pressed against the sensor. Another detection method involves a hardware and software combo that allows you to detect the fingerprint and detect veins in a sample. This combo device is known as a Multimodal Finger Capture Device. Its inner working and logic are shown in figure 6, while figure 7 shows the images captured. Moreover, here is a quote describing the illustration "As it may be observed, the camera and illumination boards are placed inside a closed box, which includes an open slot in the middle. When the finger is placed there, all ambient light is blocked, and therefore only the desired wavelengths are used to acquire the images. In particular, a Basler acA1300-60gm Near-infrared (NIR) camera is used, which captures 1280×1024 px. images, with an Edmunds Optics 35mm C Series." VIS-NIR Lens. This camera is used for both frontal visible (VIS) light images and NIR finger vein samples…" This method has shown great results and has shown to be an effective method for PAD.

Figure 6.

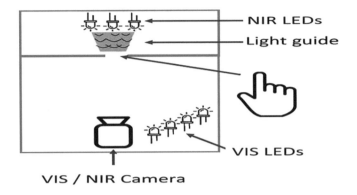

Figure 7.

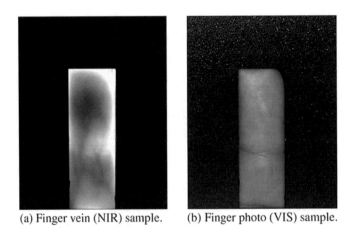

(a) Finger vein (NIR) sample.   (b) Finger photo (VIS) sample.

FACIAL RECOGNITION

Facial recognition captures an image of an individual's facial features, and an algorithm creates a signature based on the geometry of those features. Similar to fingerprint recognition, facial scanning is being equipped more and more into smartphones. Like other biometrics, its popularity comes from speed and convenience for the user.

Hardware and Algorithms

Cell phone creators and companies tend to use sensors and or software when it comes to facial recognition. A few kinds are the basic android, Samsung Intelligent Scan, Infrared assisted face unlock, and Apple Face ID and 3D scanning. The basic android facial recognition uses a basic 2D recognition algorithm and the front-facing camera. This allows this method to be cheap and easy to implement. Also, it makes this method not very secure because a mere photo can be used to unlock your device. Samsung was the first company to use more advanced facial recognition in a smartphone. Samsung Intelligent Scan uses sensors that scan the iris of a user's eye, which is hard to replicate. This is done through an infrared diode in the camera that can illuminate the eye, and the camera then gets detailed information about the iris. Infrared-assisted face recognition requires extra hardware. The additional hardware is that of an IR emitter and a camera that can detect the IR signal. This technique uses the IR camera to take a picture, but it can distinguish between a person's face and a mere picture with the signal. Lastly, the Apple Face ID and 3D scanning does not depend on the camera but rather the sensor held near the camera (See Figure 8). It works by using "an infrared floodlight to illuminate your face, which will work regardless of your surrounding lighting conditions as it's outside of the visible spectrum. A secondary 30,000-point infrared laser matrix is then beamed out, which reflects off the floodlight. Rather than snapping a picture of this infrared light, a special infrared camera detects subtle changes in the matrix point reflections as your face makes minute movements, which allows the camera to capture very accurate 3D depth data." (Dang et al., 2020) This is considered more secure than the options above and the only one used for payments.

Figure 8.

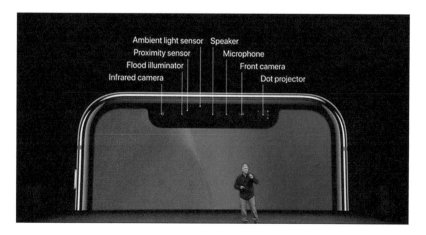

Facial Recognition Attacks

Similar to the fingerprint sensor attacks, presentation attacks focus on the biometric sensor and indirect attacks that involve attacking other parts of the device, such as cracking the system that holds your passwords and biometric signatures. The latter relates more to other cryptography, so the focus of the section will mostly be the presentation attacks. These attacks include but are not limited to photo attacks, video attacks, and 3d masks (see figure 9) (Dang et al., 2020). In photo attacks, an attacker presents a photo of the user in front of the camera, while a video is presented in a video attack. Lastly, a prosthetic mask of the user is presented in the 3D mask attack.

Figure 9.

Attack Countermeasures

There are various countermeasures for these attacks or anti-spoofing. One way is asking specific user commands such as smile, move the head back and forth, or change facial expressions. Asking real-time commands can help, especially in photo and mask attacks, since the attackers will have a harder time executing these commands. This method is known as the challenge-response method. Other prevention methods involve various algorithms, including specular feature projections, image quality assessment, and deep learning. For specular feature uses genuine projections from real images, 3d mask projections to spot spoofing. Image quality assessment compares the picture quality using various measurements and compares it to the original image stored. Deep learning "method is based on a multi-input architecture that combines a pre-trained CNN model and the local binary patterns descriptor." All these algorithms have similar implementations (See figure 10).

Figure 10.

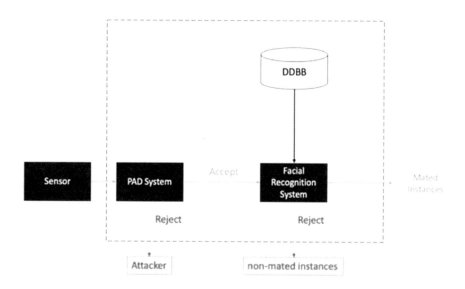

CONCLUSION

In conclusion, biometrics is becoming more and more commonplace. Biometrics are used to unlock devices and even make payments when purchasing items. This makes it extremely important to be able to guard against attacks. Biometric attacks usually fall into two categories: indirect and presentation attacks. This chapter mainly focused on the latter since indirect attacks are more related to cryptography since the attacks involve getting information already stored.

On the other hand, presentation attacks relate more to the sensors and the software used to interpret the information. The focus in this chapter is on fingerprint fabrication attacks for the fingerprint sensor, which involves 3D printing various prints onto different materials to imitate the print. One way to counter this is by having a Multimodal Finger Capture Device that can take a picture of the fingerprint and the veins in the finger, which is hard to duplicate with various materials. Also, another focus is on various facial attacks such as photo, video, and 3D mask attacks. Adding much more beefed-up hardware can be countered by even just asking users for various motion commands.

REFERENCES

Dang, T. A. (2020, October 13). *Facial Recognition: Types of Attacks and Anti-Spoofing Techniques.* Retrieved from https://towardsdatascience.com/facial-recognition-types-of-attacks-and-anti-spoofing-techniques-9d732080f91e

Facial recognition technology explained. (2019, February 8). Retrieved from https://www.androidauthority.com/facial-recognition-technology-explained-800421/

O'Rourke & Daleyn. (2017). *Front, back or side: Where should a fingerprint sensor be located?* https://mobilesyrup.com/2017/07/14/front-back-or-side-where-should-a-smartphone-fingerprint-sens or-be-located/

Chapter 4
Attacks on Voice Assistant Systems

Jie Lien
University of Louisiana at Lafayette, USA

Md Abdullah Al Momin
University of Louisiana at Lafayette, USA

Xu Yuan
University of Louisiana at Lafayette, USA

ABSTRACT

Voice assistant systems (e.g., Siri, Alexa) have attracted wide research attention. However, such systems could receive voice information from malicious sources. Recent work has demonstrated that the voice authentication system is vulnerable to different types of attacks. The attacks are categorized into two main types: spoofing attacks and hidden voice commands. In this chapter, how to launch and defend such attacks is explored. For the spoofing attack, there are four main types, such as replay attacks, impersonation attacks, speech synthesis attacks, and voice conversion attacks. Although such attacks could be accurate on the speech recognition system, they could be easily identified by humans. Thus, the hidden voice commands have attracted a lot of research interest in recent years.

INTRODUCTION

Voice assistant systems (*e.g.*, Siri, Alexa) have attracted wide research attention. However, such systems could receive voice information from malicious sources. Recent studies have demonstrated that the voice authentication system is vulnerable to

DOI: 10.4018/978-1-7998-7323-5.ch004

different types of attacks. The attacks are categorized into two main types: spoofing attacks and hidden voice commands. In this chapter, how to launch and defend such attacks is explored.

For the spoofing attack, there are four main types, including replay attacks, impersonation attacks, speech synthesis attacks, and voice conversion attacks. Although such attacks could be accurate on the speech recognition system, they could be easily identified by humans. Thus, hidden voice commands have attracted a lot of research interest in recent years (Abdullah *et al.*, 2020).

The hidden voice commands could be categorized into hardware nonlinearity, obfuscated command, and adversarial command. For example, the Dolphin attack (Zhang *et al.*, 2017) is based on the nonlinearity effect of the microphone. The nonlinearity effect (Roy *et al.*, 2017) has been considered a type of "data pollution" or a security "back door." The nonlinearity of the device could down-convert the ultrasonic command into signals with any frequency below 22 kHz. Then the ultrasonic command could be identified by the voice assistant systems. Zhang *et al.* presented an inaudible attack on the microphones of voice assistant systems (Zhang *et al.*, 2017). The command is modulated to a frequency carrier higher than 20 kHz. Although the device could not directly record such a signal, the voice command would appear at a frequency lower than 20 kHz due to the nonlinearity effect. Thus, the command would be received by the system. The attacker then could launch the attack on the system. Roy *et al.* defended the attack using the different frequency distribution of the nonlinearity and normal signals (Roy *et al.*, 2018). He *et al.* defended against such an attack by playing the ultrasonic signal in the environment to modulate the signal to several low frequencies (He *et al.*, 2019). However, the main drawback is that they need to play the ultrasonic signal continuously. Such signals sometimes might harm the human body. Zhang *et al.* showed an interesting way to defend against a Dolphin attack (Zhang *et al.*, 2021). They observed that the attenuation of the audible signal and the inaudible signal is different. Based on the different attenuations of the signals, they could identify the Dolphin attack.

The basic idea of obfuscated attack is to generate an adversarial signal like noise to the human ear. Still, it would be classified as a malicious command to the voice assistant system. For example, Cisse *et al.* and Alzantot *et al.* generated the perturbations by the deep neural networks. Such perturbations could be heard like white noise and are hard to be noticed by humans (Cisse *et al.*, 2017 & Alzantot *et al.*, 2018). But they did not consider the over-the-air transmission. That means the voice assistant system would not recognize the perturbation after the transmission in the air. Due to the sound attenuation, the perturbation would significantly change, thus not being identified by the target. Abdullah *et al.* and Chen *et al.* and Schonherr *et al.* considered the over-air transmission by modeling and processing the perturbations by the channel state information. So that their perturbations, sounds like white noise, could still be identified after the over the air transmission (Abdullah *et al.*, 2019, Chen *et al.*, 2020 & Schonherr *et al.*, 2018). However, these systems need to know the model of the target. Recent works (Abdullah *et al.*, 2019 & Chen *et al.*, 2020) successfully launch the black-box attacks on the voice assistant systems.

Now there is not a very effective way to defend against perturbation attacks. Because the perturbation is at the same frequency as the normal sound. Liveness detection (Lee *et al.*, 2020) may be a useful way to defend against such an attack. The basic idea is to identify if the sound source is a real person. Zhang et al. 2017, detected the user by the articulatory gesture. Another way is to extract features that could characterize the machine sound. The deep learning-based approaches (Kinnunen *et al.*, 2017, Lavrentyeva *et al.*, 2017 & Tom *et al.*, 2018) are accurate but introduce high computational overhead. A recent work (Ahmed *et al.*, 2020) defends the replay attack by employing the different frequency distribution of the replay signal and true signal. They extract three features to differentiate the true signal and machine signal and use an SVM as a classifier.

PRELIMINARY

In this section, the preliminary knowledge and necessary background of the voice assistant systems are presented briefly.

Voice Assistant System

A Personal Voice Assistant (PVA) records sound continuously to perform ASR for wake word detection. Once a wake-up word is detected, the PVA submits the recent audio recording to a cloud. Then the speech is analyzed, and any commands requested are executed, and a response might be formed and sent to the PVA to be played out via device speakers. Recordings are stored in the back end and can be used for continuous ASR algorithm improvements and other services.

Automatic Speech Recognition (ASR)

ASR is an interdisciplinary field of research incorporating linguistics, computer science, and electrical engineering. The goal of speech recognition is to transcribe speech into text automatically and then analyze the intent of the speech from transcribed texts. A classic ASR system simulates how humans process speech by transforming the analog acoustic signal to digital representations. Features are extracted, and machine learning methods are applied to extract phonemes (a speech sound) and finally compose text (Benesty *et al.*, 2008).

Audio Processing

The PVA usually consists of a microphone, a pre-amplifier, a low-pass filter, and an ADC. The microphone is a transducer that converts the airborne acoustic signal to an electric signal that only reacts to sound within the spectrum from 20 Hz to 20 kHz. The low-pass filter removes noise above 20 kHz, which is outside the audible sound range. The ADC converts the analog signal to digital form. The sampling frequency of the ADC usually is 44.1 kHz that restricts the maximum frequency of the analog signal to 22 kHz.

SPOOFING ATTACK

There are four different types of spoofing attacks, including replay attacks, speech synthesis attacks, and voice conversion attacks.

A replay attack refers to a playback of a legitimate user's voice sample, which is pre-recorded by an attacker. This attack (Villalba *et al.*, 2011, Lindberg *et al.*, 1999, Leon *et al.*, 2012 & Hautamaki *et al.*, 2013) is powerful and easy to be executed. However, this type of attack requires pre-recorded voice commands. In a voice synthesis attack (Alegre *et al.*, 2012 & Lindberg *et al.*, 1999), the victim's voice is generated from scratch. A voice conversion attack (Kinnunen *et al.*, 2012 & Wu *et al.*, 2013) relies on manipulating a given voice sample to match the target voice.

Although the spoofing attack could be effective on the speech recognition system, it would be easily noticed by a human.

HARDWARE NON-LINEARITY

This section discusses what hardware nonlinearity is and how an attacker could utilize the hardware nonlinearity to launch the attack and how to defend against such an attack.

Hardware Non-Linearity Background

The non-linearity of the hardware enables signal processing of voice commands transmitted in an inaudible frequency range. The inaudible voice commands could be transmitted to the audible frequency range. The non-linearity exists in the amplifier and the microphone. The effect is shown using the amplifier:

Figure 1. The non-linearity effect
(Zhang et al., 2017).

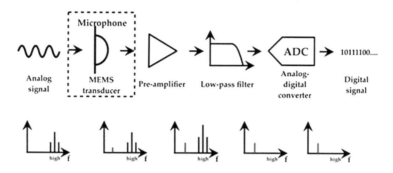

The output function of the amplifier could be expressed as:

$$S_{out} = A_1 S_{in} \tag{1}$$

Where S_{in} is the input signal, S_{out} is the output signal. However this is the ideal case, for the input signal higher than the 22 kHz, the nonlinearity of the amplifier would introduce higher-order signal components:

$$S_{out} = A_1 S_{in} + A_2 S_{in}^2 + A_3 S_{in}^3 + ... \tag{2}$$

   Most of the time the signal components above the second order can be discarded, as they are usually too weak to be detected. However, the second order of the signal need to be considered. Attackers could exploit the nonlinearity to demodulate the high-frequency attack signal to the audible band from the inaudible frequency. It is shown how this nonlinearity works.
Assume a frequency modulated signal S_{in}, which could be expressed as

$$S_{in} = \text{Cos}\left(\omega_1 t\right) + \text{Cos}\left(\omega_2 t\right) \tag{3}$$

Where ω_1 and ω_2 should be above 20 kHz, make sure S_{in} is inaudible. Consider the input function of the amplifier, then the output signal could be expressed as:

$$S_{out} = A_1 \left(\text{Cos}\,\omega_1 t + \text{Cos}\,\omega_2 t\right) + A_2 \left(\text{Cos}\,\omega_1 t + \text{Cos}\,\omega_2 t\right)^2 \tag{4}$$

Assume A$_1$ and A$_2$ to be 1 as an example, the first order would be filtered out by the low-pass filter as shown in figure 1. Because the ω_1 and ω_2 are both above the 20 kHz. However, the second order would generate complex frequency components:

$$\left(\mathrm{Cos}\,\omega_1 t + \mathrm{Cos}\,\omega_2 t\right)^2 = 1 + \frac{1}{2}\mathrm{Cos}\,2\omega_1 t + \frac{1}{2}\mathrm{Cos}\,2\omega_2 + t + \mathrm{Cos}\left(\omega_1 - \omega_2\right)t + \mathrm{Cos}\left(\omega_1 + \omega_2\right)t$$

(5)

All these frequency components, except cos ($\omega_1 - \omega_2$)t will be filtered as they are above 20kHz. The attacker only needs to ensure that $\omega_1 - \omega_2$ is below 20 kHz: to succeed in the attack. As figure 1 shows, this frequency component would not be filtered out, thus could be received by the voice recognition system. That means the malicious command could act as input to the system.

Attacks Based on Hardware Non-Linearity

Recent works studied physical-level signal injection attacks on sensors. The attacks could induce malicious signals in sensors to gain malicious control over systems without directly changing the phenomenon being sensed (Giechaskiel *et al.*, 2020 & Yan *et al.*, 2020). For instance, inaudible ultrasonic attacks can be used to inject signals into microphones to trick voice controllable systems (Zhang *et al.*, 2017), or induce targeted signals in inertial sensors to gain real-time adversarial control over actuation systems and VR/AR applications (Tu *et al.*, 2018).

Backdoor make microphones hear inaudible sounds (Roy *et al.*, 2017). This work aims to transfer the inaudible sound to the microphone's recordable sounds. At first, this work considers amplitude modulation to modulate attack signals onto a high-frequency carrier signal. By doing so, the attack signal can be demodulated without additional software and is recovered at the microphone due to the non-linearity. However, in this case, the attack signal will also be audible when the speaker plays the modulated signal because a non-linearity signal is also applied to the speaker. This work applies therefore using Frequency Modulation (FM) to address this problem. The signal is modulated with the attack signal using FM. However, that means they also need another high-frequency signal. The work further discusses how to reduce the ringing effect; the FM signal is slightly audible due to this effect.

The Dolphin Attack (Zhang *et al.*, 2017) uses a similar idea as in (Roy *et al.*, 2017). However, this work is more practical than (Roy *et al.*, 2017). As they do not need to play additional sound in the air. They only need amplitude modulation (AM) to modulate the baseband attack commands on the ultrasound carrier signal. The attack message can be demodulated to the baseband and recovered just by the nonlinearity feature of microphones. Also, no additional demodulating software is needed, so the attack could be successfully launched on the COTs device.

To ensure the recovered commands could be injected into the system, this work generates inaudible attack samples for both the wake word commands and general audio commands. Such as Amazon Echo, the activation commands can only be effective if it contains the wake word. They test their system on various systems. The result shows that both wake word detection and command recognition are all successful on all tested systems. Also, different systems need different parameters to succeed in the attack. The main limit of this work is the requirement for dedicated hardware. Also, the attack distance is limited (about 175cm).

Paper (Roy *et al.*, 2018) is based on Dolphin Attack (Zhang *et al.*, 2017) and aims to inject malicious commands into the voice assistant system. This work increases the attack range from 175cm to 750 cm and also maintains the inaudibility of commands. To increase the attack range, more power is required at the speaker. Due to the nonlinearity in speakers, attack messages using AM can be heard by the speaker when they are played. This is more obvious when more power is used for increasing the attack distance. This work addresses this by separating parts of the AM attack signal to multiple speakers, and each of them only plays a frequency segment of the original signal. By doing so, the attack message does not exist, and each microphone limits the energy and bandwidth. Also, to ensure the signal addition is still inaudible, this work applies a psychoacoustic model to ensure that sound is below the hearing threshold depending on frequency to maintain inaudibility.

Moreover, EMI attacks could also inject malicious signals into analog sensor components such as microphones, electrocardiogram (ECG) sensors (Foo Kune *et al.*, 2013), and temperature sensors (Tu *et al.*, 2019). Amplitude-modulated EMI attacks had been proposed against microphones and voice control systems. The Ghost Talk work exploited EMI signal injections on sensors and utilized the nonlinearity to convert modulated EMI signals to voice signals in the circuit (Foo Kune *et al.*, 2013). Kasmi *et al.* investigated the threats of intentional EMI attacks on voice interfaces of smartphones (Kasmi *et al.*, 2015)). Esteves *et al.* demonstrated EMI voice command injections on smartphones through a conducted propagation path (Esteves *et al.*, 2018). It is also worth noting that Rasmussen et al. observed that EM emanations could induce sound signals in microphones and pointed out adversarial usage of this effect to invalidate security properties of acoustic-based distance bounding protocols in an early work (Rasmussen *et al.*, 2009).

Additionally, the Light Commands work recently demonstrated a long-distance attack by injecting amplitude-modulated laser signals into MEMS microphones to maliciously control voice assistant systems (Sugawara *et al.*, 2020).

Defending the Hardware Non-Linearity Based Attack

Recently there are some works to be designed to defend the non-linearity-based attack on microphone sensors especially.

He *et al.* show a way to defend the attack. In their experiment, they assume an attack signal is modulated to 40 kHz. The authors introduce guard signals, placing signals at 22 kHz, 42 kHz, and 62 kHz to modulate the attack signal to be lying within 10 kHz to 20 kHz, which will be used as a reference signal to cancel the recovered attack command. However, their system relies on playing the ultrasound in the environment. The side effect of the ultrasound on the body is still questionable (He *et al.* 2019).

Zhang *et al.* show another way to defend the attack. Their design is based on the different attenuation of the audible signal and inaudible signal. The ultrasound would attenuate much faster than the audible signal. Thus, when the signals hit a microphone array, the variance of the ultrasound would be much higher than the audible sound. By this, they could identify if the incoming command is a true command or a malicious command (Zhang *et al.* 2021).

Zhang and Rasmussen 2020, proposed to detect EMI attacks on sensors such as microphones by modulating the sensor output in a way that is unpredictable to the adversary. In their protocol, the system selectively turns sensors on and off based on an encoded secret bit sequence. In this way, EMI attacks causing inconsistent or unexpected non-zero samples can be detected.

Tu *et al.* discuss a low-complexity defense method against the intentional EMI injection attacks on sensors such as the microphone in a voice-controlled device. They implement the circuit on microphones using simple common components in low-end sensing systems to defend against the EMI injection attacks. Their experimental results show that the proposed method can detect the attack with high accuracy. Moreover, it can correct corrupted sensor data with a relatively high error reduction rate, improving the reliability and usability of sensor-based systems under EMI attacks (Tu *et al.*, 2021).

OBFUSCATED COMMANDS

This section discusses the Obfuscated Commands, how an attacker launches the Obfuscated Commands attack, and how to defend against such attacks is presented.

Obfuscated Commands

The obfuscated command creates an audio signal that humans perceive as meaningless sound while the voice assistant system recognizes it as a command. The attacker starts with a target command that is gradually changed until a human could not understand it while the voice assistant system can still decode the command.

For example, the voice assistant system is to transcribe speech to the corresponding text. This process can be defined as:

$$y = \arg\max_{\tilde{y}} p\left(\tilde{y} \mid x\right) \tag{6}$$

x here is the audio input, and $\tilde{y}$ are all possible transcription candidates. The voice assistant system aims to find the most likely transcription y given the audio input x. Once the voice assistant system has been trained, its function is $y = f(x)$. A human listening to the audio signal x also would conclude the same transcription y. This process can be described as $y = f_H(x)$, with f_H describing the human's processing capability. An adversary can modify an input signal x by adding perturbation δ, resulting in $x' = x+\delta$. The following situation arises when a system decodes x':

$$y = f\left(x'\right) \tag{7}$$

y here is the obfuscated command transcription which remains the same as the one decoded from pure input x. However, a human cannot perceive the same transcription y this time from the audio signal x'. The x' could be like noise to humans. The audio input x' is called the obfuscated command.

An attack relying on internal knowledge of the voice assistant system is referred to as a white box attack. If the attacker is not able to access the internal voice assistant workings, then the attack is classified as a black-box attack. Generally, attacks assuming the black box attack are more difficult to execute.

Attacks Based on Obfuscated Commands

The Cocaine Noodles'15 (Vaidya *et al.*, 2015) may be the first work that examines the gap between the human auditory system and modern Speech recognition system. The work received its name from an interesting thing. It was posted on Reddit that the phrase 'Cocaine Noodles' is often misinterpreted by Google Now as its wake word 'OK Google'.

In this work, the researchers successfully craft speech signals recognized by the speech recognition system but are incomprehensible for humans. In this work, the acoustic features are extracted via Mel frequency cepstrum coefficient (MFCC) from the raw audio input and are then fed into the acoustic model. They found MFCC can be tuned using a variety of parameters. So, it is possible to change these parameters so that the speech recognition system still recognizes the crafted commands as the correct command. This audio signal is unintelligible for humans, but the MFCC produces a feature set that results in the desired command being recognized.

The crafted samples are tested on Google Now on a Samsung Galaxy S4 smartphone by being played over the air in a large room with 50 dB background noise. The results show that these crafted signals can activate commands while they are difficult to understand.

Carlini et al. 2016, continued the work of the Cocaine Noodles'15 (Vaidya *et al.*, 2015), exploring how the system can be attacked by hidden voice commands which are able to be interpreted by the system but unintelligible to human beings.

The work reproduces the black box attack as described in Cocaine Noodles. Furthermore, the work describes a white-box attack showing that by knowing the system's parameters, commands that are better hidden from human ears can be crafted.

The black box attack uses a similar mechanism as the work in Cocaine Noodles but considers more practical settings and targets a newer Google ASR. For the white-box attack, with the knowledge of the target ASR, first, an attack similar to the black-box attack is launched by targeting specific MFCC vectors. They did not directly use the MFCC vectors. Instead of MFCC vectors, the attack aims at attack phrases and thus target phonemes, which enables the flexibility of different MFCC.

The work in (Abdullah *et al.,* 2019) considers a much more practical scenario. They try to attack the system combined with multiple acoustic hardware configurations without knowledge of the underlying systems. To make attack samples applicable for different systems, their work focuses on the signal processing phase. Signal features that are important for the human auditory system but not critical for speech recognition are selected. This results in obfuscated commands that can still be transcribed correctly to different systems but are not understandable to humans. Four aspects of signal features are selected: Time Domain Inversion, Random Phase Generation, High-Frequency Addition, and Time Scaling.

They tested their system on various systems, showing their commands could be generalized to different systems. However, the evaluation misses quantifying how unintelligible the generated samples are.

ADVERSARIAL COMMANDS

This section discusses Adversarial Commands, how an attacker generates the Adversarial Commands, and how to defend against such attacks is presented.

Adversarial Commands Background

Adversarial commands are based on the previously described obfuscated commands. The difference is that for an obfuscated command, the added perturbation results in a signal perceived by a human as noise while the system still successfully decodes the original command as the transcription y. In the case of the adversarial command, even with the added perturbation, a human still perceives the adversarial audio input x' as original benign command transcription y, while a system recognizes the audio input x' as the adversarial command transcription y'.

There are targeted and non-targeted adversarial commands. In the case of a targeted adversarial command, the attacker is interested in one specific command transcription T, which is carefully selected (y' = T). In the case of a non-targeted adversarial command, the attacker does not care about what specific command would be decoded by the system. The attacker only wants to ensure that human and machine transcription is not the same. This may affect the performance of some systems which analyze how people speak.

Figure 2 is an example of the general adversarial command signal generation process. Adversarial commands are generated through an iterative process. In each iteration, the output y of the deep neural network (the acoustic model) is compared with the target y' using a loss function. Then the gradient of the loss function with respect to the corresponding input is calculated through back-propagation. Finally, finding the input resulting in the local/global minimum ensures that the input is transcribed as the target command. In addition, the perturbation value is constrained by a threshold, ensuring that people cannot perceive the difference between the new signal and the original audio input.

Figure 2. Workflow of the voice assistant system.

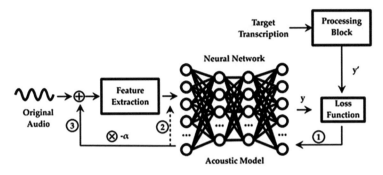

Adversarial Commands Attacks

Iter *et al.* show that it is possible to generate adversarial commands to fool Automatic Speech Recognition (ASR) systems by using methods that usually applied to image recognition. The attack assumes the ASR to be a white box, and targeting and non-targeting attacks are considered. To ensure similarity between the reconstructed audio and the original, an approximate inverse transformation function is used. However, due to the missing user study, it is unclear how "hidden" the produced adversarial commands are (Iter *et al, 2017*).

Alzantot *et al.* introduce a method for generating one-word targeted adversarial examples assuming a black-box ASR. Their attack is successful with an average rate of 87% and 89% of the participants in the user study cannot differentiate the adversarial command from the original command (Alzantot *et al.*, 2018).

Carlini *et al.* successfully construct white-box targeted adversarial commands for the DeepSpeech ASR. A small perturbation is added to the audio input, resulting in an audio signal that is over 99:9% similar to the input. This is the first robust, targeted adversarial attack study, resulting in an audio output that can be influenced such that theoretically, any chosen phrase can be transcribed (Carlini *et al.*, 2018).

Yuan *et al.* achieve an adversarial white-box attack by creating modified songs that are perceived by listeners as songs but recognized by the ASR as commands. Their commands play in the air; thus, real-world settings are considered. For the evaluation, 26 randomly picked songs with 12 common commands are directly fed to the ASR. And Over 200 songs are generated, and all of them succeed in being recognized by the ASR. The distortions range from 14 to 18.6dB, which is unlikely to be noticed (Yuan *et al.*, 2018).

DEFENDING THE ATTACKS

Recently, there have been several ways to detect the hidden voice way. There are mainly two different ways: the deep learning-based approaches and the liveness detection-based approach.

A recent work (Ahmed *et al.*, 2020) detects attacks by utilizing the different frequency distributions of the crafted and real signals. Different from the previous work, they classify the features by the SVM, which improves their efficiency. Moreover, it offers good performance on all the spoofing attacks and hidden voice commands, which shows their efficiency.

Liveness detection (Lee *et al.*, 2020) is another way. In their work, they use the smart speaker as a sonar, generating the signal to detect the direction of the people. If the direction of the source is the same as the people, then the command would be treated as a true command. Otherwise, it will be dropped. However, their system has a quite limited working range of 2 meters.

CONCLUSION

In this chapter, several different ways to attack a voice assistant system are surveyed. It is found that the research interest in recent years is concentrated on hidden voice commands. After investigating several types of hidden voice attacks, it is found that although the hidden voice attacks are accurate, how to make sure that they are imperceptible to humans is still questionable. So how to improve the imperceptibility should be studied.

REFERENCES

Abdullah, H., Garcia, W., Peeters, C., Traynor, P., Butler, K. R., & Wilson, J. (2019). *Practical hidden voice attacks against speech and speaker recognition systems.* arXiv preprint arXiv:1904.05734. doi:10.14722/ndss.2019.23362

Abdullah, H., Rahman, M. S., Garcia, W., Blue, L., Warren, K., Yadav, A. S., Shrimpton, T., & Traynor, P. (2019). *Hear no evil, see kenansville: Efficient and transferable black-box attacks on speech recognition and voice identification systems.* arXiv preprint arXiv:1910.05262.

Abdullah, H., Warren, K., Bindschaedler, V., Papernot, N., & Traynor, P. (2007). *The Faults in our ASRs: An Overview of Attacks against Automatic Speech Recognition and Speaker Identification Systems.* arXiv preprint arXiv:2007.06622.

Ahmed, M. E., Kwak, I.-Y., Huh, J. H., Kim, I., Oh, T., & Kim, H. (2020). Void: A fast and light voice liveness detection system. *29th USENIX Security Symposium (USENIX Security 20)*, 2685–2702.

Alegre, F., Vipperla, R., Evans, N., & Fauve, B. (2012). On the vulnerability of automatic speaker recognition to spoofing attacks with artificial signals. In *Proceedings of the 20th European signal processing conference (EUSIPCO)*. IEEE.

Alzantot, M., Balaji, B., & Srivastava, M. (2018). *Did you hear that? adversarial examples against automatic speech recognition.* arXiv preprint arXiv:1801.00554.

Benesty, Chen, & Huang. (2008). *Automatic speech recognition: a deep learning approach.* Academic Press.

Carlini, N., Mishra, P., Vaidya, T., Zhang, Y., Sherr, M., Shields, C., Wagner, D., & Zhou, W. (2016). Hidden voice commands. *25th USENIX Security Symposium (USENIX Security 16)*, 513–530.

Carlini, N., & Wagner, D. (2018). *Audio adversarial examples: Targeted attacks on speech-to-text. In 2018 IEEE Security and Privacy Workshops (SPW)*. IEEE.

Chen, T., Shangguan, L., Li, Z., & Jamieson, K. (2020). Metamorph: Injecting inaudible commands into over-the-air voice controlled systems. *Proceedings of NDSS.* 10.14722/ndss.2020.23055

Chen, Y., Yuan, X., Zhang, J., Zhao, Y., Zhang, S., Chen, K., & Wang, X. (2020). Devil's whisper: A general approach for physical adversarial attacks against commercial black-box speech recognition devices. *29th USENIX Security Symposium (USENIX Security 20)*, 2667–2684.

Cisse, A. Neverova, & Keshet. (2017). Houdini: Fooling deep structured visual and speech recognition models with adversarial examples. Advances in Neural Information Processing Systems, 30. doi:10.14722/ndss.2021.24551

De Leon, P. L., Pucher, M., Yamagishi, J., Hernaez, I., & Saratxaga, I. (2012). Evaluation of speaker verification security and detection of hmm-based synthetic speech. *IEEE Transactions on Audio, Speech, and Language Processing*, 20(8), 2280–2290. doi:10.1109/TASL.2012.2201472

Esteves, J. L., & Kasmi, C. (2018). *Remote and silent voice command injection on a smartphone through conducted IEMI: Threats of smart IEMI for information security.* Wireless Security Lab, French Network and Information Security Agency (ANSSI), Tech. Rep.

Giechaskiel, I., & Rasmussen, K. (2019, November 12). Taxonomy and challenges of out-of-band signal injection attacks and defenses. *IEEE Communications Surveys and Tutorials, 22*(1), 645–670.

Hautamaki, Kinnunen, Hautamaki, Leino, & Laukkanen. (2013). I-vectors meet imitators: on vulnerability of speaker verification systems against voice mimicry. Interspeech, 930–934.

He, Y., Bian, J., Tong, X., Qian, Z., Zhu, W., Tian, X., & Wang, X. (2019). Canceling inaudible voice commands against voice control systems. *The 25th Annual International Conference on Mobile Computing and Networking*, 1–15. 10.1145/3300061.3345429

Iter & Jermann. (2017). *Generating adversarial examples for speech recognition.* Stanford Technical Report.

Kasmi, C., & Esteves, J. L. (2015, August 13). IEMI threats for information security: Remote command injection on modern smartphones. *IEEE Transactions on Electromagnetic Compatibility, 57*(6), 1752–1755.

Kinnunen, T., Wu, Z.-Z., Lee, K. A., Sedlak, F., Chng, E. S., & Li, H. (2012). Vulnerability of speaker verification systems against voice conversion spoofing attacks: The case of telephone speech. In *2012 IEEE International Conference on Acoustics, Speech and Signal Processing (ICASSP)*. IEEE. 10.1109/ICASSP.2012.6288895

Kinnunen, Sahidullah, Delgado, Todisco, Evans, Yamagishi, & Lee. (2017). *The asvspoof 2017 challenge: Assessing the limits of replay spoofing attack detection.* Academic Press.

Lavrentyeva, G., Novoselov, S., Malykh, E., Kozlov, A., Kudashev, O., & Shchemelinin, V. (2017). Audio replay attack detection with deep learning frameworks. Interspeech, 82–86. doi:10.21437/Interspeech.2017-360

Lee, Y., Zhao, Y., Zeng, J., Lee, K., Zhang, N., Shezan, F. H., Tian, Y., Chen, K., & Wang, X. (2020). Using sonar for liveness detection to protect smart speakers against remote attackers. *Proceedings of the ACM on Interactive, Mobile, Wearable and Ubiquitous Technologies, 4*(1), 1–28. doi:10.1145/3380991

Lindberg, J., & Blomberg, M. (1999). Vulnerability in speaker verification-a study of technical impostor techniques. *Sixth European Conference on Speech Communication and Technology*.

Rasmussen, K. B., Castelluccia, C., Heydt-Benjamin, T. S., & Capkun, S. (2009). Proximity-based access control for implantable medical devices. *Proceedings of the 16th ACM conference on Computer and communications security*, 410-419.

Roy, N., Hassanieh, H., & Roy Choudhury, R. (2017). Backdoor: Making microphones hear inaudible sounds. *Proceedings of the 15th Annual International Conference on Mobile Systems, Applications, and Services*, 2–14. 10.1145/3081333.3081366

Roy, N., Shen, S., Hassanieh, H., & Choudhury, R. R. (2018). Inaudible voice commands: The long-range attack and defense. *15th USENIX Symposium on Networked Systems Design and Implementation (NSDI 18)*, 547–560.

Schonherr, L., Kohls, K., Zeiler, S., Holz, T., & Kolossa, D. (2018). *Adversarial ¨ attacks against automatic speech recognition systems via psychoacoustic hiding.* arXiv preprint arXiv:1808.05665.

Sugawara, T., Cyr, B., Rampazzi, S., Genkin, D., & Fu, K. (2020). Light commands: laser-based audio injection attacks on voice-controllable systems. *29th USENIX Security Symposium (USENIX Security 20),* 2631-2648.

Tom, F., Jain, M., & Dey, P. (2018). End-to-end audio replay attack detection using deep convolutional networks with attention. Interspeech, 681–685. doi:10.21437/Interspeech.2018-2279

Tu, Y., Lin, Z., Lee, I., & Hei, X. (2018). Injected and delivered: Fabricating implicit control over actuation systems by spoofing inertial sensors. *27th USENIX Security Symposium (USENIX Security 18),* 1545-1562.

Tu, Y., Rampazzi, S., Hao, B., Rodriguez, A., Fu, K., & Hei, X. (2019). Trick or heat? Manipulating critical temperature-based control systems using rectification attacks. *Proceedings of the 2019 ACM SIGSAC Conference on Computer and Communications Security*, 2301-2315.

Tu, Y., Tida, V. S., Pan, Z., & Hei, X. (2021). Transduction Shield: A Low-Complexity Method to Detect and Correct the Effects of EMI Injection Attacks on Sensors. *Proceedings of the 2021 ACM Asia Conference on Computer and Communications Security*, 901-915.

Vaidya, T., Zhang, Y., Sherr, M., & Shields, C. (2015). Cocaine noodles: exploiting the gap between human and machine speech recognition. *9th USENIX Workshop on Offensive Technologies (WOOT 15).*

Villalba, J., & Lleida, E. (2011). Detecting replay attacks from far-field recordings on speaker verification systems. In *European Workshop on Biometrics and Identity Management*. Springer. 10.1007/978-3-642-19530-3_25

Wu, Z., & Li, H. (2013). Voice conversion and spoofing attack on speaker verification systems. In *2013 Asia-Pacific Signal and Information Processing Association Annual Summit and Conference*. IEEE. 10.1109/APSIPA.2013.6694344

Yan, C., Shin, H., Bolton, C., Xu, W., Kim, Y., & Fu, K. (2020). Sok: A minimalist approach to formalizing analog sensor security. In *2020 IEEE Symposium on Security and Privacy (SP)* (pp. 233-248). IEEE.

Yuan, X., Chen, Y., Zhao, Y., Long, Y., Liu, X., Chen, K., Zhang, S., Huang, H., Wang, X., & Gunter, C. A. (2018). Commandersong: A systematic approach for practical adversarial voice recognition. *27th USENIX Security Symposium (USENIX Security 18)*, 49–64.

Zhang, G., X. L. G. Q. W. X., & Ji, X. (2011). Eararray: defending against dolphinattack via acoustic attenuation. *The Network and Distributed System Security Symposium (NDSS)*.

Zhang, G., Yan, C., Ji, X., Zhang, T., Zhang, T., & Xu, W. (2017). Dolphin attack: Inaudible voice commands. *Proceedings of the 2017 ACM SIGSAC Conference on Computer and Communications Security*, 103–117. 10.1145/3133956.3134052

Zhang, L., Tan, S., & Yang, J. (2017). Hearing your voice is not enough: An articulatory gesture based liveness detection for voice authentication. *Proceedings of the 2017 ACM SIGSAC Conference on Computer and Communications Security*, 57–71. 10.1145/3133956.3133962

Zhang, Y., & Rasmussen, K. (2020). Detection of electromagnetic interference attacks on sensor systems. In *2020 IEEE Symposium on Security and Privacy (SP)* (pp. 203-216). IEEE.

Chapter 5
Survey of Automotive Cyber–Physical System Security

Michael Arienmughare
University of Louisiana at Lafayette, USA

Andrew S. Yoshimura
University of Louisiana at Lafayette, USA

Md Abdullah Al Momin
University of Louisiana at Lafayette, USA

ABSTRACT

This chapter will provide a survey on cyber-physical systems security related to automobiles. In modern vehicles, there has been discussion on how automobiles fit into the world of cyber-physical systems, considering their interaction with both the cyber and physical worlds and interconnected systems. With many modern vehicles being connected to the outside world, there are many vulnerabilities introduced. Modern cars contain many electronic control units and millions of lines of code, which, if compromised, could have fatal consequences. Interfaces to the outside world (e.g., in-vehicle infotainment) may be used as a vector to attack these critical components.

INTRODUCTION

This chapter will provide a survey on Cyber-Physical Systems (CPS) security related to automobiles. There has been discussion on how automotive fits into the world of Cyber-Physical Systems in modern vehicles, considering their interaction with both the cyber and physical worlds and interconnected systems.

DOI: 10.4018/978-1-7998-7323-5.ch005

With many modern vehicles being connected to the outside world (*e.g.,* V2X infrastructure), there are many vulnerabilities introduced. Modern cars contain many electronic control units and millions of lines of code, which, if compromised, could have fatal consequences. Interfaces to the outside world (e.g., in-vehicle infotainment) may be used as a vector to attack these critical components.

The structure of this chapter is as follows. First, the definition of Cyber-Physical Systems will be discussed briefly. Then different components of automotive will be discussed and why they are considered CPSs. Finally, after understanding the different components of automotive CPSs, the security and threats of various components of modern vehicles will be discussed.

CYBER-PHYSICAL SYSTEMS

Cyber-Physical Systems can be defined as engineered systems built from, and depend upon, the seamless integration of computation and physical components. CPS tightly integrate computing devices, actuation and control, networking infrastructure, and sensing of the physical world".

In a survey of CPS, Khaitan, and McCalley classify existing work and identify challenges. They discuss the challenges involved in ensuring the security of cyber-physical systems and discuss work done to detect and prevent intrusions and cyber-attacks. They note that CPSs have various applications, such as in vehicular systems, medical and healthcare systems, smart homes, buildings, etc. (Khaitan *et al.*, 2015). In discussing security-related aspects of cyber-physical systems, Khaitan and McCalley describe securing a CPS as "extremely challenging" due to how interconnected the various components of CPSs are. Since many components depend on each other, if one component fails, it may have a "cascading effect" (Khaitan *et al.*, 2015).

Chattopadhyay and Lam describe a generic attack model for CPSs (Chattopadhyay *et al.*, 2017) (Figure 1). It breaks the attacks into cyber and physical components, discussing possible threats for each. While this is just a generic model and does not cover specific CPSs, the figure is essential in broadly understanding the attack capabilities on CPSs.

Figure 1. Generic CPS attack model.
Figure from (Chattopadhyay et al., 2017)

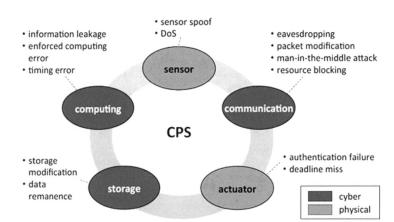

Automotive Cyber-Physical Systems

Before diving into the security threats posed to automotive CPSs, it is first needed to understand its different components. Security of automotive systems has become increasingly important with the evolution of automotive technology. Modern vehicles are now considered CPSs, "which provide enhanced displays, information, and entertainment and manage motion and energy consumption of the automotive" (Khaitan *et al.*, 2015). Khaitan *et al.* mention various examples of works on automotive CPSs, including data fusion, public transport, design of cyber-physical vehicles, electric vehicle charging, and road monitoring (Khaitan *et al.* 2015).

One increasingly popular example of automotive CPSs is autonomous vehicles. There has been much work on autonomous vehicles as cyber-physical systems. Chattopadhyay and Lam (Chattopadhyay et al. 2017) review the security objectives of Autonomous Vehicles and argue that they are a "kind of Cyber-Physical System (CPS) for control and operations of the vehicle."

Considering that modern automotive systems are becoming increasingly complex (*e.g.*, some modern vehicles have 200M+ lines of code, 200+ electronic control units (Simacsek *et al.*)), many vulnerabilities need to be considered and safeguarded against.

Scalas and Giacinto (Scalas *et al.* 2019) list the constraints of vehicle software and hardware (as summarized by Studnia *et al.* 2013 and Pike *et al.* 2017), paraphrased here:

- Hardware limitations: Car ECUs have low computing power/memory; things like public-key encryption are not completely possible; ECUs are exposed to "demanding conditions" (*e.g.*, harsh weather, vibrations, *etc.*.); ECUs must not be too heavy or physically large.
- Timing: Several ECUs operate in real-time and are "safety-critical", meaning security must be prioritized for them.
- Autonomy: The vehicle should be as autonomous as possible when protection mechanisms are active since the driver must focus on the road.
- Life-cycle: Vehicle last much longer than consumer electronics, so the hardware must be durable and the software must be easily updatable.
- Supplier integration: Suppliers provide software components without source code to protect intellectual property, making it difficult to modify for increased security.
- CAN: The Controller Area Network is the "most used protocol for the in-vehicle network" and serves as the backbone of the entire in-vehicle network. It is implemented with twisted pair wires. An essential aspect is the network topology, implemented as a bus line.
- Automotive Ethernet: Ethernet's high bandwidth is a desirable feature for modern automobiles. However, the cost and weight are key limitations.

Scalas and Giacinto also describe the OBD (on-board diagnostics), which has a physical port that allows for "self-diagnostic capabilities" for the identification of failures of specific components. It is directly connected to the CAN bus, which presents a significant security threat.

Moreover, many autonomous vehicles communicate with the outside world via a V2X infrastructure. The aim of this infrastructure is primarily related to ensuring the safety of the driver and those around them. V2X communications may reveal the danger that could not be previously sensed by onboard equipment (Mueck *et al.*, 2018). V2X includes vehicle-to-vehicle, vehicle-to-infrastructure, and vehicle-to-pedestrian communications. The V2X infrastructure presents many security concerns, considering that vehicles are connected to many aspects of the outside world.

AUTOMOTIVE CPS SECURITY

Threats Classification

Security threats for automotive have previously been classified using a three-layer hierarchical system, also known as the AutoVSCC (Autonomous Vehicular Sensing Communication and Control) framework described by El-Rewini *et al.*, 2019. Figure

2 shows the framework containing a separate layer for sensing, communication, and control. They represent the three layers as follows:

At the bottom of the hierarchy is the sensing layer, which is vulnerable to spoofing and eavesdropping attacks on vehicle sensors, such as the inertial or radar sensors. Above the sensing layer is the communication layer, which encompasses both inter-vehicular and intra-vehicular communications and is vulnerable to eavesdropping attacks and the manipulation of messages between vehicles and roadside infrastructure. The communication layer is also susceptible to threats that propagate upward from the sensing layer, which is made of vehicular sensors. Threats to both the sensing and communication layers can affect the topmost tier, the control layer, which describes automated vehicular control techniques, such as vehicle speed and steering control.

Figure 2. Autonomous vehicular sensing-communication-control (AutoVSCC) framework.
Figure from El-Rewini et al,. 2019

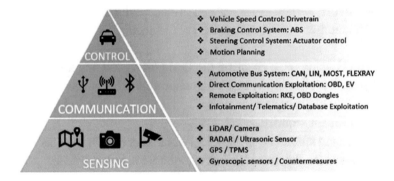

Sensing Layer

In this section, the summary of the sensing layer threats, as detailed by El-Rewini *et al.* is provided. They build on their AutoVSCC classification discussed earlier (El-Rewini *et al.*, 2020).

They state that the sensing layer is "comprised of vehicular sensors that measure the physical properties of a vehicle's state and surroundings" and state that it is critical to "smooth vehicle operation." The sensing layer contains 60-100 sensors, with a possibility for more in the future.

El-rewini *et al.* classify the sensors in the sensing layer into "environment sensors" and "vehicle dynamics sensors." Vehicle dynamics sensors sense the vehicle's state, and environment sensors look at the vehicle's physical surroundings. Vehicle dynamics sensors are described as passive sensors, which are receivers, and most environment sensors are described as active sensors, which are both emitters and receivers (El-Rewini *et al.*, 2020). Figure 3 shows the environment and vehicle dynamics sensors in a modern vehicle.

Based on information from Wang et al., 2006, El-Rewini *et al.* state that the following security requirements must be met for defending against vehicular sensor exploitation: availability, authorization, confidentiality, freshness, and integrity (El-Rewini *et al.*, 2020).

Sensing Layer: Vehicle Dynamics Sensors

Vehicle dynamics sensors include magnetic-based sensors, inertial sensors, and TPMS sensors, as shown in Figure 3.

1. **Magnetic-Based Sensors:** Shoukry *et al.* discuss disruptive and spoofing attacks for Anti-lock Braking Systems, which rely on "magnetic-based wheel speed sensors which are exposed to an external attacker from underneath the body of the vehicle." Their proposed technique places a non-intrusive, malicious actuator near the ABS wheel sensors to inject magnetic fields and tamper with sensor measurements. They explore a disruptive attack that "corrupts the measured wheel speed by overwhelming the original signal" and a spoofing attack that injects "a counter-signal such that the braking system mistakenly reports a specific velocity." They demonstrate that this type of attack can cause the ABS controller to fail to brake (via spoofed wheel speed measurements) and slip off an icy road (Shoukry *et al.*, 2013).

2. **Inertial Sensors:** Inertial sensors consist of accelerometers for measuring the acceleration of an object they are attached to and gyroscopes for measuring the rotation rate with respect to a specific axis (El-Rewini *et al.*, 2020). Spoofing attacks involve injecting sound waves to "deceive" inertial sensors: "Side-swing" attacks involve the attacker changing the injected waveform's amplitude to manipulate the vehicle's heading value (Tu *et al.*, 2018); Switching attacks involve alternating between injected waveforms of different frequencies to induce phase pacing (Tu *et al.*, 2018). Acoustic attacks involve targeting MEMS gyroscopes and accelerometers and falsifying acoustic waves with the same frequency of the load resonant frequency of the CPS (Moller *et al.*, 2018).

3. **TPMS Systems:** Rouf et al. showed that wireless Tire Pressure Monitoring Systems (TPMS) were vulnerable to reverse engineering attacks. Based

on information found in the reverse engineering attack, they were able to demonstrate an eavesdropping attack to intercept TPMS packets from a range of up to 40 m from a passing car. They were further able to spoof a TPMS message to light up the low-tire pressure warning lights on a car traveling "highway speeds." This was possible because TPMS system messages are not authenticated and the TPMS ECU doesn't use any input validation. They also managed to completely disable the TPMS ECU by repeatedly turning on and off the warning lights through the previously described method (Rouf *et al.*, 2010).

Figure 3. Vehicle dynamics sensors (Blue) and environment sensors (Green) in autonomous and connected vehicles.
Figure from (El-Rewini et al.2020)

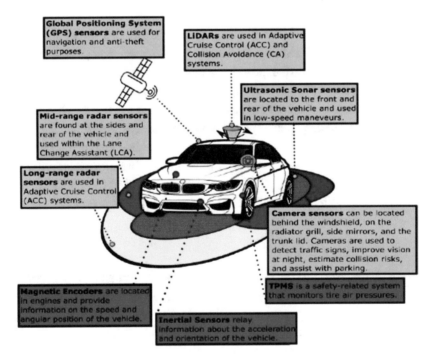

Sensing Layers: Environment Sensors

Environment sensors include LiDAR, ultrasonic sensors, camera sensors, radars, and GPS systems, as shown in Figure 3.

1. **LiDAR Systems:** Light Imaging Detection and Ranging (LiDAR) systems are used to generate 3D mappings of the vehicle's surroundings and are used for things like adaptive cruise control and collision avoidance (El-Rewini *et al.*, 2020).

Replay attacks allow attackers to replay LiDAR signals and cause them to map objects that are not there (Stottelaar *et al.*, 2015). Relay attacks are an extension of replay attacks, where attackers can relay around LiDAR signals to result in an incorrectly reported map location of nearby objects (Petit et al. 2015). Blinding attacks deny services to the vehicle by injecting a light source that has the same wavelength as the LiDAR's pulses (Shin *et al.* 2017). Spoofing attacks spoof a LiDAR system to cause it to over calculate (Petit *et al.* 2015) or under calculate (Shin et al. 2017) distance to an obstacle. Jamming attacks emit light with the same frequency band as the scanner unit on a vehicle (Parkinson *et al.* 2017). Denial of service attacks is performed by injecting many fake objects using the jamming or spoofing attacks mentioned previously (Stottelaar *et al.*, 2015).

2. **Ultrasonic sensors:** Ultrasonic sensors are used to detect nearby obstacles and calculate their distance to a vehicle by calculating the time between transmission and reception of a reflected ultrasonic signal. Ultrasonic sensors are usually used for low-speed tasks like parking (El-Rewini *et al.*, 2020).

Blind Spot Exploitation attacks are performed by placing a thin object in a reversing vehicle's blind spot so the vehicle will collide with the object (Lim *et al.*, 2018). Sensor Interference attacks are performed by placing a second ultrasonic sensor opposite to the vehicle's sensor to interfere with the signals received (Lim *et al.* 2018). Cloaking attacks conceal nearby objects from the ultrasonic sensor by placing some sound-absorbent materials around obstacles so the sensor cannot detect them (Lim *et al.* 2018 & Yan *et al.*, 2016). Physical Tampering attacks work by covering the sensor's receiver and transmitter to disable the ultrasonic sensor (Lim et al., 2018). Acoustic Cancellation attacks eliminate legitimate ultrasonic signals by transmitting an illegitimate signal with a phase that is opposite of the legitimate signal, causing the phase to become zero (Lee *et al.*, 2019). Spoofing attacks use false signals to "falsely" perceive an object that does not exist, with three different types of spoofing attacks (simple, random, advanced) (Yan *et al.*, 2016 & Xu *et al.*, 2018). Jamming attacks are performed by continually sending ultrasound pulses toward an ultrasonic sensor, causing the sensor to lose its ability to calculate the distance to other nearby objects (Yan *et al.*, 2016, Xu *et al.*, 2018 & Lee *et al.*, 2019).

3. **Cameras:** Cameras are used in automated vehicles to identify the vehicle's surroundings. They are used to identify things like traffic signs, hard-to-see objects in low-lighting conditions, showing nearby objects while parking, avoiding collisions, and verifying information from other sensors (El-Rewini *et al.*, 2020).

Blinding attacks shoot a laser beam at the camera to disable it, possibly leading to "vehicle distortion" or emergency braking (Yan *et al.*, 2016 & Petit *et al.*, 2015). Auto-Control attacks shoot bursts of light at the camera to manipulate the auto controls (rather than "maxing them out" like in the blinding attack), so the image can't stabilize (Petit *et al.*, 2015).

4. **Radars:** Radar sensors "emit electromagnetic signals and gauge the distance of nearby objects by determining the time elapsed from the moment the signal is sent to the moment the signal is detected by the radar's receiver" (El-Rewini *et al.*, 2020).

Jamming attacks jam the radar sensors with a signal on the same frequency band, causing the radar to lose its ability to detect nearby objects (Lopez *et al.*, 2019 & Yan *et al.*, 2016). Spoofing/Relay attacks involve the attacker falsifying signals and continually re-transmitting a previous legitimate signal (Lopez *et al.*, 2019 & Petit *et al.*, 2014).

5. **GPS Systems:** Global positioning systems (GPS) are used to gather geographic locations. "GPS satellites send navigation messages to on-ground receivers, which then calculate their distance to satellites by using the message's time of transmission and arrival. Receivers can determine their location by calculating their distance to at least four different satellites" (El-Rewini *et al.*, 2020).

Jamming attacks jam GPS sensor signals to prevent the sensor from locating the vehicle. It is one of the simplest attacks as GPS jammers are cheap and easy to obtain (Petit et al., 2014). Spoofing attacks involve overwhelming the GPS signal to compromise data integrity (Narain *et al.* 2019) or tampering with the GPS receiver, so it reports false locations/times (Lopez *et al.*, 2019 & Zhang et al., 2018). Black Hole attacks involve the attacker causing the loss of information that should have been forwarded from one vehicle to another in a VANET (Jadoon *et al.* 2018).

Communication Layer

This section will summarize the communication layer threats, as detailed by El-Rewini *et al.* 2019.

Vehicular communications can occur both internally and externally (El-Rewini *et al.*, 2019). In-vehicle communication occurs among Electronic Control Units (ECUs) within a vehicle's electronic subsystems (Eiza *et al.*, 2017 & Carsten *et al.*, 2015). The main features of an in-vehicle network are shown in Figure 4:

Figure 4. Main domains in a modern car.
Figure from El-Rewini et al. 2019.

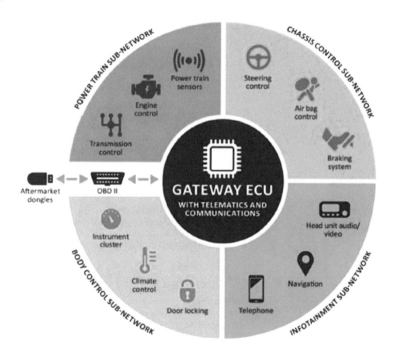

The external vehicular communication occurs from USBs, Remote Keyless Entry systems, and V2X communication. Connected and autonomous vehicles are able to operate as nodes within self-organized vehicular ad-hoc networks (VANETs) (Jadoon *et al.* 2018). According to El-Rewini *et al.* 2019, VANETs are primarily composed of On-Board Units (OBUs) and Road-Side Units (RSUs):

OBUs are wireless transmitters installed within V2X-capable vehicles. OBU-equipped vehicles can communicate with one another and with Road-Side Units

(RSUs), which are stationary devices located along roads and infrastructure that can provide internet connectivity for OBUs and report on the state of traffic. OBU and RSU nodes can transmit and receive messages over the wireless network. They are able to enter into communication with surrounding nodes and exit from these communications when the nodes are no longer in range (Jadoon et al., 2018 & Lu et al., 2019). To protect against malicious transmissions, Trust Authorities (TAs) perform authenticity checks and remove malicious nodes within VANETs (Lu et al., 2019). In this way, real-time information about vehicles and infrastructure can be transmitted to increase road safety and efficiency and ultimately work to support fully automated and driverless vehicles.

Figure 5. Cyber vulnerabilities in a vehicular ecosystem.
Figure from El-Rewini et al., 2019

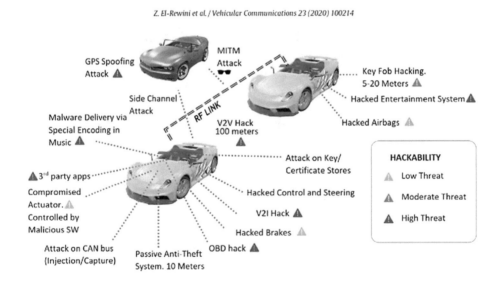

Z. El-Rewini et al. / Vehicular Communications 23 (2020) 100214

Figure 5 shows how attackers can target vehicular communication. Vehicular communications must meet the following security requirements: confidentiality, integrity, availability, non-repudiation, privacy, real-time constraints, and flexibility (Dak *et al.*, 2012).

Communication Layer: Automotive Bus System Exploitation

Automotive bus systems in the in-vehicle network enable ECUs in one electronic subsystem to communicate with one another and with other subsystems. Fig. 6 shows a common architecture for the in-vehicle network, where "different subsystems are connected to one another and to external networks through the use of a gateway" (El-Rewini *et al.* 2019).

Figure 6. A common in-vehicle network architecture based on (Deng et al. 2017, Petit et al. 2015 & Henniger et al., 2009).
Figure from El-Rewini et al., 2019

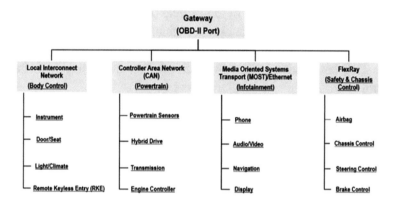

Communication protocols transmit messages within each subsystem and between different subsystems (El-Rewini *et al.* 2019). CAN is the most used network protocol and serves as the backbone of the entire in-vehicle network.

1. **CAN:** CAN broadcasts packets to all nodes in the network. Each node must then accept or reject packets based on if the message is relevant to it (Carsten et al. 2015 & Liu et al. 2017). Ueda et al. 2015, identify use cases for CAN attacks: replacing an authorized ECU program with a malicious program and using an unauthorized device to connect to the CAN bus. One major downside of the CAN frame is that it is generally unable to support Message Authentication Code (MAC) (El-Rewini *et al.* 2019).
2. **CAN Security Threats:** CAN security threats include masquerading, eavesdropping, injection, replay, Denial of Service (DoS), and bus-off attacks.

For masquerading attacks, an attacker masquerades as a legitimate node. Liu et al. 2017 and Choi *et al.* 2018, discuss two CAN vulnerabilities that allow masquerading attacks: CAN frames are not encrypted and can be studied by attackers to find system entry points. Message authentication is not supported (Liu *et al.* 2017 & Choi *et al.* 2018).

Eavesdropping attacks allow unauthorized users to gain access to vehicular messages. CAN's broadcast transmissions allow attackers to gain access to the in-vehicle network and eavesdrop on CAN transmissions. This lets the attackers identify patterns in legitimate CAN frames (Liu et al. 2017).

In injection attacks, fake messages are injected into the automotive bus system. Some common entry points to the in-vehicle network include: OBD-II ports, compromised ECUs, or infotainment and telematics systems (Liu *et al.*, 2017).

In replay attacks, an attacker re-sends valid frames over and over in order to impede the real-time functioning of the vehicle (Liu *et al.*, 2017).

Bus-off attacks occur when attackers continually send bits in the identifier and other fields. This causes the ECU's transmit error counter (TEC) to be incremented. When the TEC has a value greater than 255, the corresponding ECU has to shut down (Choi *et al.*, 2018).

In terms of denial of service (DoS) attacks, Liu et al. 2017, show a DoS attack when an attacker sends high priority messages that block legitimate low priority messages. This is because the identifier segment of a CAN packet determines message priority. Thus attackers can easily assign their identifier segment a low value and gain high priority status. Carsten et al., 2015, also showed that DoS attacks could be used as a means to carry out control override attacks.

Communication Layer: Infotainment and Telematics Exploitation

Jaisingh *et al.* 2016, stated that information that is provided by infotainment systems could include "voice calls, text messages, emails, social networking, personal contacts," and other forms of data that can be received by connecting to a mobile phone. Bernardini *et al.* 2017, discussed security and privacy in vehicular communications and found that some advanced infotainment systems enable mirroring, which enables a mobile device's screen to be shown on a vehicle's screen. According to Jaisingh *et al.* 2016, telematics systems complement infotainment systems by providing information on internal vehicular systems, which includes "fuel efficiency, engine failures, brake pad wear, transmission issues, oil life, climate control, biometric sensors, vehicle speed, acceleration, direction, braking, cornering, ignition, steering, seat belts, door locking, tire pressure and recently visited destinations including routes traveled."

1. **Infotainment and Telematics Threats:** Infotainment and telematics systems are susceptible to control override attacks and injection attacks.

For control override attacks, an attacker may override the vehicle operator's attempts to take corrective action. In one instance, Jo *et al.* 2017, show security risks in Android OS-based telematics systems that let drivers remotely unlock and lock car doors, start and stop the car engine using low-speed CAN, and access diagnostic information using high-speed CAN.

Injection attacks let an attacker inject illegitimate and malicious messages within the In-Vehicle network. Mazloom *et al.* 2016, show that the Mirror Link protocol, which links smartphones to vehicular infotainment systems, has security vulnerabilities that could allow an attacker to gain access to the in-vehicle network and inject malicious messages.

Communication Layer: Vehicular Port Exploitation

Vehicles now come equipped with ports that enable access to various data such as maintenance information, entertainment, and synchronizing of mobile devices and charging of electric cars. These ports also serve as attack points to gain access to the In-Vehicle Network (IVN). Hence, vulnerabilities of the On-Board Diagnostics port, USB port, and the electric vehicle charging port is considered for discussion.

1. **OBD-II Ports:** OBD-II is an onboard computer that monitors emissions, mileage, speed, and other data about your car. It's connected to the Check Engine light, which illuminates when the computer detects a problem. The OBD-II onboard computer features a 16-pin port located under the driver's side dash. It allows a mechanic or anyone else to read the error code using a special scan tool. OBD-II ports are vulnerable to IVN access attacks and dongle exploitation attacks.

    Carsten et al. 2015, studied OBD vulnerabilities and found that it allows access to the IVN and installation of malware. Valasek *et al.* 2014, were able to connect to the OBD-II port using an ECOM cable and proceeded to transmit and receive messages over CAN.

    For dongle exploitation attacks, Eiza *et al.* 2017 found that dongles plugged into OBD-II ports can be exploited via remote control. Kovelman *et al.* 2017, reported a remote attack on the bosch drive log connector dongle, which connects to a vehicle's OBDII port. A brute force attack enabled the attackers to connect to the dongle via Bluetooth and send malicious transmissions over the CAN, which led to the engine failure of the vehicle.

2. **USB Ports:** Security Research Labs showed that USB peripherals could be exploited by attackers. They were able to reprogram USB controller chips and install malware, spoof network cars, and small viruses that targeted the operating

system. Cai *et al.* 2019, showed that the USB port could be used to create a backdoor within the BMW Next Best Thing (NBT) vehicle entertainment system.

3.   **Electric Vehicle Charging Infrastructure:** According to Mustafa *et al.* 2013, EV charging is susceptible to masquerading, tampering, eavesdropping, DOS attacks, privacy concerns, and charging thievery. Fries and Falk *et al.* 2012, discuss EV charging susceptibility to eavesdropping, man-in-the-middle, and tampering attacks on the payment price and the amount of energy that the meter believes the EV has received. They also discuss the potential for malicious software within the vehicle to affect a charging station or a compromised charging station to affect an EV.

Sun *et al.* 2015, show that an EV location's privacy can be compromised when it is close to a charging station.

Alcaraz *et al.* 2017, identify security threats within the Open Charge Point Protocol (OCPP), which is used in communications between charging stations and a smart grid's central energy management system. Sun et al. 2015, show that an EV location's privacy can be compromised when it is close to a charging station.

Lee et al. 2014, show that some protocols used within EV charging are not secure. Attackers can take advantage of vulnerabilities within the ISO/IEC 15188 protocol to assume another vehicle's identity by manipulating an identification number, which is stored in the EV's internal storage. They can also manipulate message properties to illegally charge more than the EV requires. Other identified threats to ISO/IEC 15188 include manipulating meter statuses, payment types, and tariff table type messages. Attackers can reduce/eliminate the charging price or even shut off a charging station's service.

CONCLUSION

Cyber-Physical Systems are ubiquitous in our everyday lives. Applications of CPSs range from health care systems to smart homes to modern vehicles (Khaitan *et al.*, 2015). Detailed discussions on the threats applicable to automotive Cyber-Physical Systems are discussed throughout the chapter. Due to their complex and interconnected nature, most modern vehicles are now considered CPSs.

The threats to the sensing and communication aspects of automotive cyber-physical systems as described by El-Rewini *et al.* 2019 & 2020, are summarized. They define a three-tier framework for security threats in modern vehicles, known as the AutoVSCC (Autonomous Vehicular Sensing Communication and Control) Framework. This framework breaks down security threats into three tiers: sensing, communication, and control.

It is clear that automotive Cyber-Physical Systems are susceptible to many types of threats, with some even having fatal consequences. Therefore, it should be the top priority to ensure the security of the various components of modern vehicles. As suggested by Scalas and Giacinto, following secure-by-design practices when designing vehicles is likely the best way to ensure the safety of modern vehicles (Scalas *et al.* 2019). As seen in the framework described by El-Rewini *et al.* 2020, threats are able to propagate through different components of the vehicle, which means attackers could even compromise crucial control components of a vehicle by attacking other components that were not previously thought of as security threats.

In conclusion, it is observed that there is much prior work on automotive CPS security, and possibly it is headed in the right direction. As vehicles become even more complex, more threats are bound to appear. But following more secure protocols for the design of vehicles may help mitigate this.

REFERENCES

Alcaraz, C., Lopez, J., & Wolthusen, S. (2017). *OCPP protocol: Security threats and challenges* (Vol. 8). IEEE.

Bernardini, C., Asghar, M., & Crispo, B. (2017). Security and privacy in vehicular communications: Challenges and opportunities. *Vehicular Communications*, *10*, 13–28.

Cai, Wang, & Zhang. (2019). *0-days and mitigations: roadways to exploit and secure connected bmw cars*. Academic Press.

Carsten, P., Yampolskiy, M., Andel, T. R., & Mcdonald, J. T. (2015). In-vehicle networks: Attacks, vulnerabilities, and proposed solutions. CISR, 1, 1–8.

Chattopadhyay, A., & Lam, K. (2017). Security of autonomous vehicle as a cyber-physical system. *2017 7th International Symposium on Embedded Computing and System Design (ISED)*, 1–6.

Choi, W., Joo, K., Jo, H., Park, M., & Lee, D. (2018). *Voltageids: lowlevel communication characteristics for automotive intrusion detection system* (Vol. 13). IEEE.

Cyber-physical systems (CPS). (n.d.). Available: https://www.nsf.gov/pubs/2021/nsf21551/nsf21551.htm

Cyber security and resilience of smart cars. (2016). Available: https://www.enisa.europa.eu/publications/cyber-security-and-resilience-of-smart-cars

Dak, A. Y., Yahya, S., & Kassim, M. (2012). A literature survey on security challenges in vanets. *International Journal of Computer Theory and Engineering*, *4*(627).

Deng, J., Yu, L., Fu, L., Oluwakemi, H., & Brooks, R. (2017). *Security and data privacy of modern automobiles, in: Data analytics for intelligent transport systems*. Elsevier.

Eiza, M. H., & Ni, Q. (2017). Driving with sharks: rethinking connected vehicles with vehicle cybersecurity. IEEE.

El-Rewini, Sadatsharan, Selvaraj, Plathottam, & Prakash. (2019). Cybersecurity challenges in vehicular communications. *Vehicular Communications*, *23*.

El-Rewini, Sadatsharan, Sugunaraj, Selvaraj, Plathottam, & Ranganathan. (2020). Cybersecurity attacks in vehicular sensors. *IEEE Sensors Journal*, *20*(22), 752–767.

Fries & Falk. (2012). Electric vehicle charging infrastructure-security considerations and approaches. *INTERNET 2012*.

Henniger, O., Apvrille, L., Fuchs, A., Roudier, Y., Ruddle, A., & Weyl, B. (2009). *Security requirements for automotive on-board networks*. ITST.

Jadoon, Wang, Li, & Zia. (2018). Lightweight cryptographic techniques for automotive cybersecurity. *Wireless Communications and Mobile Computing*, 1–15.

Jaisingh, R. A. K., & El-Khatib, K. (2016). Paving the way for intelligent transport systems (its): Privacy implications of vehicle infotainment and telematics systems. DIVANet, 25–31.

Jo, H., Choi, W., Na, S., Woo, S., & Lee, D. (2017). Vulnerabilities of android os-based telematics system. *Wireless Personal Communications*, 1512–1530.

Khaitan, S. K., & McCalley, J. D. (2015). Design techniques and applications of cyberphysical systems: A survey. *IEEE Systems Journal*, *9*(2), 350–365.

Kovelman. (2017). *A remote attack on the bosch drivelog connector dongle-argus cyber security*. Academic Press.

Lee, Choi, & Lee. (2019). Securing ultrasonic sensors against signal injection attacks based on a mathematical model. *IEEE Access*, *7*, 716–729.

Lee, S., Park, Y., Lim, H., & Shon, T. (2014). Study on analysis of security vulnerabilities and countermeasures in iso/iec 15118 based electric vehicle charging technology. *International Conference on IT Convergence and Security*.

Lim, B., Keoh, S., & Thing, V. (2018). Autonomous vehicle ultrasonic sensor vulnerability and impact assessment. *2018 IEEE 4th World Forum on Internet of Things (WF-IoT)*, 231–236.

Liu, J., & Zhang, S. (2017). In-vehicle network attacks and countermeasures: Challenges and future directions. *IEEE Systems Journal*, *31*(5), 50–58.

Lopez, A., Malawade, A. V., Al Faruque, M. A., Boddupalli, S., & Ray, S. (2019). Security of emergent automotive systems: A tutorial introduction and perspectives on practice. *IEEE Design Test*, *36*(6), 10–38.

Lu, Z., Qu, G., & Liu, Z. (2019). A survey on recent advances in vehicular network security, trust, and privacy. IEEE.

Mazloom, S., Rezaeirad, M., Hunter, A., & Mccoy, D. (2016). *A security analysis of an in-vehicle infotainment and app platform*. WOOT.

Moller, D., Jehle, I. A., & Haas, R. E. (2018). Challenges for vehicular cyber-security. *2018 IEEE International Conference on Electro/Information Technology (EIT)*, 428–433.

Mueck, M., & Karls, I. (2018). *Networking vehicles to everything: evolving automotive solutions*. Walter de Gruyter Inc.

Mustafa, M., Zhang, N., Kalogridis, G., & Fan, Z. (2013). *Smart electric vehicle charging: Security analysis*. IEEE PES.

Narain, S., Ranganathan, A., & Noubir, G. (2019). Security of gps/ins based on-road location tracking systems. *2019 IEEE Symposium on Security and Privacy (SP)*, 587–601.

Parkinson, Ward, Wilson, & Miller. (2017). Cyber threats facing autonomous and connected vehicles: Future challenges. *IEEE Transactions on Intelligent Transportation Systems*, *18*, 1–18.

Petit & Shladover. (2014). Potential cyberattacks on automated vehicles. *Intelligent Transportation Systems, IEEE Transactions on*.

Petit, Stottelaar, & Feiri. (2015). *Remote attacks on automated vehicles sensors: Experiments on camera and lidar*. Academic Press.

Petit, S. S. J. (2015). *Potential cyberattacks on automated vehicles*. IEEE.

Pike, L., Sharp, J., Tullsen, M., Hickey, P. C., & Bielman, J. (2017, May). Secure automotive software: The next steps. *IEEE Software*, *34*(03), 49–55.

Rouf, I., Miller, R., Mustafa, H., Taylor, T., Oh, S., Xu, W., Gruteser, M., Trappe, W., & Seskar, I. (2010). Security and privacy vulnerabilities of in-car wireless networks: A tire pressure monitoring system case study. In *Proceedings of the 19th USENIX Conference on Security.* USENIX Association.

Scalas, M., & Giacinto, G. (2019). Automotive cybersecurity: Foundations for next-generation vehicles. Academic Press.

Shin, H., Kim, D., Kwon, Y., & Kim, Y. (2017). Illusion and dazzle: Adversarial optical channel exploits against lidars for automotive applications. In W. Fischer & N. Homma (Eds.), *Cryptographic Hardware and Embedded Systems – CHES 2017* (pp. 445–467). Springer International Publishing.

Shoukry, Y., Martin, P., Tabuada, P., & Srivastava, M. (2013). Non-invasive spoofing attacks for anti-lock braking systems. *Cryptographic Hardware and Embedded Systems - CHES 2013*, 55–72.

Simacsek, B. (n.d.). *Can we trust our cars?* Available: https: //www.nxp.com/docs/en/white-paper/AUTOSECWP.pdf

Stottelaar, B. G. (2015). *Practical cyber-attacks on autonomous vehicles.* Available: http://essay.utwente.nl/66766/

Studnia, I., Nicomette, V., Alata, E., Deswarte, Y., Kaaniche, M., & Laarouchi, Y. (2013). Survey on security threats and protection mechanisms in embedded automotive networks. *2013 43rd Annual IEEE/IFIP Conference on Dependable Systems and Networks Workshop (DSN-W)*, 1–12.

Sun, X., Xia, L., & Jia, S. (2015). *Enhancing location privacy for electric vehicles by obfuscating the linkages of charging events.* IEEE.

Tu, Y., Lin, Z., Lee, I., & Hei, X. (2018). *Injected and delivered: Fabricating implicit control over actuation systems by spoofing inertial sensors. In 27th USENIX Security Symposium (USENIX Security 18).* USENIX Association. Available https://www.usenix.org/conference/usenixsecurity18/presentation/tu

Ueda, Kurachi, Takada, Mizutani, Inoue, & Horihata. (2015). Security authentication system for in-vehicle network. *SEI, 81.*

Valasek & Miller. (2014). *Adventures in automotive networks and control units.* Technical Report.

Wang, Y., Attebury, G., & Ramamurthy, B. (2006). A survey of security issues in wireless sensor networks. *IEEE Communications Surveys and Tutorials, 8*(2), 2–23.

Xu, Yan, Jia, Ji, & Liu. (2018). Analyzing and enhancing the security of ultrasonic sensors for autonomous vehicles. *IEEE Internet of Things Journal.*

Yan. (2016). *Can you trust autonomous vehicles: Contactless attacks against sensors of self-driving vehicle.* Academic Press.

Zhang, Y., Shi, P., Dong, C., Liu, Y., Shao, X., & Ma, C. (2018). Test and evaluation system for automotive cybersecurity. *2018 IEEE International Conference on Computational Science and Engineering (CSE)*, 201–207.

Chapter 6

Handwritten Signature Spoofing With Conditional Generative Adversarial Nets

Md Fazle Rabby
University of Louisiana at Lafayette, USA

Md Abdullah Al Momin
University of Louisiana at Lafayette, USA

Xiali Hei
University of Louisiana at Lafayette, USA

ABSTRACT

Generative adversarial networks have been a highly focused research topic in computer vision, especially in image synthesis and image-to-image translation. There are a lot of variations in generative nets, and different GANs are suitable for different applications. In this chapter, the authors investigated conditional generative adversarial networks to generate fake images, such as handwritten signatures. The authors demonstrated an implementation of conditional generative adversarial networks, which can generate fake handwritten signatures according to a condition vector tailored by humans.

INTRODUCTION

With the tremendous growth of the world, banking is getting more and more available to the mass people. People are generally getting more and more information and available options to have the banking activity quickly done than is previously possible.

DOI: 10.4018/978-1-7998-7323-5.ch006

With the increasing activity of money flow, there is also a concern for forging in banking activity. One type of forging is check spoofing, and in this chapter, an approach to spoof signatures on the checks is discussed.

As the growing banking activity, people now focus on comparatively easy and short time spending banking activity. For the past few decades, people are mainly focusing on depositing money to the bank using checks. In the money deposit system, checks have an identification process, which is the signature of the person who intends to deposit the money (Graeve et al., 2007). Previously, the system only used in-hand or physical methods. But, with the advent of technology, many banks try to make their system more accessible and comfortable to the users. In the prospect of this, banks like Chase bank introduced a new system called Chase QuickDeposit.

Figure 1. A general checkbook page from a bank with rounded mark indicates the account holder signature.

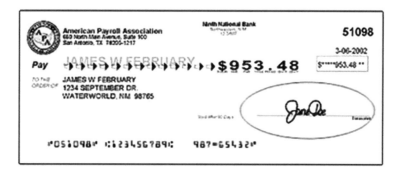

Deposit of electronic system uses two potential positions to write by the account holder in the check. The account holder needs to write down the amount of money and the unique signature that the banks will check when updating the system after depositing for verification (Pennacchi et al., 2006). Every individual has a different handwritten system that can be identified using the character pattern and the pressure point of any handwritten materials. By using this concept of difference in handwritten systems, banks like Chase bank introduced Chase QuickDeposit.

In the prospect of forgery, an adversary can spoof the amount written in the check or spoof the signature using the deep learning approach and specifically using Generative Adversarial Networks (GANs).

In this chapter, implementing an adversarial neural network model to spoof the signatures of any individual is discussed, and the model tries to regenerate the signature for forging purposes.

Related Works

Ferrer et al. 2013, proposes a novel methodology to generate static/offline signatures of new identities. The signature of the new synthetic identity is obtained, particularizing the random variables of a statistical distribution of global signature properties. The results mimic real signature shapes and writing style estimated properties from static signature databases. Shin et al. 2020, propose a technique for generating an English signature. They introduce a cubic Bezier curve for cursive connection and affine transform for customization to generate a signature. The system proposed the essential features that depict the signature generation using the following parameters for customization and decoration: scale, slant, rotation, skew, translation, the character's position, circles in the signature, horizontal lines, and the underline. Melo et al. 2018 proposed generating synthetic offline signatures by using dynamic and static (real) ones. The synthesis is here faced under the perspective of supervised training: the learning model is trained to perform the task of online-to-offline signature conversion. The approach is based on a deep convolutional neural network. The main goal is to enlarge the offline training dataset to improve the performance of the offline signature verification systems. Galbally et al. 2009, presented the algorithm to generate online signatures. The algorithm uses a parametrical model to generate the synthetic Discrete Fourier Transform (DFT) of the trajectory signals, which are then refined in the time domain and completed with a synthetic pressure function. Multiple samples of each signature are created so that they may produce synthetic databases. Quantitative and qualitative results are reported, showing that, in addition to presenting a very realistic appearance, the synthetically generated signatures have very similar characteristics to those that enable the recognition of genuine signatures.

THREAT MODEL

As the operation progress, the authors check the possibility of forging the check as it is observed that spoofing the checks can be done by faking the signatures. As previously mentioned, a check can have an account number, the amount in words, and a signature. In the system of QuickDeposit, a user needs to put amounts in words and their signature for authentication. This work aims to spoof the signature as it is the only authentication for the online deposit of money.

For depositing online using mobile, one needs to capture an image of the check and then let the system work the rest by itself. There are two possibilities of an attack vector here. If mobile security is compromised, then the system can be vulnerable. But this is not the attack scope in this work. Instead, the work focuses on spoofing the signature of the check using GANs. An attacker can modify the amounts in words or the signature in any check. Forgery checking can be possible by manipulating one or more fields in the checks, as mentioned.

Figure 2. Chase bank QuickDeposit of money using the mobile app to capture the image of the check

BACKGROUND

In this section, some essential conceptual topics are discussed, which are under the project's hood. For example, Neural Networks, Generative Adversarial Networks, Conditional Generative Adversarial Networks, etc., are discussed.

Neural Network

In the past ten years, the best performing artificial-intelligence systems, such as the speech recognizers on smartphones or Google's latest automatic translator, have resulted from a technique called "deep learning."

Deep learning is a new name for an approach to artificial intelligence called neural networks, which have been going in and out of fashion for more than 70 years. Neural networks were first proposed in 1944 by Warren McCullough and Walter Pitts.

Neural nets are a means of doing machine learning, in which a computer learns to perform some task by analyzing training examples. Usually, the examples have been hand-labeled in advance. An object recognition system, for instance, might be fed thousands of labeled images of cars, houses, coffee cups, and so on, and it would find visual patterns in the images that consistently correlate with particular labels. Artificial neural networks (ANNs) or connectionist systems are computing systems vaguely inspired by the biological neural networks that constitute animal brains. Such systems learn to perform tasks by considering examples, generally without being programmed with any task-specific rules.

A neural net consists of thousands or even millions of simple processing, densely interconnected nodes. Most of today's neural nets are organized into layers of nodes, and these are ——feed-forward, meaning that data moves through them in only one direction. So, for example, an individual node might be connected to several nodes in the layer beneath it, from which it receives data, and several nodes in the layer above it, to which it sends data.

Figure 3. Simple artificial neural network

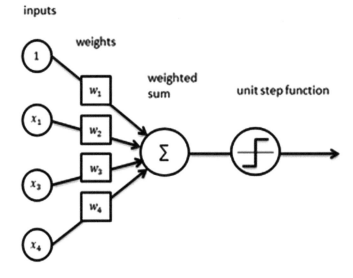

ANN is a set of connected neurons organized in layers:

- **Input Layer:** Brings the initial data into the system for further processing by subsequent layers of artificial neurons.
- **Hidden Layer:** A layer in between input layers and output layers, where artificial neurons take in a set of weighted inputs and produce an output through an activation function.
- **Output Layer:** The last layer of neurons that produces given outputs for the program.

A Multi-layer ANN (e.g., Convolutional Neural Network, Recurrent Neural Network, etc.) can solve more complex classification and regression tasks thanks to its hidden layer(s).

Figure 4. Multi-layer artificial neural network

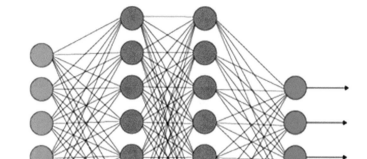

In artificial neural networks, *the Activation Function* of a node defines the output of that node given an input or set of inputs. There are several types of activation functions.

A *Sigmoid Function* is a mathematical function having a characteristic, S-shaped curve or sigmoid curve. Often, the sigmoid function refers to the particular case of the logistic function, which generates a set of probability outputs between 0 and 1 when fed with a set of inputs. For example, the sigmoid activation function is widely used in binary classification.

Instead of the sigmoid activation function, most recent artificial neural networks use *Rectified Linear Units (ReLUs)* for the hidden layers. A rectified linear unit has output 0 if the input is less than 0 and raw output otherwise. That is, if the input is greater than 0, the output is equal to the input.

The loss function is an integral part of artificial neural networks, which measure the inconsistency between predicted value ($\hat{y}$) and actual label (y). It is a non-negative value, where the robustness of the model increases along with the decrease of the loss function value.

Forward Propagation is the process of feeding the Neural Network with a set of inputs to get their dot product with their weights, then feeding the latter to an activation function and comparing its numerical value to the actual output called "the ground truth."

Back Propagation is a method used in artificial neural networks to calculate a gradient needed to calculate the weights to be used in the network.

Generative Adversarial Networks

Generative adversarial networks (GANs) are deep neural network architectures comprising two nets, pitting one against the other. GANs were introduced in a paper by Ian Goodfellow et al. 2014.

GANs' potential is enormous because they can learn to mimic any distribution of data. That is, GANs can be taught to create worlds eerily similar to our own in any domain: images, music, speech, prose. They are robot artists in a sense, and their output is impressive – poignant even.

One neural network, called the *generator*, generates new data instances. The discriminator evaluates them for authenticity. For example, the discriminator decides whether each instance of data it reviews belongs to the actual training dataset or not.

The generator creates new images that it passes to the discriminator. It does so in the hopes that they, too, will be deemed authentic, even though they are fake. The goal of the generator is to generate passable hand-written digits to lie without being caught. The goal of the discriminator is to identify images coming from the generator as fake. Here are the steps a GAN takes:

- The generator takes in random numbers and returns an image.
- This generated image is fed into the discriminator alongside a stream of images taken from the actual dataset.

The discriminator takes in both real and fake images and returns probabilities, a number between 0 and 1, with 1 representing a prediction of authenticity and 0 representing fake.

Figure 5. GANs architecture

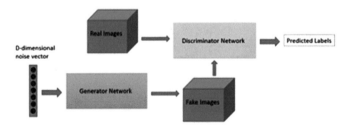

The discriminator network is a standard convolutional network that can categorize the images fed to it, a binomial classifier labeling images as real or fake. In a sense, the generator is an inverse convolutional network. While a standard convolutional classifier takes an image and down-samples it to produce a probability, the generator takes a vector of random noise and up-samples it to an image. The first throws away data through down-sampling techniques like max-pooling, and the second generates new data.

Both nets try to optimize a different and opposing objective function, or loss function, in a zero-sum game. This is essentially an actor-critic model. As the discriminator changes its behavior, so does the generator, and vice versa. As a result, their losses push against each other.

Figure 6. The discriminator training for MNIST dataset.

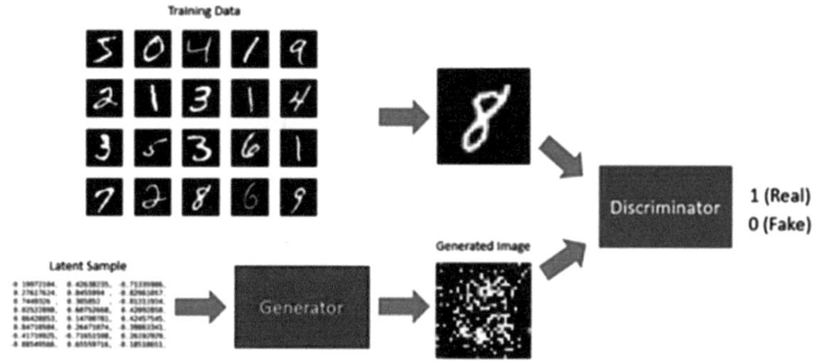

Theoretically, the adversarial modeling framework is most straightforward to apply when the models are both multilayer perceptions. To learn the generator's distribution pg over data x, they define a prior on input noise variables $pz(z)$, then represent a mapping to data space as $G(z; \theta g)$, where G is a differentiable function represented by a multilayer perception with parameters θg. They also define a second multilayer perception $D(x; \theta d)$ that outputs a single scalar. $D(x)$ represents the probability that x came from the data rather than pg. Finally, they train D to maximize the probability of assigning the correct label to both training examples and samples from G. They simultaneously train G to minimize $log(1 - D(G(z)))$. In other words, D and G play the following two-player mini-max game with value function $V(G; D)$:

Conditional Generative Adversarial Networks

Generative adversarial nets can be extended to a conditional model if both the generator and discriminator are conditioned on some extra information y. y could be any auxiliary information, such as class labels or data from other modalities.

Conditioning is performed by feeding *y* into both the discriminator and generator as an additional input layer.

In the generator, the prior input noise *pz(z)*, and *y* are combined in joint hidden representation. The adversarial training framework allows for considerable flexibility in how this hidden representation is composed.

In the discriminator *x* and *y* are presented as inputs and to a discriminative function (embodied again by a MLP in this case).

The objective function of a two-player mini-max game would be as:

ortega

$$\min_{G} \max_{D} V(D,G) = \mathbb{E}_{x \sim p_{data}(x)}\left[\log D(x \mid y)\right] + \mathbb{E}_{z \sim p_z(z)}\left[\log\left(1 - D(G(z \mid y))\right)\right]$$

Figure 7 illustrates the structure of a simple conditional adversarial net.

Figure 7. Conditional adversarial net

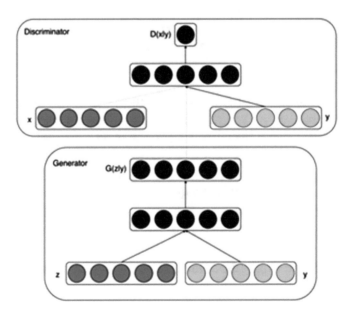

In contrast with the architecture of GAN, There is an additional input layer in both discriminator net and generator net.

Figure 8 shows some of the generated MNIST Digit samples with CGAN. Each row is conditioned on one label, and each column is a different generated sample.

Figure 8. Generated MNIST digits, each row conditioned on one label

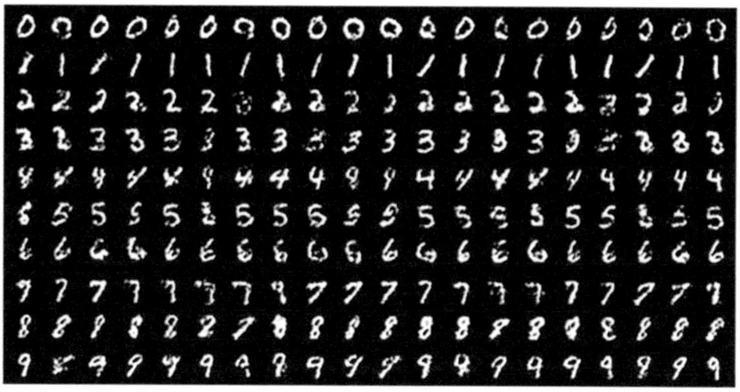

IMPLEMENTATION OF HANDWRITTEN SIGNATURE GENERATION

First, a conditional adversarial network is trained using the collected handwritten signature images conditioned on their class labels, encoded as one-hot vectors.

In the generator network, a prior noise z with dimensionality *100* was drawn from a uniform distribution within the unit hypercube. Next, both z and y are mapped to hidden layers with Rectified Linear Unit (ReLu) activation with layer sizes *200* and *1000*, respectively, before both being mapped to second, combined hidden ReLu layer of dimensionality *1200*. Then a final sigmoid unit layer is obtained as the output for generating the *22500*-dimensional collected signature samples.

The model is trained using stochastic gradient descent with mini-batches of size *64. Three hundred* samples are drawn in *30000* iterations. And the initial learning rate of *0:1,* which is exponentially decreased down to:*000001* with a decay factor of *1:00004*. Also, momentum is used with an initial value of:*5* which is increased up to *0:7*. Then, dropout (Ortega-Garcia et al. 2003) with a probability of *0.5* is applied to both the generator and discriminator. And the best estimate of log-likelihood on the validation set is used as a stopping point.

EXPERIMENT SETUP AND RESULTS

In the implementation, a CGAN with collected signature images is trained. The number of train signature images is around *60* from around *20* individuals. Every *100* iteration of training, *16* images are drawn, which are generated by Generator. The model is trained with train datasets around *30000* times. It takes around *1* hour

20 minutes for *30000* iterations. Some train sample signature images are given in Figure 9.

Figure 9. Some signature images (Train data)

Conditioning is performed by feeding *y* (label of signature images) into the discriminator and generator as additional input layers.

Figure 10. (a) Train images for a particular label "Momin". (b) Fake signature generated by Our CGANs Model

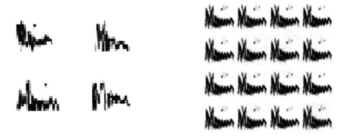

Some other samples are provided in Figures 11 and 12.

Figure 11. (a) Train images for a particular label "Sumit". (b) Fake signature generated by Our CGANs Model

Figure 12. (a) Train images for a particular label "Xiali Hei". (b) Fake signature generated by Our CGANs Model

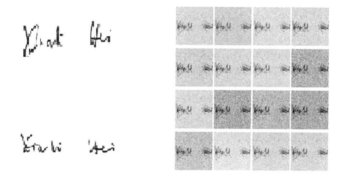

LIMITATIONS OF THE APPROACH

Neural Nets work better when the training data is significant. But this work has a minimal number of train images. The CGANs model is trained with only 60 images. So it is expected that the generated fake image quality would not be so good. However, after the experiment, it was found that the image quality is up to the mark. So one of the reasons for bad image quality might be the small training data set.

Another limitation of the work is that generated fake images often lack enough sharpness, which is very noisy. Therefore, a deeper look into CGANs parameters and structure are required so that fine-tuning the model for less noisy output is possible.

In the future, more signatures need to be collected to increase the size of the training dataset to enhance the quality and realism of generated images. It could be better to use MCYT baseline corpus: a bimodal biometric database by Ortega Garcia, Javier, et al. 2003.

CONCLUSION

The work demonstrated a CGAN Model for generating fake handwritten signatures. However, it suffers from generating practical and acceptable handwritten signatures because of the small training data set. Furthermore, as the realism and quality of the generated images are not enough, further investigations are required to fine-tune the nets.

REFERENCES

De Graeve, F., De Jonghe, O., & Vander Vennet, R. (2007). Competition, transmission and bank pricing policies: Evidence from Belgian loan and deposit markets. *Journal of Banking & Finance*, *31*(1), 259–278. doi:10.1016/j.jbankfin.2006.03.003

Ferrer, M. A., Diaz-Cabrera, M., & Morales, A. (2013). *Synthetic off-line signature image generation. In 2013 international conference on biometrics (ICB)*. IEEE.

Galbally, J. (2009). Synthetic generation of handwritten signatures based on spectral analysis. In *Optics and Photonics in Global Homeland Security V and Biometric Technology for Human Identification VI* (Vol. 7306). International Society for Optics and Photonics.

Goodfellow, I. (2014). Generative adversarial nets. *Advances in Neural Information Processing Systems*.

Melo. (2019). Deep learning approach to generate offline handwritten signatures based on online samples. *IET Biometrics*, *8*(3), 215-220.

Ortega-Garcia, J. (2003). MCYT baseline corpus: A bimodal biometric database. *IEE Proceedings. Vision Image and Signal Processing*, *150*(6), 395–401.

Pennacchi, G. (2006). Deposit insurance, bank regulation, and financial system risks. *Journal of Monetary Economics*, *53*(1), 1–30. doi:10.1016/j.jmoneco.2005.10.007

Shin, J., Rahim, M. A., Islam, M. R., & Yun, K. S. (2020). A novel approach of cursive signature generation for personal identity. *International Journal of Computer Applications in Technology*, *62*(4), 384.

Smithies & Newman. (1996). *Method and system for the capture, storage, transport and authentication of handwritten signatures*. U.S. Patent No. 5,544,255.

Chapter 7

Generating Device Fingerprints for Smart Device Pairing Using the Unique Spectrum Characteristic From LEDs

Md Imran Hossen
University of Louisiana at Lafayette, USA

Md Abdullah Al Momin
University of Louisiana at Lafayette, USA

Xiali Hei
University of Louisiana at Lafayette, USA

ABSTRACT

Currently, the vast majority of smart devices with LEDs are on the rise. It has been observed that the lights emitted by each LED have unique spectral characteristics. Despite the fact that there are a number of methods out there to generate fingerprints, none seem to explore the possibility of generating fingerprints using this unique feature. In this chapter, the method to perform device fingerprinting using the unique spectrum emitted from the LED lights is discussed. The generated fingerprint is then used in device pairing.

INTRODUCTION

Currently, the vast majority of intelligent devices with LEDs are on the rise. However, it has been observed that the lights emitted by each LED have unique spectral

DOI: 10.4018/978-1-7998-7323-5.ch007

characteristics. Although there are several methods to generate fingerprints, none seem to explore the possibility of generating fingerprints using this unique feature (Tom et al., 2016; Mayrhofer et al., 2009; Bojinov et al., 2014; Han et al., 2018; Pan et al., 2018). This chapter discusses a new way to perform device fingerprinting using the unique spectrum emitted from the LED lights. The generated fingerprint is then used in device pairing.

BACKGROUND

What happens when two devices want to become paired? First, the devices need to identify each other uniquely. Second, the devices must use some method to do that. This method should be unique so that the device does not recognize the wrong device. This process is known as fingerprinting.

The fingerprint could be a vast, random number. It can be other unique characteristics such as the spectrum of the light emitted by LEDs, as the spectrum of rays emitted by LEDs is unique. So, this feature can be used to identify each LED individually. Once the fingerprint is generated by one device, the other device can verify and recognize the device generating the fingerprint. Then the device initiates the pairing protocol.

CONCEPTUAL MODEL

In this chapter, the method to perform the LED-based device fingerprinting is discussed. In LED-based device fingerprinting, the unique spectrum information of one LED mounted on the first device is saved inside itself. Then, when another device wants to connect, it takes the photo of the light of the LED of the first device, extracts the spectrum from the image, and sends the spectral information to the first device. Next, the first device compares the received spectral data with the one stored inside it. If the information matches, the device generates the pairing protocol, and the two devices become paired. This process is shown in figure 1.

Figure 1. Conceptual model

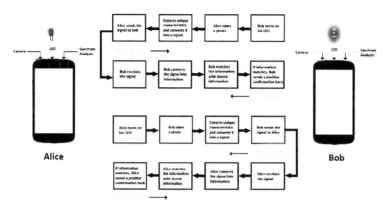

METHODOLOGY

Several methods to achieve the goal are followed. Zhu et al., 2017 discuss how they use the characteristics of light such as Spatial Radiance Pattern (SRP) to identify a light. SRP is defined as the radiance intensity distribution across a light's body. SRP is some unique characteristics of light due to the inevitable manufacturing variations of the materials that are used to produce the light. This SRP feature is resilient to the camera's viewing angle or distance and highly diverse among lights. So, this feature can be used to uniquely identify light and, in turn, the device the light is mounted on. Then the devices can generate a pairing protocol. So, to perform the fingerprinting, the first task is to extract the SRP of a light. Several approaches are followed to extract the SRP. The methods to extract the SRP are discussed in the experiments section.

EXPERIMENTS

The process described in (Li et al., 2018) is followed to extract the spectrum information of the light emitted by the LEDs. The method followed in their work exploits the characteristics of birefringence material. Birefringence is the optical property of a material having a refractive index that depends on light's polarization and propagation direction. These optically anisotropic materials are said to be birefringent (or birefractive). The birefringence is often quantified as the maximum difference between refractive indices exhibited by the material. Crystals with non-cubic crystal structures are often birefringent, as are plastics under mechanical stress. Some examples of birefringence materials are the plastic, thin film that is present on a Compact Disk (CD) or the transparent, adhesive tape. It is found that the spectrum information extracted by exploiting a birefringence material may not be accurate. Hence, the idea of using a birefringence material in this method is dropped, and employ a handheld mobile spectrum analyzer because spectrum analyzers are highly precise in extracting the spectrum information of light. This way, the process will be able to identify a specific LED more accurately. The experiment has three main parts. In what follows is a short description of each step involved.

Figure 2.

Figure 3.

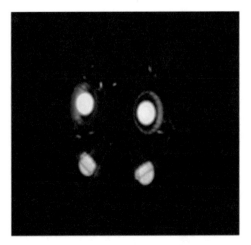

Figure 4.

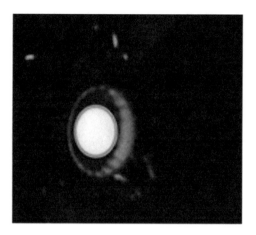

Capturing Images of the LEDs

This part discusses capturing images of the LEDs using three different smartphones – Google Pixel2, Samsung J2, and Samsung Core Prime. First, an app called OpenCamera, which allows to adjust and tweak many different camera settings not usually available in built-in camera app provided by mobile phone manufacturers, is used. Then images are taken from varying orientations and distances and ensured that the LED body is visible enough in the photos.

Figure 5.

Figure 6.

Figure 7.

Figure 8.

Figure 9.

Figure 10.

Preprocessing

As mobile phone cameras are not perfect, they induce noise in the images taken by them. Consequently, some preprocessing needs to be done before jumping on to the next stage. Experimentation with various filters is done, such as mean filter, median filter, and Gaussian filters. What is being noticed is that the Gaussian filter seemed to provide a relatively good result compared to the other two.

Extracting the Spatial Radiance Pattern (SRP)

Once preprocessing is done, the LED body (where SRP is visible) is extracted from the images. This process is essential because it reduces computational overhead.

Moreover, it would be impractical to work with the whole image as the only thing to care about is its SRP. Hence filtering out the unnecessary parts of the image is efficient. Open source Computer Vision library or OpenCV is utilized for this purpose. First, a threshold is applied to find the brightest part in the images. Then this threshold image is fed into the contour detection algorithm available in OpenCV. Finally, the SRP part from the original grayscale image is cropped out using the coordinates determined to BoundingRect method in OpenCV.

Figure 11. Extraction of SRP image

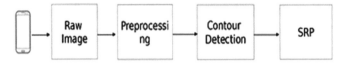

Figure 12. Original image (LED1)

Figure 13. Radiance image

Figure 14. Original image

Figure 15. Radiance image

Classification

The last and final step is to classify the images. The goal is to investigate whether it is possible to identify each LED uniquely by exploiting the LED light's visual feature (SRP). The SRP could be calculated directly from the pixel values in the images. Still, a deep learning model such as Convolutional Neural Network (Convnets or CNN) seemed to make more sense in this scenario. In the next section, a brief description of CNN is provided.

Convolutional Neural Networks (Convnets or CNNs)

CNN's do take biological inspiration from the visual cortex. The visual cortex has small regions of cells that are sensitive to the specific areas of the visual field. This idea is expanded upon by a fascinating experiment by Hubel and Wiesel in 1962. They showed that some individual neuronal cells in the brain responded (or fired) only in the presence of edges of a particular orientation. For example, some neurons fired when exposed to vertical edges and some when shown horizontal or diagonal edges. Hubel and Wiesel found out that all of these neurons are organized in a columnar architecture and that together, they can produce visual perception. This idea of specialized components inside a system having specific tasks (the neuronal cells in the visual cortex looking for particular characteristics) is one that machines use and is the basis behind CNNs.

Convolutional Neural Networks have a different architecture than regular Neural Networks. Regular Neural Networks transform an input by putting it through a series of hidden layers. Every layer is made up of a set of neurons, where each layer is fully connected to all neurons in the layer before. Finally, there is a last fully connected layer — the output layer — that represents the predictions. ConvNets are also used for object detection, scene recognition, human pose estimation, video caption generation, speech recognition, language translation, among other tasks.

CNN Architecture

ConvNets usually have three main types of layers 1) Convolutional layer, 2) Pooling layer, and 3) Fully Connected layer.

Convolution Layer

The convolutional layer is the core building block of a CNN. The layer's parameters consist of a set of learnable filters (or kernels), which have a small receptive field but extend through the full depth of the input volume. During the forward pass, each filter is convolved across the width and height of the input volume, computing the dot product between the entries of the filter and the input and producing a 2-dimensional activation map of that filter. As a result, the network learns filters that activate when it detects a specific feature at some spatial position in the input.

Stacking the activation maps for all filters along the depth dimension forms the total output volume of the convolution layer. Every entry in the output volume can thus also be interpreted as an output of a neuron that looks at a small region in the input and shares parameters with neurons in the same activation map.

Pool Layer

Pool Layer performs a function to reduce the spatial dimensions of the input and the computational complexity of the model. And it also controls overfitting. It operates independently on every depth slice of the input. There are different functions such as Max pooling, average pooling, or L2-norm pooling. However, Max pooling is the most used type of pooling, which only takes the most critical part (the value of the brightest pixel) of the input volume.

Figure 16. CNN architecture

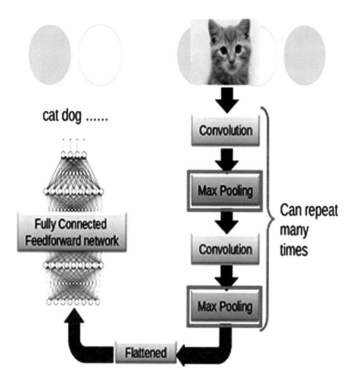

Figure 17. Convolution

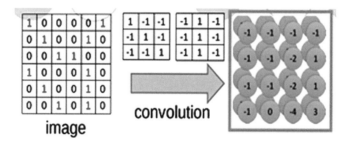

Example of a Max pooling with 2x2 filter and stride = 2. So, for each of the windows, max-pooling takes the max value of the 4 pixels.

The pooling layer doesn't have parameters (the weights and biases of the neurons) and no zero padding, but it has two hyper-parameters: Filter (F) and Stride (S). More generally, having the input W1×H1×D1, the pooling layer produces a volume of size W2×H2×D2 where:

$$W2 = (W1-F)/S+1$$

$$H2 = (H1-F)/S+1$$

$$D2 = D1$$

Figure 18. Max-pooling with 2x2 filter and stride = 2. Ref: Wikipedia

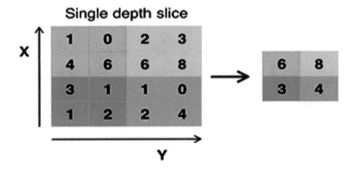

A common form of Max pooling is filters of size 2x2 applied with a stride of 2. The Pooling sizes with larger filters are too destructive, and they usually lead to worse performance.

Fully Connected Layer (FC)

Fully connected layers connect every neuron in one layer to every neuron in another layer. The last fully-connected layer uses a softmax activation function to classify the input image's generated features into various classes based on the training dataset.

EXPERIMENT SETUP

A CNN model is built using a python deep learning library called Keras. Three different smartphones are used – Google Pixel2, Samsung J2, and Samsung Core Prime G2 for capturing images. Ninety-seven images are used to train the model, and validation is done on 42 images. In summary, the experimental setup is as follows,

Training Dataset Size: 97
Validation Dataset: 42

RESULTS

The CNN model is run on an Arch Linux machine with Intel Core i7 8th Gen. CPU, 16GB RAM, and NVIDIA GTX150 GPU. For training the model, it took around 53 minutes. Below is the list of the parameters of the CNN model,

Number of Train Samples: 7000
Number of Validation Samples: 500
Epochs: 40
Batch Size: 10

Figure 19. Accuracy of CNN model

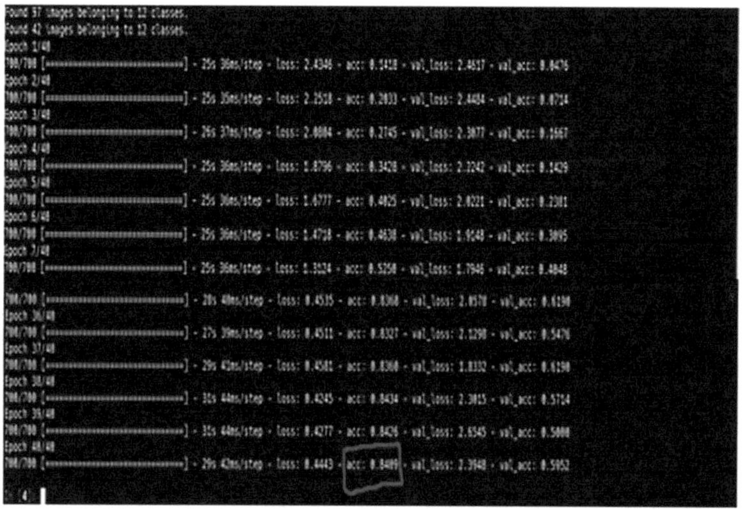

The final accuracy after running the model is 84.09%. The figure shows that the loss is pretty high, and the model seemed to be overfitted. Different parameters of this model are tweaked, and its performance is observed.

LIMITATIONS AND FUTURE WORK

The main limitation of this approach is that the focus is only on a single feature to fingerprint the LEDs. For robust fingerprinting, combining more features should be done. Therefore, future works should include more features. In addition, the number of the dataset used in this work is not large enough. Thus, in the future, the work needs to be done with large-scale datasets.

CONCLUSION

LEDs are being increasingly available in commodity devices. Fingerprinting devices have many practical applications in numerous domains. In this work, a unique visual feature of LED is exploited called LED for fingerprinting devices. Convolutional Neural Network is used to classify images of 12 different LEDs. Although, some of these images look very similar with naked eyes. The CNN model can distinguish the images with 84% accuracy.

REFERENCES

Bojinov, H. (2014). *Mobile device identification via sensor fingerprinting.* arXiv preprint arXiv:1408.1416.

Han, J. (2018). Do you feel what I hear? Enabling autonomous IoT device pairing using different sensor types. In *2018 IEEE Symposium on Security and Privacy (SP)*. IEEE. 10.1109/SP.2018.00041

Li, X., & Wang. (2018). Rainbowlight: Towards low cost ambient light positioning with mobile phones. *Proceedings of the 24th Annual International Conference on Mobile Computing and Networking.*

Mayrhofer, R., & Gellersen, H. (2009). Shake well before use: Intuitive and secure pairing of mobile devices. *IEEE Transactions on Mobile Computing, 8*(6), 792–806. doi:10.1109/TMC.2009.51

Pan, S. (2018). Universense: Iot device pairing through heterogeneous sensing signals. *Proceedings of the 19th International Workshop on Mobile Computing Systems & Applications.* 10.1145/3177102.3177108

Van Goethem, T. (2016). Accelerometer-based device fingerprinting for multi-factor mobile authentication. In *International Symposium on Engineering Secure Software and Systems.* Springer. 10.1007/978-3-319-30806-7_7

Zhu, S., & Zhang, X. (2017). Enabling high-precision visible light localization in today's buildings. *Proceedings of the 15th Annual International Conference on Mobile Systems, Applications, and Services.*

Chapter 8
Deep Learning Approach for Protecting Voice–Controllable Devices From Laser Attacks

Vijay Srinivas Srinivas Tida
University of Louisiana at Lafayette, USA

Raghabendra Shah
University of Louisiana at Lafayette, USA

Xiali Hei
University of Louisiana at Lafayette, USA

ABSTRACT

The laser-based audio signal injection can be used for attacking voice controllable systems. An attacker can aim an amplitude-modulated light at the microphone's aperture, and the signal injection acts as a remote voice-command attack on voice-controllable systems. Attackers are using vulnerabilities to steal things that are in the form of physical devices or the form of virtual using making orders, withdrawal of money, etc. Therefore, detection of these signals is important because almost every device can be attacked using these amplitude-modulated laser signals. In this project, the authors use deep learning to detect the incoming signals as normal voice commands or laser-based audio signals. Mel frequency cepstral coefficients (MFCC) are derived from the audio signals to classify the input audio signals. If the audio signals are identified as laser signals, the voice command can be disabled, and an alert can be displayed to the victim. The maximum accuracy of the machine learning model was 100%, and in the real world, it's around 95%.

DOI: 10.4018/978-1-7998-7323-5.ch008

INTRODUCTION

Human interaction with devices such as Amazon Echo, Google Home, Apple HomePod, and Xiaomi AI became more prominent which can be helpful to users to control their smart home appliances, adjust the temperature, home security systems, online shopping, making phone calls, and many other tasks. In recent days most smartphones are equipped with Siri, Google Now, Cortana which provide users more flexible interface to control many IoT systems (Yuan Gong 2018) (Abdullah et al. 2019). Further advancements of these devices made not only normal individuals interact but also disabled and elderly people purely rely on them (H.Stephenson n.d.) (C. Martin n.d.). Security of these devices has become more important because of more sensitive information available from the user like payment information, car device control, etc. However, development in machine learning played a crucial role in handling a large amount of data with less effort and helped to have a better user experience. Even though they rapidly developed but these devices have a major security problem by taking the audio samples in the nearby environment and process it whether intentionally or unintentionally (Maheshwari n.d.)(Ramirez, M., and C. 2007). Speech recognition devices mainly consist of hardware components that show some non-ideal characteristics. There is the possibility of other kinds of attacks and these things can be broadly classified further. Attackers exploit these non-ideal characteristics of the devices to steal sensitive information or control the device. Attackers can attack voice-controllable systems using various sources like laser light(Sugawara et al. 2020), long-range attacks (Roy et al. 2018), ultrasonic waves(G. Zhang et al. 2017), solid materials(Q. Yan et al. 2020), electromagnetic interference signals(Kune et al. 2013)(Tu, Yazhou and Tida, Vijay Srinivas and Pan, Zhongqi and Hei 2021), etc. In the paper(Sugawara et al. 2020), they proposed how to attack various voice assistant systems from far away distances using laser light as the source of medium. In (Giechaskiel and Rasmussen 2020) clearly explained how the working of various sensors are manipulated using out-of-band signal injections. To avoid unsolicited access to the voice assistant systems, they proposed various hardware or software solutions. They briefly discussed various attacks and recommended certain solutions by taking all cross research areas into account. Further in (C. Yan et al. 2020) analog sensor security is explained through analyzing the security properties in a meaningful way. This work makes a systematic process to analyze the security properties of sensors which can provide a better understanding of devices helps to prevent future attacks. In (Tu et al. 2018), the authors clearly explained how inertial sensors can malfunction through means of using out-of-band acoustic signals. Also proposed two solutions to handle these attacks utilizing digital amplitude adjusting and phase pacing. In (Tu et al. 2019) temperature sensor measurement manipulation can be demonstrated by adversary attacks made using hardware used in devices like operational amplifiers, instrumental amplifiers, etc. Also, they showed the defense method using the prototype design of a low-cost anomaly detector. Modern smartphones are susceptible to various attacks which can be seen in (Kasmi and Lopes Esteves 2015). They took electromagnetic signals as a source to induce the attack by exploring the properties of electronic devices and proposed a notable solution using a new silent remote voice command injection method. In medical field applications, these kinds of attacks pose a serious threat which can be seen in (Rasmussen et al. 2009). Here the authors tried to solve the attacks using proximity-based access control technique with the help of ultrasonic distance bounding protocols. Electromagnetic interference attacks on sensor devices constitute a major threat in this physical world and the detection of these signals has more importance which can be observed in (Y. Zhang and Rasmussen 2020). They proposed a simple technique by measuring the value on the sensor when it's at rest should be zero volts with the help of a little amount of extra hardware. Deep learning approaches showed higher efficiency towards the usage of voice-based assistant devices, however, attackers use the vulnerabilities in the model to perform unsolicited activities. In (Abdullah H, Warren K, Bindschaedler V, Papernot N n.d.) proposed how the attacks can be performed and proposed the future research directions to avoid these attacks. In (Chen Y, Zhang J, Yuan X, Zhang S, Chen K, Wang X n.d.) mentioned the above problems clearly by classifying them into various classes like out-of-band signal attack, adversarial attack, etc with various solutions. They provide some insights on how we align the research related to security in the Image Recognition System (IRS) as the base. In (Z. Xu et al. 2021) proposed an inaudible attack method for increased distance of 2.5m using Electromagnetic Interference on smart speakers with the help of non linear property of microphones. By using deep learning algorithms will help to protect these devices to some extent without having additional costs. Since voice assistant devices contains microphone and more sensitive information is present inside it, adding more hardware components might cause more problems. Instead of solving problems the added components might create new problems. Since many devices are already purchased it is difficult to change the physical characteristics of the devices more efficient deep algorithms are necessary. Although there are cases where attackers used white box knowledge of the deep learning models which can create audio samples that can be understood by the voice assistant devices but difficult for humans to interpret (Carlini et al. 2016; Yuan et al. 2018). A typical block diagram of the Voice Controlled Systems (VCS) is shown in Figure1 how the machine learning model will make to process the malicious signal can be seen. In the first step, the input signal might be in the form of the recorded human voice or any other manipulated signals from various sources which can be considered as a spoofing process. The second step making the voice system accept the malicious command by hacking the operating system.

After that, the malicious analog signals are converted to a digital signal in the third step, and in the final step, the machine learning model will execute the adversarial command by deception process (Yuan Gong 2018).

Figure 1. General block diagram of voice controlled system. (1) spoofing (2) hacking (3) analog to digital conversion (4) deception
[adapted from (Yuan Gong 2018)]

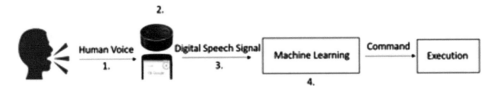

There is rapid growth in voice-driven IoT devices which makes them have more sensitive information which can lead to theft activities like unauthorized entry to the home, purchases, credit card usage, etc (Alepis and Patsakis 2017; Diao et al. 2014; Lei et al. 2018). These attacks can be broadly classified into five categories namely 1) basic voice replay attack 2) operating system-level attack 3) hardware-level attack 4) machine learning level attack and 5) adversary's knowledge from (Yuan Gong 2018).

- Basic Voice Replay Attack: In this type of attack, the intruder will replay the recorded voice to ensure the desired malicious activity is performed. This kind of attack can be seen in (Chen et al. 2017)(Lei et al. 2018; Petracca et al. 2015). The major disadvantage of this attack is that it is easy to identify but these attacks play a crucial role in many other dangerous attacks.
- Operating System-Level Attack: In this type of attack, the intruder will use vulnerabilities in the operating system to make desired malicious activity These attacks can be seen in (Alepis and Patsakis 2017; Diao et al. 2014; Jang et al. 2014). These attacks are performed by changing permissions in malware from zero to high. These attacks are performed either by no user in the proximity range or by making the import an audio file to the microphone directly without playing it.
- Hardware Level Attack: In this type of attack, the intruder had information about the vulnerabilities of the hardware used. These attacks can be seen in (G. Zhang et al. 2017)(Kune et al. 2013; Roy et al. 2018; Sugawara et al. 2020; Q. Yan et al. 2020)(Tu, Yazhou and Tida, Vijay Srinivas and Pan, Zhongqi and Hei 2021)s. By using the different mediums with the help of

different hardware settings these attacks can be performed. These attacks can be usually performed using non-linear characteristics of devices using different modulation techniques. There are major limitations like distance range, the microphone should be powered, etc. which makes these attacks not easy. In our experiments, we majorly focused on detecting the laser light signal from the real audio samples since it has a large distance range in which users might not be able to identify.

- Machine Learning Level Attack: In this type of attack, adversarial samples play a crucial role for the intruder. These adversarial samples behave the same as the human voice, but the operation performed might be different. For instance, the open the garage door command might work as changing the temperature by speech recognition device. These attacks can be seen in (Carlini et al. 2016; Carlini and Wagner 2018; Cisse et al. 2017; M. Alzantot, B. Balaji 2018; Poellabauer 2017; Vaidya et al. 2015). The adversarial samples generated have been advanced over time. Initially, Mel-Frequency Cepstral Coefficients (MFCC) were used to generate malicious samples but later developed by using some advanced mathematical optimization techniques.

- Adversary's Knowledge: In this type, based on the information of the device it was classified. If the intruder has domain knowledge about the experiment setup that it is considered a white box attack. If the intruder does not have any information, then it is considered a black box attack. Usually, hardware and operating system level attacks come under the white box group since the intruder has some knowledge of the system. Practical machine learning level attacks are usually considered under the black-box group because the algorithms and datasets used are unknown. Another major problem that can be seen in the attacks is combined using responding like normal speech but underlying the attack is performed which was unknown by the user (Alepis and Patsakis 2017).

The deep learning process has been adopted in various applications on audio signals (Vera-Diaz, Pizarro, and Macias-Guarasa 2018), (Lavner et al. 2018). While some applications such as audio recognition (speech recognition, sound detection, localization, and tracking) and synthesis and transformation (Purwins et al. 2019) are positive implementations, adversaries can find ways to impact the classification system to perform negatively (Kereliuk, Sturm, and Larsen 2015). In this project, we observe the use of deep learning in classifying the incoming audio signals from the microphone as either normal audio signals or is it the result of the amplitude-modulated laser signal and analyze the performance of using various optimizers.

LITERATURE REVIEW

Voice Processing System (VPS)

Voice processing tools that have machine learning models can be called VPS. They can be classified into two types Automatic Speech Recognition (ASR) and Speaker Identification models.

1. **ASRs:** An ASR used to convert the raw audio file by humans to text. ASRs will complete this conversion using three steps. 1) Pre-processing, 2) signal processing, and 3) model inference.
2. **Speaker Identification model:** Initially this model was trained on voice samples of the speakers from which it will identify the speaker. Based on voting information of the model the audio is processed to a text file.

Preprocessing

In the preprocessing, step filtering of the audio signal is made to remove any noise in the input signal. Some signal processing algorithms are used to extract the important features thereby reducing the dimensionality of the audio signal. Using the signal processing step feature vectors are generated. Mostly used algorithm for feature extraction is Mel Frequency Cepstrum Coefficient (MFCC) algorithm. This feature vector will become input to the model during the subsequent phases like training and testing.

MFCC Features of Audio Signals

Mel Frequency Cepstrum (MFC) is a short-term representation of the power spectrum of a sound based on a linear cosine transform of a log power spectrum on a nonlinear Mel scale of frequency. Mel-frequency Cepstral Coefficients (MFCC) are coefficients that collectively make up an MFC (M. Xu et al. 2004). The main advantage of using this is a better representation of sound using frequency wrapping. Mel-Cepstral Distortion (MCD) is used as a measure for checking the quality of the demodulated signal. Preferred signals are usually MCD less than 8.

MFCC features have been effective to use for machine learning models (Yang et al. 2020), (Logan 2000). They have been a dominant feature for speech recognition application and their ability to represent speech amplitude spectrum in a compact form has made them successful (Logan 2000). Figure 2 shows the process to extract MFCC features from an audio waveform.

First, we divide the waveform into frames (usually 20ms intervals). Each frame goes through four major steps. Then Discrete Fourier Transform (DFT) of each frame is taken. The amplitude information is more important than the phase information, and the loudness of a signal is logarithmic. Therefore, in the next step, we retain the log of amplitude. The next step is smoothing the spectrum and emphasizing perpetual meaningful frequencies using Mel scaling. Finally, the Discrete Cosine Transform (DCT) is applied to decorrelate the components of Mel-spectral vectors to get 13 (or so) cepstral features for each frame.

Figure 2. Extracting MFCC features

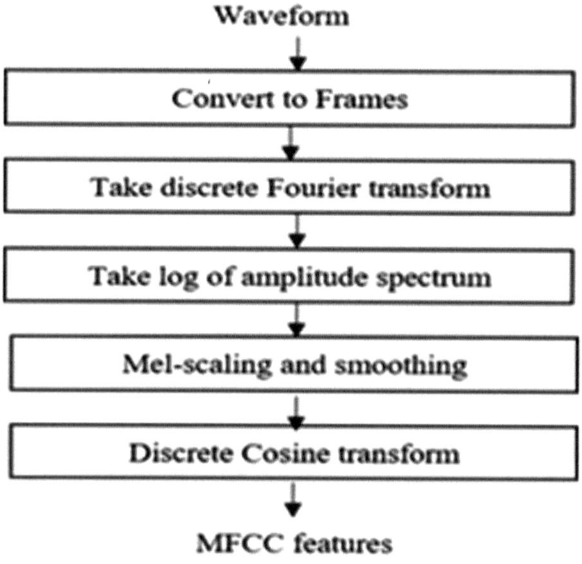

Other Methods

Although MFCC is used widely for audio signal processing for machine learning applications there are some other processing techniques used in modern VPSes such as Mel-Frequency Spectral Coefficients (MFSC), Linear Predictive Coding (LPC), and Perceptual Linear Prediction (PLP)(Zue 1980). While some other VPSes uses probabilistic techniques like transfer learning. Transfer learning (L. Torrey and J. Shavlik n.d.) involve extracting the features from the model which was already trained for inference implemented in (Venugopalan et al. 2015). Some additional models are also proposed which are called an end to end systems using replacing intermediate modules between the raw input and the model by removing pre-processing and signal processing steps which can be observed in (Amodei et al. 2016).

Model Inference

From signal processing steps features are selected after that these are features are passed to machine learning algorithms for inference. For speech recognition tasks use of machine learning algorithms can be observed in VPSes. Features observed from the trained models play a crucial role in predicting the classes belongs to different test samples. Earlier features are extracted base done based on the specific domain but due to the availability of a huge amount of data, this extraction process can be made automatic. Because of this automatic extraction of features has more general knowledge than domain-specific. Present-day deployed models extract features automatically which can learn required features such that it creates relevant mapping by applying cost function for error reduction. Because of this automatic extraction, they have more flexibility utilizing dividing into independent modules which can be used for different applications.

Feed Forward Neural Network

Feed-forward networks will satisfy the following properties:

1. It consists of the input layer, output layer, and multiple hidden layers. Through the input layer which can be considered as the first layer that has fed the preprocessed data is given as input and from the output, the layer will get the outputs of the model designed. The hidden layers have no connections to the external world. Each layer consists of multiple neurons.
2. Each layer is connected to the next layer through means of weights assigned for every connection. Here the information flows in the forward and input fed in the first layer.
3. Each layer of neurons will not have any connections among them.

Loss Function

It is known as cost function which helps to evaluate the model performance by given weights (Janocha and Czarnecki 2016). Here we used simple error which can be written as below:

Error = True value – Predicted value

where True value is the real output label either '0' or '1' in our case mean whether the signal is the real audio signal or laser-generated signal. The predicted value is the output value of the neural network designed to train the model.

Activation Function

Activation functions are placed at corresponding neurons output to have a smoother experience of the training process. Usually, activation used here is the sigmoid function.

$$f\left(x\right) = \frac{1}{1 + \exp\left(-x\right)}$$

where f(x) is the sigmoid function

Feed Forward Process

In this process, the weights of the neural networks are initialized with random weights and the input is sent through the input layer and the corresponding neuron calculates the values from which we get the output value from the output layer.

Backpropagation Process

In this process, the weights of the neural networks are updated with the loss function calculated from the output of the feedforward process based on the derivatives obtained from the backward process through every neuron in the reverse direction.

Optimizers

Optimizers play a crucial role in making the model train faster and having better accuracy. The selection of optimizers is important for the specific application. Usually, for most applications, the Adam optimizer will work with the learning rate of 3e-4 for better performance.

Light Commands

Amplitude modulated laser signal can act as an audio signal for a microphone (Sugawara et al. 2020). Laser light commands can be used from a large distance (up to 110 m) and do not require physical contact with the victim device. However, a stable line of sight is essential. Since most of the devices are always-listening devices and the microphone perceives laser light signals as audio signals, they are prone to such attacks. The adversary can unlock victim smart devices such as phones, garages, door locks, shop on commercial websites, or hack vehicles.

The research (Sugawara et al. 2020) suggests many hardware and software solutions prevent laser-signals attacks such as the use of shields over the microphone, change microphone architecture, use extra authentication layers, or use multiple microphones. However, each of these solutions has some vulnerabilities. They either increase the complexity of the hardware or hamper the user experience.

Figure 3. Experimental setup block diagram

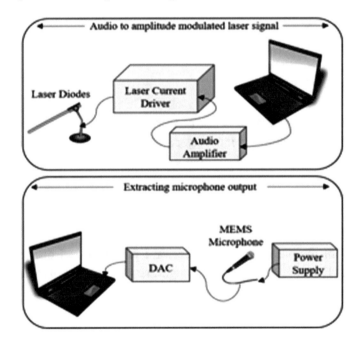

METHODOLOGY

Experimental Setup

The experimental setup is represented by the model shown in figure 3. In the first block, the audio signals from the laptop are fed into an audio amplifier which is then fed to the laser current driver. The laser is mounted with holders and can be repositioned as desired. In the second block, a mems microphone is powered by the power supply, and the output from the microphone is fed to DAC. It is important to align and focus the laser to the microphone aperture for proper signal injection. The larger the distance between the microphone and laser, it becomes difficult to align the laser to the microphone aperture.

Dataset

For every Deep learning project, we need to have a dataset, model, and type of optimizer. In our project dataset is prepared using recording audio signals from the original microphone using two different inputs:

- Voice commands played on the laptop
- Amplitude modulated laser signals projected on the microphone aperture

Table 1. List of voice commands

List of Commands	Voice Users
Call 1234567890 UK Male FaceTime 1 2 3 4 5 6 7 8 9 0 Open dolphinattack.com Turn on airplane mode Open the back door Navigation Hey Siri Ok Google Hi Galaxy Hello Huawei Alexa What Time Is It? Set the Volume to Zero	UK Male UK Female UK Hazel US G US David US Zira

We used a text-to-speech converter provided by https://ttsreader.com/ to generate different audio commands using different users shown in Table 1. Since the commands are short and it is difficult to extract samples for each command separately, all the commands were run in a single loop. First, the audio sample was run simply over a laptop speaker and the microphone output was recorded. Then the audio samples were used to drive the laser and the laser signal was used as input to the microphone. A single stream of audio signals was extracted as microphone outputs for each input signal. These audio signals were sliced into 10 seconds of equal parts to generate145 samples for each audio sample.

Audio Signal Classification

The model training and testing were done on a Dell laptop (Intel i7-7th generation 2.7 GHz, 8GB RAM, 64-bit Windows OS). For the model selection, the number of layers and the activation functions used are very important for determining the accuracy of the model. In our model, we used four fully connected layers and the first three layers with Rectified Linear Unit activation and with last layer sigmoid function is used for classifying whether the signal is a laser or not. For optimization purposes, we used different optimizers and found Adam optimizer as the most effective for training the model. The corresponding neural network is shown in figure 4.

Figure 4. Experimental setup block diagram

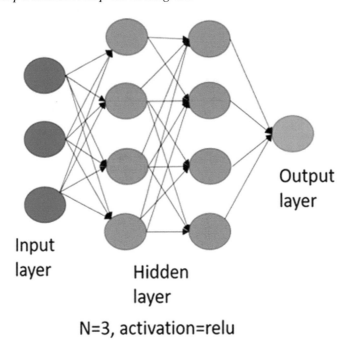

So in this experiment first we further increase the size of the signal using splitting the signal further into five segments which will help the model to have enough information about the signal. The main reason for this process is to avoid the underfitting of data. After this, the MFCC coefficient for each segment is derived from using the popular audio machine learning library Librosa. 40% of the data is solely used for testing and among the 60%, 20% of data is used for validation purposes to avoid overfitting.

Results

These MFCC are used as input to our model and found that validation and test accuracy of the recorded signals were 100% on validation data. To further improve the training, we randomly selected signals and apply the same process for testing and found them to be an average of 80% accurate.

Table 2. Accuracy result for different optimizers

Optimizer Used	Testing Accuracy 1st Case	Testing Accuracy 2nd Case
Adam	100	95
SGD	99.65	80
RMSprop	100	82
Adadelta	79.26	32
Adagrad	98.40	85
Adamax	99.65	75
Nadam	99.82	90
Ftrl	98.4	85

Table 2 shows the result for two different testing samples. The 1st case testing includes the samples drawn from the microphone output and therefore the accuracy is higher for all kinds of optimizers used. The 2nd case testing includes random audio samples used to test how the model would respond and therefore we can see accuracy has dropped.

FUTURE RESEARCH DIRECTIONS

Human interaction with devices is almost everywhere this kind of detection will be helpful in various real-time applications like self-driving cars. This application is further extended to the detection of various Electromagnetic Interference signals which can be helpful for the protection of sensors in physical devices. Cybersecurity attacks can also be minimized by replicating the same work to the time-varying signals like audio signals used in this project. This can be helpful for various sensitive industries such as nuclear power plants which can be saved from explosions from malicious attacks. In medical applications, also help determine the analog signals such as ECG signals by feed into machine learning models such that the health of the patient can be monitored without the need of an assistant. At money withdrawal stations we can assist using analyzing the audio signals which are not common can help identify the thieves and protect the individual lives with less effort instead of recording videos which consume a lot of memory.

CONCLUSION

Deep learning provides an alternative to detect malicious signals which can protect various types of sensors. We can use simple models to classify signals from malicious signals. While amplitude modulated laser signals were explored in this project, other attacks can also be explored for applying deep learning models for identification.

REFERENCES

Abdullah, H. (2019). *Practical Hidden Voice Attacks against Speech and Speaker Recognition Systems*. Academic Press.

Abdullah, H., Warren, K., Bindschaedler, V., Papernot, N., & Traynor, P. (2020). *The Faults in Our ASRs: An Overview of Attacks against Automatic Speech Recognition and Speaker Identification Systems*. arXiv preprint arXiv:2007.06622.

Alepis, E., & Patsakis, C. (2017). Monkey Says, Monkey Does: Security and Privacy on Voice Assistants. *IEEE Access: Practical Innovations, Open Solutions*, 5, 17841–17851. doi:10.1109/ACCESS.2017.2747626

Alzantot, M., Balaji, B., & Srivastava, M. (2018). *Did You Hear That? Adver-Sarial Examples against Automatic Speech Recognition*. arXiv preprintarXiv:1801.00554.

Amodei, D. (2016). Deep Speech 2: End-to-End Speech Recognition in English and Mandarin. *33rd International Conference on Machine Learning, ICML 2016*.

Carlini, N. (2016). Hidden Voice Commands This Paper Is Included in the Proceedings of the Hidden Voice Commands. *USENIX Security Symposium*.

Carlini, N., & Wagner, D. (2018). Audio Adversarial Examples: Targeted Attacks on Speech-to-Text. *Proceedings - 2018 IEEE Symposium on Security and Privacy Workshops, SPW 2018*. 10.1109/SPW.2018.00009

Chen, S. (2017). You Can Hear but You Cannot Steal: Defending Against Voice Impersonation Attacks on Smartphones. *Proceedings - International Conference on Distributed Computing Systems*. 10.1109/ICDCS.2017.133

Chen, Y., Zhang, J., Yuan, X., Zhang, S., Chen, K., Wang, X., & Guo, S. (2021). *SoK: A Modularized Approach to Study the Security of Automatic Speech Recognition Systems.* arXiv preprint arXiv:2103.10651.

Cisse, M., Adi, Y., Neverova, N., & Keshet, J. (2017). *Houdini: Fooling Deep Structured Visual and Speech Recognition Models with Adversarial Examples.* Advances in Neural Information Processing Systems.

Diao, W., Liu, X., Zhou, Z., & Zhang, K. (2014). Your Voice Assistant Is Mine: How to Abuse Speakers to Steal Information and Control Your Phone. *Proceedings of the ACM Conference on Computer and Communications Security.* 10.1145/2666620.2666623

Giechaskiel, I., & Rasmussen, K. (2020). Taxonomy and Challenges of Out-of-Band Signal Injection Attacks and Defenses. *IEEE Communications Surveys and Tutorials*, *22*(1), 645–670. doi:10.1109/COMST.2019.2952858

Gong, Y., & Poellabauer, C. (2018). An Overview of Vulnerabilities of Voice Controlled Systems. *1st International Workshop on Security and Privacy for the Internet-of-Things.*

Jang, Y. (2014). A11y Attacks: Exploiting Accessibility in Operating Systems. *Proceedings of the ACM Conference on Computer and Communications Security.* 10.1145/2660267.2660295

Janocha, K., & Czarnecki, W. M. (2016). *On Loss Functions for Deep Neural Networks in Classification.* Schedae Informaticae.

Kasmi, C., & Esteves, J. L. (2015). IEMI Threats for Information Security: Remote Command Injection on Modern Smartphones. *IEEE Transactions on Electromagnetic Compatibility*, *57*(6), 1752–1755. doi:10.1109/TEMC.2015.2463089

Kereliuk, C., Sturm, B. L., & Larsen, J. (2015). Deep Learning and Music Adversaries. *IEEE Transactions on Multimedia*, *17*(11), 2059–2071. doi:10.1109/TMM.2015.2478068

Kune, D. F. (2013). Ghost Talk: Mitigating EMI Signal Injection Attacks against Analog Sensors. *Proceedings - IEEE Symposium on Security and Privacy.* 10.1109/SP.2013.20

Lavner, Y., Cohen, R., Ruinskiy, D., & IJzerman, H. (2018). Baby Cry Detection in Domestic Environment Using Deep Learning. SSRN *Electronic Journal.*

Lei, X. (2018). The Insecurity of Home Digital Voice Assistants - Vulnerabilities, Attacks and Countermeasures. *2018 IEEE Conference on Communications and Network Security, CNS 2018.* 10.1109/CNS.2018.8433167

Logan, B. (2000). Mel Frequency Cepstral Coefficients for Music Modeling. *International Symposium on Music Information Retrieval.*

Maheshwari, S. (2017). *Burger King 'O.K. Google' Ad Doesn't Seem O.K. With Google.* www.nytimes.com/2017/04/12/business/burger-king-tv-ad-google-home.html

Martin. (n.d.). *72% Want Voice Control In Smart-Home Products.* https://www.mediapost.com/publications/article/292253/72-want-voice-control-in-smart-home-products.html?edition=993

Petracca, G., Sun, Y., Jaeger, T., & Atamli, A. (2015). AuDroid: Preventing Attacks on Audio Channels in Mobile Devices. *ACM International Conference Proceeding Series.* 10.1145/2818000.2818005

Poellabauer, Y., & Gong, C. (2017). *Crafting Adversarial Examples for Speechparalinguistics Applications.* arXiv preprint arXiv:1711.03280.

Purwins, H. (2019). Deep Learning for Audio Signal Processing. *IEEE Journal of Selected Topics in Signal Processing.*

Ramirez, J. J. M., & J. C. (2007). Voice Activity Detection. Fundamentals and Speech Recognition System Robustness. Robust Speech Recognition and Understanding.

Rasmussen, K. B., Castelluccia, C., Heydt-Benjamin, T. S., & Capkun, S. (2009). Proximity-Based Access Control for Implantable Medical Devices. *Proceedings of the ACM Conference on Computer and Communications Security.* 10.1145/1653662.1653712

Roy, N. (2018). Inaudible Voice Commands : The Long-Range Attack and Defense. *Proceedings of the 15th USENIX Symposium on Networked.*

Stephenson, H. (n.d.). *UX design trends 2018: From voice interfaces to a Need to Not Trick People.* https://www.digitalartsonline.co.uk/features/interactive-design/ux-design-trends-2018-from-voice-interfaces-need-not-trick-peop

Sugawara, T. (2020). Light Commands: Laser-Based Audio Injection Attacks on Voice-Controllable Systems. *Proceedings of the 29th USENIX Security Symposium.*

Torrey, L., & Shavlik, J. (2010). Transfer Learning. In *Handbook of Researchon Machine Learning Applications and Trends: Algorithms, Methods,and Techniques* (pp. 242–26). IGI Global. doi:10.4018/978-1-60566-766-9.ch011

Tu, Y. (2019). *Trick or Heat?* Academic Press.

Tu, Y., Lin, Z., Lee, I., & Hei, X. (2018). Injected and Delivered: Fabricating Implicit Control over Actuation Systems by Spoofing Inertial Sensors. *Proceedings of the 27th USENIX Security Symposium.*

Tu, Y., Tida, V. S., Pan, Z., & Hei, X. (2021). Transduction Shield: A Low-Complexity Method to Detect and Correct the Effects of EMI Injection Attacks on Sensors. *Proceedings of the 2021 ACM Asia Conference on Computer and Communications Security.* 10.1145/3433210.3453097

Vaidya, T., Zhang, Y., Sherr, M., & Shields, C. (2015). Cocaine Noodles: Exploiting the Gap between Human and Machine Speech Recognition. *9th USENIX Workshop on Offensive Technologies, WOOT 2015.*

Venugopalan, S. (2015). Translating Videos to Natural Language Using Deep Recurrent Neural Networks. *NAACL HLT 2015 - 2015 Conference of the North American Chapter of the Association for Computational Linguistics: Human Language Technologies, Proceedings of the Conference.* 10.3115/v1/N15-1173

Vera-Diaz, J. M., Pizarro, D., & Macias-Guarasa, J. (2018). *Towards End-to-End Acoustic Localization Using Deep Learning: From Audio Signals to Source Position Coordinates.* Sensors.

Xu, M. (2004). HMM-Based Audio Keyword Generation. Lecture Notes in Computer Science (including subseries Lecture Notes in Artificial Intelligence and Lecture Notes in Bioinformatics). doi:10.1007/978-3-540-30543-9_71

Xu, Z., Hua, R., Juang, J., Xia, S., Fan, J., & Hwang, C. (2021). Inaudible Attack on Smart Speakers with Intentional Electromagnetic Interference. *IEEE Transactions on Microwave Theory and Techniques*, 69(5), 2642–2650. doi:10.1109/TMTT.2021.3058585

Yan, C. (2020). SoK: A Minimalist Approach to Formalizing Analog Sensor Security. *Proceedings - IEEE Symposium on Security and Privacy.* 10.1109/SP40000.2020.00026

Yan, Q. (2020). *SurfingAttack: Interactive Hidden Attack on Voice Assistants Using Ultrasonic Guided Waves.* Academic Press.

Yang, N., Dey, N., Sherratt, R. S., & Shi, F. (2020). Recognize Basic Emotional Statesin Speech by Machine Learning Techniques Using Mel-Frequency Cepstral Coefficient Features. *Journal of Intelligent & Fuzzy Systems*, 39(2), 1925–1936. doi:10.3233/JIFS-179963

Yuan, X. (2018). CommanderSong: A Systematic Approach for Practical Adversarial Voice Recognition. *Proceedings of the 27th USENIX Security Symposium.*

Zhang, G. (2017). DolphinAttack: Inaudible Voice Commands. *Proceedings of the ACM Conference on Computer and Communications Security.*

Zhang, Y., & Rasmussen, K. (2020). Detection of Electromagnetic Interference Attacks on Sensor Systems. *Proceedings - IEEE Symposium on Security and Privacy.* 10.1109/SP40000.2020.00001

Zue, V. W. (1980). Digital Processing of Speech Signals, by L. R. Rabiner and R. W. Schafer. *The Journal of the Acoustical Society of America, 67*(4), 1406–1407. doi:10.1121/1.384160

Chapter 9
Teleoperated Surgical Robot Security:
Challenges and Solutions

Md Abdullah Al Momin
University of Louisiana at Lafayette, USA

Md Nazmul Islam
University of Louisiana at Lafayette, USA

ABSTRACT

Technology has greatly increased the availability of medical procedures in remote locations that are difficult to access, such as battlefields. Teleoperated surgical robots can be used to perform surgeries on patients over the internet in remote locations. A surgeon can remotely operate the robot to perform a procedure in another room or in a different continent. However, security technology has not yet caught up to these cyber-physical devices. There exist potential cybersecurity attacks on these medical devices that could expose a patient to danger in contrast to traditional surgery. Hence, the security of the system is very important. A malicious actor can gain control of the device and potentially threaten the life of a patient. In this chapter, the authors conduct a survey of potential attack vectors a malicious actor could exploit to deny service to the device, gain control of the device, and steal patient data. Furthermore, after the vulnerability analysis, the authors provide mitigation techniques to limit the risk of these attack vectors.

DOI: 10.4018/978-1-7998-7323-5.ch009

INTRODUCTION

In recent years, Tele-operated Surgical Robots (TSRs) have become more and more popular for diagnosis and surgery. TSRs such as da Vinci and RAVEN I/II have popularized using robots for minimally invasive surgeries (Chang, Lum & Hannaford *et al.*) TSRs have been designed to perform minimally invasive surgeries in remote locations such as battlefields, underwater, and disaster territories over ad-hoc wireless and satellite networks (Tozal *et al.*, 2011).

TSRs are categorized as real-time interactive network applications and are constrained with maximum delay and loss requirements while still being capable of service in extreme environments. Many TSRs have adopted the Interoperable Telesurgery Protocol (ITP) as a standard. The ITP protocol uses light-weight UDP to achieve the lowest possible latency for communication between the endpoint devices. Figure 1 shows the communications diagram for the RAVEN I. This protocol, however, has several disadvantages when considering the safety and privacy of the patient. In addition, there consists of a lack of remote software attestation of TSRs and are susceptible to an endpoint-based attack.

Background Information on Tele-Operated Surgical Robots

Telesurgery is an emerging technology that connects surgeons and patients remotely—combining advances in the medical field, network communications, and robotics. Telesurgery can overcome the shortage of local medical experts and the general inaccessibility of medical care in remote locations. In addition, it could potentially reduce the overall cost of medical care of fielding surgical specialists in remote geographical areas while still providing high-quality surgical care.

The RAVEN I/II is an open-source platform for research in tele-operative robotic surgery. As shown in Figure 2, it is composed of a master console, a network communications channel, and a surgical robot. The master console provides the surgeon's tool manipulators to issue commands to the surgical robot and contains a 2D/3D display for video feedback. The commands issued by the master console are converted into user command packets and sent over the network communications channel. Next, they are translated into motor commands by the robotic control software and sent to the control hardware, which enables the movement of the robotic arms and instruments. Video feedback is then sent back towards the master console to allow the surgeon visual confirmation of the current state.

Security Protocols of Tele-Operated Surgical Robots

There is a safety Programmable Logic Controller (PLC) that operates in a state machine that consists of four states: a) emergency stop ("E-STOP"), b) initialization ("Init"), c) foot pedal released ("Pedal Up"), and d) foot pedal pressed ("Pedal Down"). The control software state is synced with the PLC state every 1 millisecond (Alemzadeh *et al.*, 2015). In the "Pedal Up" state, the brakes are engaged, and the robot does not move. The "Pedal Down" state is initiated when the surgeon pushes the foot pedal down and allows the master console to control the robot directly. The "E-STOP" state immediately stops the robot. The control software detects and corrects any unsafe motor commands. During regular operation, the software continuously sends a square-wave watchdog signal to the PLC. Upon detecting a motor command that deviates too far time-wise from the last known command or the motor command position deviates too far from the robotic hardware's current position, it terminates sending the watchdog signal. Upon loss of the signal, the PLC immediately puts the system into the "E-STOP" state.

Figure 1. RAVEN I communications diagram

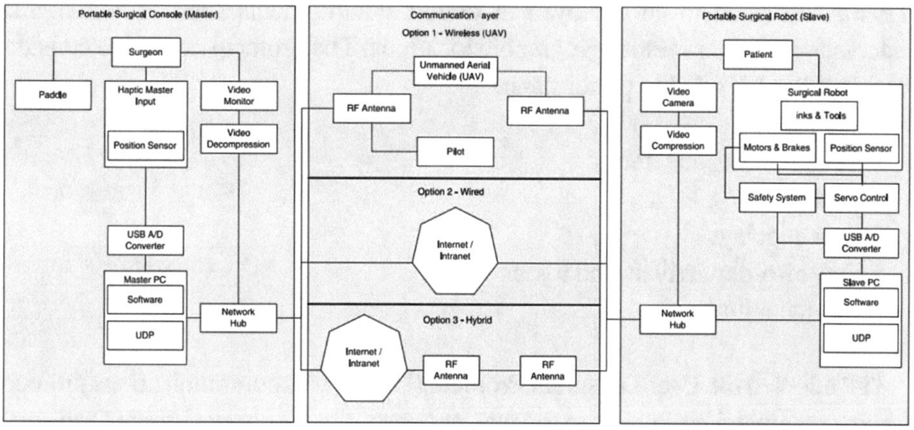

Figure 2. Robotic telesurgery using RAVEN II surgical platform

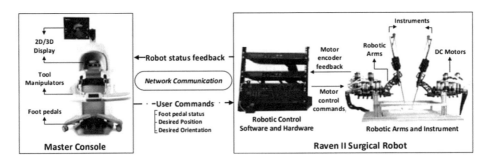

Interoperable Telesurgery Protocol

Most current-generation TSRs use a communications protocol called the Interoperable Telesurgery Protocol to communicate between the master console and the surgical robot. ITP allows heterogeneous surgical consoles (masters) and manipulators (slaves) to communicate regardless of the individual hardware and software (King *et al.*, 2010). It also allows any brand or vendor master console and surgical robot to be used interchangeably as long as they adhere to the communications standard. ITP was designed to be deployed in remote environments such as battlefields, underwater, or other remote geographic locations. The protocol needed to consider the following for reliable performance:

- Communication latency
- Jitters
- Packet delays
- Out-of-order arrivals and losses
- Device failures

ITP adopted the User Datagram Protocol (UDP) as its communications protocol to carry command packets from the master console to the surgical robots and carry the video feedback from the surgical robot to the master console due to the low latency a real-time medical device like TSRs requires and its ability to handle communication latency and packet loss.

VULNERABILITIES

Attacks on the TSRs can be labeled in one of two categories: Network-based attacks and endpoint-based attacks. Network-based attacks on TSRs try to observe or intercept data while en route from the master console and surgical robot. The endpoint-based attacks happen when one of the end machines is compromised.

Table 1 shows potential attacks, examples of the attack, and if that attack is a threat to either security or privacy (Lera *et al.* 2017).

Table 1. Types of attacks

Attack	Type	Example
Stealth attack	2	Modification/Substitution of sensor reading
Replay attack	1,2	Attacker impersonating roles
Covert attack	1	Third-party apps sharing personal data
False-data injection	1,2	Medical robots
DoS attack	2	Robot not working at all
Remote access	1,2	Robot controlled by an attacker
Eavesdropping	1	Attacker monitoring robot-user messages

Type 1 indicates a privacy concern. Type 2 indicates a security concern

Network-Based Attacks

TSRs are designed to be usable in remote locations and potentially even perform transcontinental surgery. However, there is a significant tradeoff between the operability and availability of TSRs and their security. Many TSRs have adopted the Interoperable Telesurgical Protocol (ITP), which employs the lightweight UDP protocol. UDP-Lite is designed to serve applications in error-prone networks that a malicious actor could take advantage of.

Network-based attacks on TSRs can be categorized as Man in the Middle (MITM) attacks. They take advantage of the insecure, high loss, and high delay tolerance afforded by UDPLite to conduct attacks such as eavesdropping or denial of service, which threaten security and privacy.

To launch a MITM attack on a TSR a network observer initially eavesdrops on the exchange between the two endpoints. This task is trivial if an attacker can compromise a node along the network communications path because the UDP packets are not encrypted. Once enough information is gained about the status of the connection, further attacks can be launched:

- **Stealthy attacks:** There is no detection in place to verify the source of a packet. All network-based attacks on TSRs using ITP can be considered stealthy attacks. Injecting malicious packets and legitimate packets will be processed the same.
- **Replay attack:** The TSR assumes the steam of UDP packets coming from the host computer to itself is continuous. As such, it uses a sequence number on each packet to determine the order as they are received. If packets are received out of order, only the highest numbered packet is considered legitimate and processed. The replay attacks resend captured packets and should not be a threat to the system since they will by default be lower-numbered and thrown out. Although, there exists the possibility of a replay attack succeeding where the sequence number counter hits its maximum threshold and resets back to 0. Where a replay attacks packets would then be considered legitimate.
- **Denial of Service attack:** A denial of service attack can be performed by sending a sequence leading packet to the TSR client that triggers the E-Stop mechanism. This mechanism triggers if the movement of the robotic arms is too great from the current packet and the most recent packet or the current packet commands the robot to move into a forbidden region. This attack can be done continuously, rendering the device inoperable.
- **Remote access/Hijacking:** This attack can be performed by abusing the information gained from the sequence number. The system accepts the highest-numbered packets to be processed. To gain full remote access to the robot, an attacker can just add an offset when injecting packets. The legitimate packets from the surgeon will always be lower-numbered and rejected.
- **Eavesdropping:** Packets sent by the host computer to the TSR are not encrypted, and they can be intercepted and post a great concern to privacy and security.

Endpoint-Based Attacks

Most of the focus for finding vulnerabilities for TSRs is in the network communications domain. However, there exists a potential for attacks from compromising the endpoint computers that pose severe consequences. Not much research has been done for mitigating these types of attacks because they are assumed to be secure.

There are plenty of ways an attacker can gain remote access to the robot control system. An attacker can exploit vulnerable services, unpatched medical devices, stolen credentials, or insider attacks to penetrate the hospital network. From there, the attacker can move laterally across devices until the target robot control system is penetrated.

If the host computer is compromised, an attacker can gain full remote access to the RAVEN by performing the following steps (Alemzadeh *et al.*, 2016):

1. Attacker downloads a malicious shared library, which implements a write or read system call wrapper.
2. Attacker modifies LD PRELOAD or /etc/ld.so/preload to force future Linux processes to link to the malicious library.
3. The system call wrapper sniffs USB traffic sent by the TSR and forwards the USB packet contents to the attacker listening on a remote server.
4. Attacker performs off-line analysis on sniffed USB data from several runs to find a field in the USB packet that represents the state of the robot.
5. Based on the analysis, the attacker modifies the malicious wrapper to trigger an attack when the robot is in an operational ("Pedal Down") state.
6. Attacker downloads the modified shared library to the RAVEN system by repeat
7. Attack will be triggered automatically when the RAVEN control software reaches the "Pedal Down" state.
8. The control command/feedback sent over the USB channel is modified to cause a sudden jump of the robotic arm or cause the control software to stop.

Figure 3. Typical control structure in surgical robots

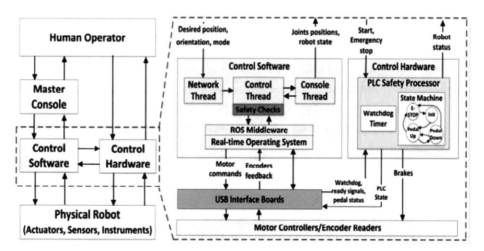

149

The real danger of the endpoint attack is the software-designed safety checks that cause the E-Stop feature in network-based attacks don't work here as the control software performs the safety checks before they are sent to the USB interface boards. This attack can circumvent all known safety protocols and cause total destruction of the machine or the patient.

Detection of an attack like this is difficult because no shared processes are created to run the malware, no system-wide malicious activities are performed, no changes are made to the control flow of the target process, and there is no anomaly in the syntax of robot control commands (Alemzadeh *et al.*, 2016). Current malware detection methods are insufficient in detecting this kind of attack.

Sensor-Based Attacks

It is a very reasonable security concern for the researchers as there have been many sensors present in the telesurgical robots. Also, teleo-perated robots do not use any encryption mechanism to communicate between patient consoles and doctor consoles. So, an adversary might capture data in the intermediate path and initiate attacks against the system. In this section, a brief discussion about all the sensors present in the telesurgical robots is presented, and the respective possible vulnerabilities are also explored. Our goal is to establish a ground from which to start exploring attacks on the tele-operated systems and suggest possible countermeasures for the respective security concern.

- **Sensors Present in the Telerobotic Machines and Their Vulnerabilities:** Sensors can be either internal or external to the robotic manipulator. The former is directly mounted on the manipulator (*e.g.*, joint position sensors, force sensors). The latter is separated from the manipulator (*e.g.*, external camera systems) and integrated into the control system.
- **Inertial Sensor:** Inertial sensors are sensors based on inertia and relevant measuring principles. Typically known as Inertial Measurement Unit (IMU), an IMU sensor consists of accelerometers, gyroscopes, and sometimes also magnetometers.
  - **Vulnerabilities in Inertial Sensor:** (Tu *et al.*, 2018) demonstrated that by injecting acoustic signals into inertial sensors, an attacker can control the output of an inertial sensor. The authors described slight sample rate drifts could be amplified and cause deviations in the frequency of digital signals. Such deviations result in fluctuating sensor output.
- **Strain Gauge Force Sensor:** Embedded in the probe holder, measures the contact force between the real probe and the patient's skin.

- ○ **Vulnerabilities in Strain Gauge Force Sensor:** A strain gauge is a sensor whose resistance varies with applied force; It converts force, pressure, tension, weight, etc., into a change in electrical resistance that can then be measured. When external forces are applied to a stationary object, stress, and strain are the result. Stress is defined as the object's internal resisting forces and strain is defined as the displacement and deformation that occurs. Faulty wiring in the surgical machine and wrong impact settings make the sensor vulnerable at the time of measuring stress in a stationary object. This problem also can be crucial for telesurgical robots also.

- **Force Sensor:** Present at the master site or doctor site. This hands-free input device allows the medical expert to perform natural medical gestures as in conventional conditions. These sensors provide the setpoints for robot control.
  - ○ **Vulnerabilities in the Force Sensor:** Remote attack in the force sensor might occur problems in the sensing material. In the master site, there presents a monitor screen that shows the force pressured with the pedal from the foot. Force value could have tampered with the change remotely from the remote site. The effect is too severe as sensing material could cause a huge change at the time of the operation.

- **6D Localization Magnetic Sensor:** Giving the attitude and position of the fictive probe in real time; this system also integrates an actuator that can be controlled to render to the expert the effort sensed by the robot end-effector on the patient.
  - ○ **Vulnerabilities in 6D Localization Magnetic Sensor:** To track the movement of a wireless capsule and get the 6D localization and with the magnetic sensor array arranged out of the human body, it is very urgent to have exact measurement and localization at the time of surgical procedures. Passive magnetic attack on localization sensor creates false localization and make it harder for the tele-operational procedures.

- **Range Sensor:** To determine the physical distance at the time of the operation.
  - ○ **Vulnerabilities in Range Sensor:** Transmission in a wireless network might be in lag for the range sensor. The communication range in the range sensor is limited, and a lag of response could happen for the faulty sensor configuration. For example, if the master side and the patient side have a long distance between them, then the range sensor could not act properly at the time of distance measurement. Also, operational procedures might face lag in communication for faulty range measurement by the range sensor.

- **Torque Sensor:** A torque sensor, torque transducer or torque meter is a device for measuring and recording the torque on a rotating system, such as an engine, crankshaft, gearbox, transmission, rotor, a bicycle crank, or cap torque tester. Static torque is relatively easy to measure.

- ○ **Vulnerabilities in Torque Sensor:** Torque sensors or torque transducers use strain gauges applied to a rotating shaft or axle. So, the vulnerabilities found in the strain gauge sensors can be applied in the torque sensors too.

- **Vibration Sensor:** The vibration sensors measure the high-frequency accelerations of the tool arms, and the central receiver drives the voice coil actuators on the master handles to let the surgeon feel these vibrations. The gain control knob adjusts the magnitude of the vibration feedback.

  - ○ **Vulnerabilities in Vibration Sensors:** The vibration sensor and intrusion sensor acts as same. Both the sensors could be affected by the change in the surface. A physical-injection attack on the vibration sensor could change the effect of the normal vibration and could dampen the effect in the normal operational procedure. Surface-aided and aerial vibration could also be affected by the physical attack in the process.

- **Acceleration Sensor:** The basic underlying working principle of an accelerometer is such as a dumped mass on a spring. When acceleration is experienced by this device, the mass gets displaced till the spring can easily move the mass, with the same rate equal to the acceleration it sensed.

  - ○ **Vulnerabilities in Acceleration Sensors:** Acceleration sensors are susceptible to acoustic attacks. Analog acoustic injection attacks can damage the digital integrity of the capacitive MEMS accelerometer. Spoofing such sensors with intentional acoustic interference enables an out-of-spec pathway for attackers to deliver chosen digital values to microprocessors and embedded systems that blindly trust the invalidated integrity of sensor outputs.

- **Laser Range Finder (LRF) Sensor,** (*i.e.*, a lidar), which is installed on the robot to map and perform precise localization; a technique known as Simultaneous Localization and Mapping (SLAM).

- **Distal Sensor:** To obtain realistic force information, a sensor is preferably placed close to the instrument tip, minimizing the errors due to friction between the instrument and the point of incision. The sensor should be separated from the drive mechanism to prevent the influence of backlash and friction on the sensor's performance.

  - ○ **Vulnerabilities in the Distal Sensor:** A distal sensor is related to motion feedback. The master side of the operational process has a distal sensor in the operation room, and it is used to measure and categorize the motion feedback. So, the problem may arise at the time of master to patient feedback if the communication has some lag and distal sensor data does not deliver from the patient to the master side. Change in the position of the distal sensor also could affect hugely at the time of operational procedures. Physical access also could change with the distal sensor with the heating and environmental factor.

MITIGATION

Network-Based Attacks

ITP is the standard communication protocol for telesurgery developed by Washington BioRobotics Laboratory (BRL) at SRI International. The protocol did not consider security measures, and the data is transmitted in plaintext. It is widely adopted in telesurgery robots; thus, securing it is crucial. Most of the proposed solutions involve updating the ITP protocol that uses UDP to communicate to a more secure communication platform. Protocols such as:

- Secure and Statistically Reliable UDP (SSR-UDP): SSR-UDP is a lightweight protocol that provides confidentiality and reliability for the system while conveying the requirements of Telesurgical Robot Systems (TRSs). This protocol layer is built on top of UDP and is located between transport and application layers of the Internet Protocol Suite. Instead of using encryption, the protocol is using a coding scheme based on a secure key generation function. The function takes a pre-shared key and arbitrary length input and generates the message-authentication key. Also, it relies on forwarding Error Correction (FEC). In TRSs, the controller sends messages continuously; and the robot will process the messages at the application layer. However, SSR-UDP will accumulate 'k' messages encode them into 'n' packets. The receiver will collect k packets to be able to decode the whole message. The security achieved using SSR-UDP is the same as the AES-128 security level with less overhead; that also holds when compared SSR-UDP to standard DTLS, TLS/SSL (Tozal *et al.*, 2013 & 2015).
- Secure ITP: Secure ITP enhanced security by introducing an independent framework on top of ITP. In IPT specification, two communication channels are defined: TCP Transmission Control Protocol (TCP) and User Datagram Protocol. (UDP). Transport Layer Security (TLS) and Datagram TLS (DTLS) are protocols suggested by NIST to secure TCP and UDP, respectively. TLS and DTLS to Secure ITP communication on the corresponding channels. Secure ITP used TLS and DTLS, but by implementing only one cipher Algorithm, which is AES, to encrypt the communication channel and thus

provide data integrity and privacy. Moreover, authentication and level of authorization are achieved by implementing certificates based on the X.509 standard.

- Encryption: Iqbal *et al.* developed a security framework called (SecureSurgiNET) based on standard cryptography primitives in addition to a tele-surgical authority (TSA) infrastructure. The model is divided into three phases: pre-operative, intra-operative, and post-operative phases (Iqbal *et al.* 2019). In the first phase, a secure connection is initiated between the master and slave based on the X.509 and the patients' biometric identities. In the intra-operative phase, TCP and UDP connections are active. The communication is encrypted using Advanced Encryption Standard (AES) to provide confidentiality and integrity of the data in both directions. During the last stage, all data are stored in TSA for future use. Worth mentioning that TSA maintains security components such as local certification authority, authentication server, and records of participating entities. The framework assures a strong security level while adhering to the TRS delay limit.

Endpoint-Based Attacks

- Dynamic model-based detection: Add in anomaly detection at the USB Interface level before the commands reach the physical robot to detect motor and robot arm positions if beyond safety limit. A study done by (Alemzadeh *et al.*, 2016) showed that some types of attacks are hard to detect for several reasons, including having the same command syntax of legit one, the same control flow, and unnoticed overhead in terms of the delay and performance. They developed a dynamic model framework to assess the attack by simulating its impacts on software, not physically. The model will check every command dynamically before implementing it on the physical system. The simulation estimates the motor position, precisely the motor acceleration, the motor velocities, and the joint velocities. Then the system will raise an alert if the value exceeds a pre-defined threshold (more than 1mm per 1-2 ms). The simulation process and the detection should be done within one millisecond to avoid a lag in a real-life situation. As figure 4 shows, the framework consists of:

  ◦ A master console emulator imitates the tele-operation console functionality, responsible for sending packets to the RAVEN control software.
  ◦ A graphic simulator to show a 3-D movement of the robots.

○ A dynamic model of the RAVEN II physical system: to model the robot behavior.

○ An attack injection engine: used to generate different attack scenarios.

The model succeeded at 90% in detecting malicious commands before they manifested in the physical system (Alemzadeh *et al.*, 2016).

Figure 4. (a) Simulation framework for assessment of the impact of attacks. (b) Dynamic-model based detection and mitigation mechanisms

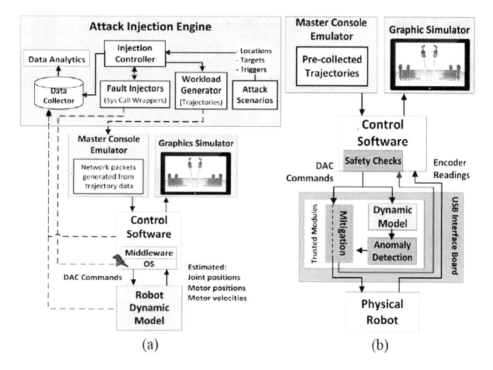

(a)   (b)

• Secure software attestation: It introduces a way to verify the integrity of the system software remotely. This form of verification verifies malicious commands are not injected by measuring latency between the endpoints. All attacks add latency to the system and would be found using this method. Three entities are involved in the protocol: a control component (the verifier), TRS (prover), and a smart card to be inserted into TRS; the TRS works as a router between the other two entities. The protocol depends heavily on asymmetric key encryption to perform encryption and digital signature. When the medical personnel inserts the smart card into TRS, an attestation request is sent to the verifier. The verifier will use the public key of the smart card to send encrypted values of seed and an ounce. Then the smart card will retrieve the values and hand them to the TRS to perform the attestation function. The smart card will start its clock, which depends on the GPS. Then TRS sends back the function's results to the smart card. The smart card will generate a digital signature to send the hash result along with the time duration to perform the function back to the verifier. Finally, the verifier will compare the value with its calculation to check the integrity of the system (Coble *et al.*, 2010).

Figure 5. Smart card assisted software attestation of the TRS

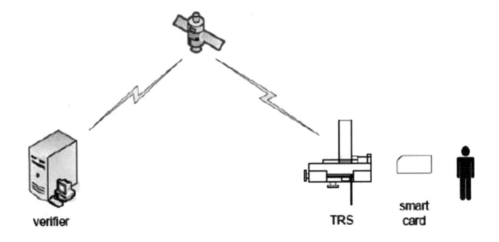

Sensor-Based Attacks

To protect MEMS inertial sensors without compromising their advantages in size, weight, power, and cost (SWaP-C (Kranz *et al.*, 2017)), recent studies have been dedicated to using micro-level techniques for acoustic isolation. Dean *et al.* proposed using micro-fibrous metallic cloth as an acoustic damping material to protect MEMS gyroscopes (Dean et al., 2011). Soobramaney et al. evaluated the mitigation effects of micro-fibrous cloth on noise signals induced in MEMS gyros under acoustic interferences (Soobramaney *et al.*, 2015). They tested 7 MEMS gyros and showed that by surrounding the sensor with 12 mm of the media, 65% reduction in the amplitude of noise signals can be easily obtained, and up to 90% reduction could be achieved (Soobramaney *et al.*, 2015). Additionally, Yunker et al. suggested using MEMS fabricated acoustic meta-material to mitigate acoustic signals at frequencies close to the resonant frequency of the MEMS gyroscope (Yunker *et al.*, 2013). Furthermore, Kranz et al. showed that a MEMS-fabricated micro-isolator could be applied within the sensor packaging, but their work mainly focused on isolating mechanical vibrations (Kranz *et al.*, 2017).

- **Filtering:** As suggested in (Trippel *et al.*, 2017), a low-pass filter (LPF) should be used to eliminate the out-of-band analog signals. According to the datasheets (STMicroelectronics L3GD20 datasheet), (STMicroelectronics LSM330 datasheet.), we find that many inertial sensors have an analog LPF in their circuits but are still vulnerable to acoustic attacks, which could be due to a cut-off frequency that is set too high. We also find that most programmable inertial sensors use a digital LPF for bandwidth control (STMicroelectronics L3G4200D datasheet.), (InvenSense MPU-6500 datasheet). However, filters in digital circuits will not alleviate the problem because out-of-band analog signals have already been aliased to in-band signals after sampling.
- **Sampling:** Trippel *et al.* proposed randomized sampling and 180∘ out-of-phase sampling methods for inertial sensors with analog outputs and software-controlled ADCs (Trippel *et al.*, 2017). These approaches were designed to eliminate an attacker's ability to achieve a DC signal alias and limit potential adversarial control. However, adding a randomized delay to each sampling period or computing the average of two samples at a 180∘ phase delay could degrade the accuracy of inertial measurements. Minor errors in the measurements could accumulate in a long time and might affect the system's performance.

An alternative sampling method to mitigate potential adversarial control without degrading the performance is using a dynamic sample rate. The frequency of the induced digital signal depends on both the frequency of resonant sound waves and the sampling frequency. With a dynamic sampling frequency, attackers may not induce a digital signal with a predictable frequency pattern. In this case, the ability of attackers will be limited, and it could be difficult for attackers to accumulate a large heading angle in a target direction. This might be a general mitigation method for ADCs subject to out-of-band signal injections.

Additionally, redundancy-based approaches could enhance the resilience of the system. For example, multiple sensors could still provide trustworthy information when one of them is under attack. It might still be possible to attack or interfere with several sensors simultaneously to affect the system's functioning, but such attacks could be more challenging to implement.

CONCLUSION

Teleoperated robots play an essential role in the medical field, especially in remote locations such as battlefields or third-world countries. ITP is the standard communication protocol for TRSs, which depends on UDP for fast communication. However, several security issues have been found in TRSs, exploits such as MITM and DoS. Since using standard security primitives add computation overhead and latency, researchers investigate different mitigation strategies to enhance security. Without securing TRSs, the potential benefits of the system are limited.

REFERENCES

Alemzadeh, Chen, Lewis, Kalbarczyk, Raman, Leveson, & Iyer. (2015). *Systems-theoretic safety assessment of robotic telesurgical systems*. Academic Press.

Alemzadeh, H., Chen, D., Li, X., Kesavadas, T., Kalbarczyk, Z. T., & Iyer, R. K. (2016). Targeted attacks on teleoperated surgical robots: Dynamic model-based detection and mitigation. *2016 46th Annual IEEE/IFIP International Conference on Dependable Systems and Networks (DSN)*, 395–406.

Chang, Raheem, Rha. (2018). Novel robotic systems and future directions. *Indian Journal of Urology*, *34*, 110.

Coble, Wang, Chu, & Li. (2010). Secure software attestation for military telesurgical robot systems. *MILCOM 2010 Military Communications Conference*, 965–970.

Dean. (2011). Microfibrous metallic cloth for acoustic isolation of a MEMS gyroscope. In *Proceedings of Industrial and Commercial Applications of Smart Structures Technologies*. Society of Photo-Optical Instrumentation Engineers.

Hannaford, B., Rosen, J., Friedman, D., King, H. I., Roan, P., Cheng, L., Glozman, D., Ma, J., Kosari, S. N., & White, L. W. (2013). Raven-ii: An open platform for surgical robotics research. *IEEE Transactions on Biomedical Engineering*, *60*(4), 954–959. doi:10.1109/TBME.2012.2228858 PMID:23204264

InvenSense MPU-6500 datasheet. (2013). https://store. invensense.com/datasheets/ invensense/MPU_6500_ Rev1.0.pdf

Iqbal, S., Farooq, S., Shahzad, K., Malik, A. W., Hamayun, M. M., & Hasan, O. (2019). Securesurginet: A framework for ensuring security in telesurgery. *International Journal of Distributed Sensor Networks*, *15*(9), 1550147719873811.

King, H. H., Hannaford, B., Kwok, K.-W., Yang, G.-Z., Griffiths, P., Okamura, A., Farkhatdinov, I., Ryu, J.-H., Sankaranarayanan, G., Arikatla, V., Tadano, K., Kawashima, K., Peer, A., Schauß, T., Buss, M., Miller, L., Glozman, D., Rosen, J., & Low, T. (2010). Plugfest 2009: Global interoperability in telerobotics and telemedicine. *2010 IEEE International Conference on Robotics and Automation*, 1733–1738. 10.1109/ROBOT.2010.5509422

Kranz, M., Whitley, M., Rudd, C., Craven, J. D., Clark, S. D., Dean, R. N., & Flowers, G. T. (2017). Environmentally isolating packaging for MEMS sensors. In *International Symposium on Microelectronics*. International Microelectronics Assembly and Packaging Society.

Lum, Friedman, Sankaranarayanan, King, Fodero, Leuschke, Hannaford, & Rosen. (2009). The raven: Design and validation of a telesurgery system. *I. J. Robotic Res.*, *28*, 1183–1197.

Rodriguez Lera, Fernandez, Guerrero, & Matellan. (2017). *Cybersecurity of Robotics and Autonomous Systems: Privacy and Safety*. Academic Press.

Soobramaney, P., Flowers, G., & Dean, R. (2015). Mitigation of the effects of high levels of high002Dfrequency noise on MEMS gyroscopes using microfibrous cloth. *ASME 2015 International Design Engineering Technical Conferences and Computers and Information in Engineering Conference*.

STMicroelectronics L3G4200D datasheet. (2011). https://www. elecrow.com/download/L3G4200_AN3393.pdf

STMicroelectronics L3GD20 datasheet. (2013). http://www.st.com/en/mems-and-sensors/l3gd20.html

STMicroelectronics LSM330 datasheet. (2012). www.st.com/resource/en/datasheet/dm00037200.pdf

Tozal, M. E., Wang, Y., Al-Shaer, E., Sarac, K., Thuraisingham, B., & Chu, B.-T. (2013, October). Adaptive information coding for secure and reliable wireless telesurgery communications. *Mobile Networks and Applications*, *18*(5), 697–711.

Tozal, M. E., Wang, Y., Al-Shaer, E., Sarac, K., Thuraisingham, B., & Chu, B.-T. (2011). On secure and resilient telesurgery communications over unreliable networks. *IEEE Conference on Computer Communications Workshops (INFOCOM WKSHPS)*, 714–719. 10.1109/INFCOMW.2011.5928905

Trippel, T., Weisse, O., Xu, W., Honeyman, P., & Fu, K. (2017). Walnut: Waging doubt on the integrity of MEMS accelerometers with acoustic injection attacks. *Proceedings of IEEE European Symposium on Security and Privacy.*

Tu, Y. (2018). Injected and delivered: Fabricating implicit control over actuation systems by spoofing inertial sensors. *27th USENIX Security Symposium (USENIX Security 18).*

Yunker. (2013). Sound attenuation using microelectromechanical systems fabricated acoustic metamaterials. *Journal of Applied Physics.*

Chapter 10
Brain–Computer Interface:
Attack Surface Analysis

Anthony Triche
University of Louisiana at Lafayette, USA

Md Abdullah Al Momin
University of Louisiana at Lafayette, USA

ABSTRACT

Launched in 2017 to widespread publicity due to the involvement of tech magnate and outspoken futurist Elon Musk, Neuralink Corp. aims to develop an advanced brain-computer interface (BCI) platform capable of assisting in the treatment of serious neurological conditions with longer-term goals of approaching transhumanism through nonmedical human enhancement to enable human-machine "symbiosis with artificial intelligence." The first published description of a complete prototype Neuralink system, detailed by Muskin the company's only white paper to date, describes a closed-loop, invasive BCI architecture with an unprecedented magnitude of addressable electrodes. Invasive BCI systems require surgical implantation to allow for directly targeted capture and/or stimulation of neural spiking activity in functionally associated clusters of neurons beneath the surface of the cortex.

INTRODUCTION

Launched in 2017 to widespread publicity due to the involvement of tech magnate and outspoken futurist Elon Musk (Winkler *et al.*, 2017), Neuralink Corp. aims to develop an advanced brain-computer interface (BCI) platform capable of assisting in the treatment of serious neurological conditions (Masunaga *et al.*, 2017), with

DOI: 10.4018/978-1-7998-7323-5.ch010

longer-term goals of approaching trans-humanism through nonmedical human enhancement to enable human-machine "symbiosis with artificial intelligence" (Newitz *et al.*, 2017).

The first published description of a complete prototype Neuralink system, detailed by (Musk et al., 2019) in the company's only white paper to date, describes a closed-loop, invasive BCI architecture with an unprecedented magnitude of addressable electrodes. Invasive BCI systems require surgical implantation – (Musk *et al.*, 2019) further describes an advanced surgical robotic system for insertion of flexible interfacing probes – to allow for directly targeted capture and/or stimulation of neural spiking activity in functionally associated clusters of neurons beneath the surface of the cortex.

Non-invasive approaches to BCI, such as electroencephalograms (EEGs), use external sensors placed against the skin over the cranium to capture neural activity patterns at a coarse and superficial granularity not considered suitable for fine motor control or intensive medical therapies. Closed-loop, invasive BCI systems are bi-directional, making direct contact with target neural populations to sense and, if necessary, electrically stimulate to induce neuron spiking. Stimulation in closed-loop systems occurs as a function of recorded neural activity and associated feedback logic under specified parameters.

Motivations

The prototype system unveiled by Neuralink (Musk *et al.*, 2019) contains a significant quantity of electrodes in comparison to medically available invasive BCI systems currently approved for use in treatment. The described implant contains a series of individual neural processing ASICs, with each individual unit interfacing with a series of up to 96 implantable polymer threads, which each contain 32 independent electrodes. This entails a system capable of recording and stimulating thousands of distinct neural clusters with relatively low latency. The implant device further includes real-time temperature, accelerometer, and magnetometer sensors, packaged in a titanium enclosure with a moisture barrier coating.

While the first Neuralink system utilized a wired USB-C style connection for power and data transfer, media releases and official demonstrations of the technology at company determined milestones have illustrated a far more modern system that employs Bluetooth Low Energy (BLE) at the link layer and an unspecified form of wireless induction for power transfer through human skin – the implanted device is no longer physically accessible without surgery. This anticipated transition to a wireless architecture may not only create a series of novel vulnerabilities which must be addressed prior to the public release of the system but also a serious advantage in the capability of BCI systems to aid in the treatment of serious neurological disorders.

Deep brain stimulation by BCI systems has been successfully used to address a number of such maladies, ranging in severity from epileptic disorders and Parkinson's disease to more typically psychological concerns like Obsessive Compulsive Disorder and anorexia (Drew *et al.*, 2019). Neural recordings from targeted cortical clusters using invasive BCI have further been employed as input to enable speech synthesis and motor control software, among other uses (Drew *et al.*, 2019).

Reliance on stimulation or monitoring systems like these, even when only for transient medical treatment, can have profound psychological impacts on implant recipients. The level of "symbiosis" felt towards the implant and its efficacy can lead to intense feelings of reliance in some cases. In contrast, others have reported anxiety over feelings over dependency and confusion about the extent to which their autonomy remains intact (Drew *et al.*, 2019), (Pugh *et al.*, 2018). Deep brain stimulation, even when under conscious control through user input, breaches the relatively closed system that composes the brain; beyond considering factors of mental state and environmental triggers, electrical stimulation functions as a third factor that modulates the neural activity and may have far-reaching impacts due to the highly complex and often reciprocal structuring of the cortex. These concerns will likely grow more prominent in regulations of BCI systems for medical and non-medical use cases as the technology scales.

More practical motivations for assessing the potential vulnerabilities in the system proposed and under active development by Neuralink relate to consumer privacy, both medical and personal, as well as human safety. BCI data about neural activity over time has been used as input in numerous machine learning models to make inference about highly sensitive personal information, including emotional states, sexual preferences, and religious beliefs, among others (Agarwal *et al.*, 2019). Inference about neurological conditions would likely be far more trivial, as the use of BCI in their treatment is well documented. Such information could undoubtedly be used with malicious intent when combined with the scale and wireless interoperability projected of a future Neuralink system.

A simple example of such an attack, assuming unprotected access to neural signatures as they are transmitted by the implant, falls under a class of so-called subliminal attacks and involves measuring the P-300 visually evoked wave response to familiar stimuli; roughly 300ms after a visual stimulus is observed, either consciously or subliminally depending on presentation duration, a reliably identifiable pattern of neural activity is generated if the subject is familiar with the targeted stimulus. This information has been documented to reveal highly sensitive personal details about the subject, such as user passwords, bank PINs, familiarity with faces, and the like (Marin *et al.*, 2018). Possession of such data, when combined with application and link-layer vulnerabilities, may enable a range of violations to patients – the concept of "targeted advertising" could take on an entirely different meaning, among other far more potent transgressions against consumers and patient rights.

Beyond the potential for human-level manipulation through highly targeted neural stimulation, made far more severe by the scale of electrodes on the Neuralink BCI system under development as well as by the related robotic surgical system designed to facilitate more accurate interfacing with neural populations, are concerns about the physical safety of implant recipients. Deep brain stimulation via electrodes can cause permanent neurological damage when abused, literally cauterizing the affected volume of neurons. For implant recipients who rely on the BCI system to manage a potentially life-threatening brain condition such as epilepsy, targeted denial or alteration of this service could have severe irreversible consequences. Similar attacks have been proposed for less severe conditions such as impulse control disorders, where maltreatment may aggravate rather than treat the condition underlying the patient's drive to engage in inappropriate behaviors such as gambling or risky sexual practices – an issue of both autonomy and personal integrity (Drew *et al.*, 2019).

Given the proposed scale of the Neuralink system, both in a breadth of access and variety of intended end uses, the numerous motivations which may drive the development of advanced methods to breach its security deserve to be considered with serious study. Neural information may be the most private data that a person can produce, and unauthorized wireless access to manipulate the brain could be the most severe invasion of human privacy and integrity imaginable given current technology.

Attack Model

The authors first consider the potential attack model, which they later use to characterize the attack surface of the proposed Neuralink BCI system. The model presented draws from both previous kinds of research in BCI security and from details confirmed by Neuralink through publications and media releases. Further assumptions about system specifications, architectural design, or protocols employed are made only as necessary and kept to a minimum.

Victim

The authors consider the potential target or victim to be a human implant recipient of the finalized Neuralink N1 Link. They assume this victim is not immobilized by paralysis or confinement and that the device may be used to treat a neurological condition. However, this does not preclude other uses enabled by the variety of applications expected in the public release of the system by Neuralink.

Figure 1. Illustration of the flow of information and commands in a closed-loop invasive BCI approach. Blue/clockwise direction represents the flow during the capture of neural activity and red/counterclockwise direction represents the process of actualizing targeted neural stimulation. Adapted with minor alterations from (Bernal et al., 2021) to reflect the Neuralink N1 system intended for use with a mobile smartphone control periphery.

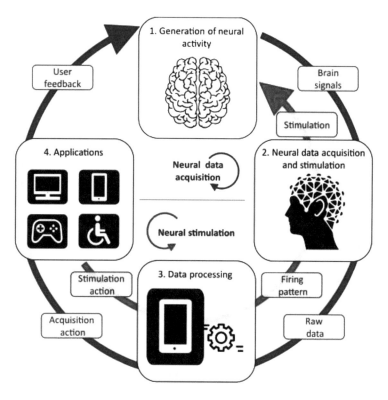

Figure 1 illustrates a combined flow model of the capture and stimulates processes of closed-loop invasive BCI. The implant identified in phase 2 of this diagram communicates wirelessly with the victim's smartphone, assumed to be running some modern release of either iOS or Android operating system.

Based on comments both by Neuralink engineers as well as details provided on their public website, it is assumed that the latest version of BLE (v5.2) is employed as the link-layer protocol. The scope of this analysis is further limited by assuming that all recordings and commands are communicated solely between the implant and peripheral smartphone controller, with no transmission of relevant data onto public channels like the Internet – latency requirements for processing this data in a useful way for most intended applications make on-peripheral processing of real-time data an obvious choice where feasible.

Attacker

As physical contact with the victim or their personal peripheral devices cannot be reasonably accomplished without detection given a non-immobilized attack victim, a man-in-the-middle (MitM) approach is the most likely scenario to be effective for attacks on the communication between implant and control device. It is assumed that the attacker operates within reasonable wireless communication range of the victim and that noticeably close proximity may only be maintained for brief periods.

Attack Surface Characterization

Given the established attacker and victim models, the authors characterize the attack surface of the proposed Neuralink system into two major components: physical attacks and BLE stack attacks. For physical level attacks, the authors primarily consider the case of EMI – physical contact is not considered a feasible means of attack under our model. The BLE stack may be sub-divided into BLE and application layer components. The current BLE protocol divides many security responsibilities primarily between the BLE chip implementation and authorized control by the application making use of the link-layer connection.

ATTACKS

In this section, each attack vector and present known vulnerabilities that may impact them are described, including a non-exhaustive explication of some example attacks.

Intentional EMI

EMI, which may impact an invasive BCI system, can occur in three common forms (Rahimpour *et al.* 2021). Interference via radiation can be caused by electromagnetic waves transmitted from one device interacting with electronic components of a secondary device, generating unwanted electrical currents in the latter. Inductive interference can also occur when there is electromagnetic coupling between two devices. This same phenomenon enables wireless charging for the proposed Neuralink device; readers may be more familiar with the effects of inductive coupling from the wireless charging pads used by some modern smartphones. Variations in a nearby magnetic field, amplified by any coils in conductive wiring, allow for one device to generate an electric current in the other without direct physical connectivity. Conductive forms of EMI require a direct physical connection between the devices. This connection may either involve only the devices having physical, and the conductive contactor may include an additional conductive medium – human tissue is a good conductor for some frequencies of this type of EMI, and this is the same principle that enables cardiac defibrillation as well as nonlethal electroshock weapons (tasers).

The EMI attack vector would be the more challenging approach to induce malicious impacts on victim implants. One cause for concern could be the aforementioned electroshock weaponry to overload the implant, though this has not been studied in BCI systems to date. Research specific to these types of implants, as recommended by (Rahimpour *et al.*, 2021), may clarify the feasibility of such attacks given the complex interactions between the human body and applied currents.

Induction-based EMI has been better studied in the literature, though not primarily focusing on implants (either BCI or other). (Selvaraj *et al.*, 2018) explored this possible attack vector in-depth and devised a theory of attack which shows how arbitrary inductive waveforms can be devised to induce random voltage readings in the analog portion of embedded systems sensor inputs and outputs. Their experimental attacks employed commercially available hardware and only required access to an example of the target device to tune the attack parameters. This method used magnetic near-field coupling, tuned to account for the unique heightened response properties of the victim circuitry to particular frequencies of EMI. The demonstrated attacks were shown to enable false data injection and false output (command) injection.

In the experiments conducted by (Selvaraj *et al.*, 2018), the attacker generates a sinusoidal EM signal to induce an AC voltage in the analog portion (sensor and its connection to chip) of the victim device circuitry. Due to clipping effects at the analog-to-digital conversion, the AC voltage is converted to DC. The authors were able to achieve a 50% bit-flip rate in targeted induction. Targeted attacks utilizing this particular vector may be difficult without advanced knowledge of the inner workings of the system (or sufficient access to reverse engineer its operation); blind attacks, either to manipulate the readings provided by implant electrodes or to cause direct neural stimulation by inducing a current in the implant threads, maybe a concern that future research should anticipate.

BLE Stack

BLE uses a different physical layer, link layer, application layer, and security architecture from Bluetooth (BT). Among other differences, the BLE standard employs frequency hopping at the physical layer, a master-servant medium access protocol at the link layer, and an entirely distinct security profile. BLE offers Secure

Connections Pairing, which operates as follows: peripheral (servant) devices advertise metadata in the clear; the master devices initiate a connection; both devices negotiate and establish a Long-Term Key (LTK) using authenticated Elliptic Curve Diffie-Hellman; this LTK is then used to derive session keys for encrypted data transfer during active connections using 128-bit AES in CCM mode.

While the latest versions of the BLE protocol have included numerous techniques to protect the integrity and privacy of communications between master and servant devices, many known passive and active attacks against the standard exist in the literature. We describe a few such techniques below which may apply to the future Neuralink BCI system, beginning with passive attacks and followed by active methods.

One class of passive attacks is digital fingerprinting. As reported in (Celosia *et al.,* 2019), unreported application-initiated scans of nearby BLE devices can be used to identify and potentially track the behavior of victim users. This allows attackers to circumvent the anti-tracking measures implemented by iOS and Android mobile platforms. iOS and Android enable applications to perform background scans of available BLE devices while Bluetooth connectivity is enabled. BLE advertisements by servant devices include (potentially randomized) addressing identifiers, plaintext names, manufacturer data, and optional service identification numbers, among other attributes. While the value corresponding to many of these fields can be encrypted, their headers are not. Unprotected visibility of field information, which may contain unique string identifiers such as owner names or device manufacturer details (Neuralink is a fairly trivial name for which to infer the corresponding device), represents a non-trivial violation of user privacy when accessed by applications that do not have a legitimate use for scan data, such as to initiate connections to a particular class of BLE peripheral.

A more helpful version of such fingerprinting attacks is to perform cross-app tracking. When two or more applications collect background peripheral advertisements simultaneously, similarity scoring to compare their results has been shown to be effective for identifying unique targets using completely disjointed application accounts (Korolova *et al.*, 2018). The constant presence of a nearby connected BLE device such as the Neuralink implant may make such passive attacks more trivial to conduct, as both iOS and Android permit applications to query the lists of available, saved, and active BLE connections. For Android devices, data communicated between the master device and peripheral servant over BLE is accessible to all applications, requiring application-level security to protect sensitive information acquired by or sent from the application actively using the BLE connection.

Active attacks represent a more pressing threat under the BLE stack attack surface. In contrast, passive attacks may violate certain aspects of user privacy and communications confidentiality, breaching link and/or application-level authentication and encryption – which we should assume any application interfacing with the Neuralink system will implement to the highest current standards – poses more severe risks to the integrity of communications as well as the privacy and safety of the implant recipient.

Bluestaking is an attack that may be used to force a MitM condition (Hensler *et al.*, 2019). This cache poisoning attack targets the Advertising Name cache on master devices to induce attacker-selected address-to-name mappings before pairing. For the Neuralink system under consideration, this entails a significant vulnerability when a new master device is being established – mobile phone upgrades and replacements are not infrequent. The attack leverages poor handling of conflicting peripheral servant device advertisements in the BLE standard to manipulate cache entries stored in the master device. A Disputed Advertisement Condition may be defined as when two advertising packets contain contradictory information about what appears to be the same device (to the master device), and an Undisputed Advertisement Condition may be defined as when information is absent from one of the advertising packets but present in the falsified but nearly identical second packet. The master device assumes that additional information in the second advertisement is correct by default.

When packets from multiple sources contain conflicting address-to-name advertisements, the master device may accept a false device mapping. Two advertisements containing the same device address but differing device names can introduce a false name record for the actual servant device. Further, the actual servant device being spoofed by the attacker can be forced into a non-discoverable state by inducing a Disputed Advertisement Condition where the attack device advertises itself as non-discoverable but with identical information to the victim peripheral. The master device accepts the falsified non-discoverable flag and removes the target servant device from a list of available connections at the user level. This second capability of Bluestaking could allow an attacker to both insert their attack device as an intermediary between target master and servant and present the attack device to the target master as the only apparent match for a desired available pairing by advertising a similar name string.

Another potentially severe active attack targets the BLE pairing process. For interoperability, the BLE standard dictates an essential negotiation phase during connection establishment (pairing), which includes negotiating the strength (known as entropy) of the LTK to be established. As documented by (Antonioli *et al.*, 2020), the BLE standard allows for entropy reduction from a default 16 bytes down to 7 bytes, with no established authentication or encryption for the negotiations between master and servant devices. The highest security setting available in BLE, Mode 1 Level 4, mandates 16-byte entropy but lacks any enforcement mechanism; similar attacks on BT reduce entropy down to 1 byte (256 candidate keys trivial), making BLE the more secure choice still. A MitM attack on the unprotected essential entropy negotiation phase allows the minimum value to be accepted with no alert to the victim.

Once both devices accept an LTK, session keys generated from this reduced entropy LTK are similarly low entropy. An attacker may then eavesdrop on all transmitted session ciphertexts to break the encryption of the LTK, which was confirmed by (Antonioli *et al.*, 2020) to be computationally feasible for all BLE implementations tested (over 30 systems). (Antonioli et al., 2020) strongly recommends that revisions to the protocol establish a minimum value of 14-byte entropy for BLE, as this strength remains secure against known practical decryption attacks.

CONCLUSION

While our initial attack surface analysis of the invasive BCI system under development at Neuralink is highly theoretical and is able to draw from few confirmed specifications of their system, there are some takeaways that warrant consideration both by the engineers at Neuralink and the research community, which must inevitably conduct a more thorough inspection for potential risks to implant recipients.

While the possibility of intentional EMI has been considered (and shown to be potentially problematic for implanted devices), experimental analysis specific to invasive BCI should be conducted. This research focus should also assess the potential for misuse of the recharging periphery in induction-based EMI attacks, as this unknown power-transfer source may be vulnerable to manipulation.

The current BLE standard has been shown to be vulnerable to numerous active and passive attacks, which may severely impact implant recipient privacy and safety. Future research will undoubtedly uncover new security holes in the specification of this link layer protocol, requiring constant vigilance from manufacturers. Relying on the security implementation of the link layer will be insufficient, mainly when the application layer operates on the Android mobile OS but potentially for iOS as well – the Apple developer documentation is vaguer about application layer risks. We could not find a similar recommendation for application-layer authentication and encryption as recommended in the Android documentation to protect against unwanted data access by other applications on the device.

Given the attack vectors assessed above, the most effective recommendation for minimum acceptable security should be for all user applications that process data related to the Neuralink implant to employ robust authentication and encryption of all recorded device information and all communications to the implant device that passes through the OS. To quote (Drew *et al.*, 2019), "brain information is probably the most intimate and private of all information," and the scale and projected consumer market for systems like those proposed by Neuralink require that the security of these implants and their control periphery be considered with complete thoroughness.

REFERENCES

Agarwal, A., Dowsley, R., McKinney, N. D., Wu, D., Lin, C.-T., De Cock, M., & Nascimento, A. C. (2019). Protecting privacy of users in brain-computer interface applications. *IEEE Transactions on Neural Systems and Rehabilitation Engineering*, *27*(8), 1546–1555. doi:10.1109/TNSRE.2019.2926965 PMID:31283483

Android developers: Bluetooth low energy. (2021). Available: https://developer.android.com/guide/topics/connectivity/bluetooth-le

Antonioli, D., Tippenhauer, N. O., & Rasmussen, K. (2020). Key negotiation downgrade attacks on bluetooth and bluetooth low energy. *ACM Transactions on Privacy and Security*, *23*(3), 1–28.

Apple core bluetooth programming guide. (n.d.). Available: https://developer.apple.com/library/archive/documentation/NetworkingInternetWeb/Conceptual/CoreBluetoothconcepts/CoreBluetoothOverview/CoreBluetoothOverview.html#//appleref/doc/uid/TP40013257-CH2-SW1

Bernal, S. L., Celdran, A. H., Pérez, G. M., Barros, M. T., & Balasubramaniam, S. (2021). Security in brain-computer interfaces: State-of-the-art, opportunities, and future challenges. *ACM Computing Surveys*, *54*(1), 1–35. doi:10.1145/3427376

Celosia, G., & Cunche, M. (2019). Fingerprinting bluetooth-low-energy devices based on the generic attribute profile. *Proceedings of the 2nd International ACM Workshop on Security and Privacy for the Internet of-Things*, 24–31. 10.1145/3338507.3358617

Drew. (2019). The ethics of brain-computer interfaces. *Nature, 571*(7766), S19–S19.

Hensler, C., & Tague, P. (2019). Using bluetooth low energy spoofing to dispute device details. *Proceedings of the 12th Conference on Security and Privacy in Wireless and Mobile Networks*, 340–342.

Korolova, A., & Sharma, V. (2018). Cross-app tracking via nearby Bluetooth low energy devices. *Proceedings of the Eighth ACM Conference on Data and Application Security and Privacy*, 43–52. 10.1145/3176258.3176313

Marin, E., Singelee, D., Yang, B., Volski, V., Vandenbosch, G. A., & Nuttin, B. (2018). Securing wireless neurostimulators. *Proceedings of the Eighth ACM Conference on Data and Application Security and Privacy*, 287–298.

Masunaga, S. (2017). A quick guide to elon musk's new brain-implant company, neuralink. *Los Angeles Times*.

Musk. (2019). An integrated brain-machine interface platform with thousands of channels. *Journal of Medical Internet Research, 21*(10).

Newitz. (2017). Elon musk is setting up a company that will link brains and computers. *Ars Technica.*

Pugh, J., Pycroft, L., Sandberg, A., Aziz, T., & Savulescu, J. (2018). Brainjacking in deep brain stimulation and autonomy. *Ethics and Information Technology, 20*(3), 219–232. doi:10.100710676-018-9466-4 PMID:30595661

Rahimpour, S., Kiyani, M., Hodges, S. E., & Turner, D. (2021). Deep brain stimulation and electromagnetic interference. *Clinical Neurology and Neurosurgery, 203*, 106577. doi:10.1016/j.clineuro.2021.106577 PMID:33662743

Selvaraj, J., Dayanıklı, G. Y., Gaunkar, N. P., Ware, D., Gerdes, R. M., & Mina, M. (2018). Electromagnetic induction attacks against embedded systems. *Proceedings of the 2018 on Asia Conference on Computer and Communications Security*, 499–510. 10.1145/3196494.3196556

Winkler, R. (2017). Elon musk launches neuralink to connect brains with computers. *The Wall Street Journal.*

Chapter 11
Medical Device Security

Md Abdullah Al Momin
University of Louisiana at Lafayette, USA

ABSTRACT

Implantable medical devices (IMDs) are miniaturized computer systems used to monitor and treat various medical conditions. Examples of IMDs include insulin pumps, artificial pacemakers, neuro-stimulators, and implantable cardiac defibrillators. These devices have adopted wireless communication to help facilitate the care they provide for patients by allowing easier transferal of data or remote control of machine operations. However, with such adoption has come exposure to various security risks and issues that must be addressed due to the close relation of patient health and IMD performance. With patient lives on the line, these security risks pose increasingly real problems. This chapter hopes to provide an overview of these security risks, their proposed solutions, and the limitations on IMD systems which make solving these issues nontrivial. Later, the chapter will analyze the security issues and the history of vulnerabilities in pacemakers to illustrate the theoretical topics by considering a specific device.

INTRODUCTION

Implantable Medical Devices (IMDs) are miniaturized computer systems used to monitor and treat various medical conditions. Examples of IMDs include insulin pumps, artificial pacemakers, neuro-stimulator, and implantable cardiac defibrillators. These devices have adopted wireless communication to help facilitate the care they provide for patients by allowing easier transferal of data or remote control of machine operations. However, with such adoption has come exposure to various

DOI: 10.4018/978-1-7998-7323-5.ch011

security risks and issues that must be addressed due to the close relation of patient health and IMD performance.

Because IMDs are implanted inside the human body, there exist several limitations on these devices. For example, size, battery power, computational power, and inadaptability are issues associated with the physical devices themselves that prove troublesome for implementing security measures. Along with this, there also exist situational limitations or limitations related to the use of these devices, which also cause problems for security. Such as requirements of availability and desires for unobtrusive operation.

It has been shown before that IMDs are incredibly vulnerable to malicious attacks by outside agents. Rios and Butts et al. evaluated the security protocols on pacemaker devices in 2017 and found over 80 thousand security vulnerabilities. Radcliffe et al., 2011 displayed his ability to remotely gain complete control over an audience member's insulin pump during a conference. These security risks often exist because manufacturers are reluctant to include security measures to avoid bugs or problems which would slow down production or regulatory approval and ultimately beat their competition to the market.

In response to these attacks, a body of research has been done on methods with which to secure IMDs and IMD systems despite the restrictions in place. These solutions primarily involve controlling access to the IMD through the use of authentication, key generation, or key distribution, managing communication with an IMD, detecting unauthorized or malicious attacks, and keeping them from influencing the IMD.

With patient lives on the line, these security risks pose ever increasingly real problems. This chapter hopes to provide an overview of these security risks, their proposed solutions, and the limitations on IMD systems which make solving these issues nontrivial. Later, the chapter will analyze the security issues and the history of vulnerabilities in pacemakers to illustrate the theoretical topics by considering a specific device.

LIMITATION AND RESTRICTIONS

Because of the implantable nature of IMDs, there exist several restrictions which limit the ability of IMDs to perform traditional or even adequate security measures. Chief among these is that the devices must be small enough to be implanted in a human body without the body rejecting them. This size restriction is one of the causes of a limitation in the amount of computational power available to the device. Along with this size restriction, should computational power increase to the point of unrestricted usage, there is also the idea of the heat produced by these computations causing harm to the body with which it is implanted.

Because these devices are implanted using invasive surgeries, they are designed with longevity in mind. The idea is to limit the number of times throughout the patient's life to replace or adjust the device. This is one of the reasons that wireless modules have become so pervasive in IMDs recently, as they allow modification of parameters and collection of data without the use of invasive surgeries. However, one method that wireless communication cannot improve is battery life. Because these devices are designed with longevity in mind, they are given batteries that, with appropriate usage, would last a decade or more. The idea of recharging a battery inside an IMD comes with a series of problems and issues in and of itself, namely the element of the battery heating up during power conference. This restriction on battery life also affects computational power, as heavy computational activities can wear down an IMDs battery, leading to unwanted surgeries and a lower quality of life for the patient. The size limitations mentioned earlier also put a subsequent limitation on battery size and lifetime, which further affects computational availability. With these things in mind, it is easy to see how the usage of IMDs informs its physical properties, which in turn inform the limitations placed on it. These limitations are interconnected, with each affecting another in some way.

Additionally, with new security schemes and solutions being introduced regularly, backward compatibility is essential. Similar to the idea behind long battery life, invasive surgeries are almost universally unwanted. Because of this, new security mechanisms should take into consideration backward compatibility with older models already implanted. Though this is not a necessary limitation, should large-scale vulnerabilities be found, such as the outdated libraries of (Rios and Butts et al.), patients with old IMDs would need to consider undergoing surgery to update their model or be at risk of attack.

Along with physical limitations imposed by usage, there are also limitations on IMDs due to other factors. As Zheng et al. interestingly point out, one crucial factor when designing security systems for IMDs is psychological acceptance of the proposed methodology. As we will see later, the one proposed solution for security measures is wearable external devices or WEDs. Because these devices must be kept track of and worn at all times to provide adequate security, there is a psychological toll taken from the patient who must carry this burden. Similarly, there should be an effort to limit the intrusiveness of security solutions in a patient's life. Patients may be likely to forsake practical security solutions but will get in the way of everyday living. This is, of course, the purpose of IMDs in the first place: to make day-to-day life more tolerable to patients. In the same vein, security solutions should not get impaired by the functionality of the device. This ties in with limited computational power, but the primary responsibility of IMDs is to provide medical assistance to patients. Any security scheme that degrades an IMDs ability to do so should not be considered applicable.

Lastly, there exists an additional tradeoff to consider when developing security solutions for IMDs. We have already discussed the tradeoff of limited resources vs. security, but the tradeoff of security vs. accessibility comes with this. In the event of an emergency, the nearest medical professional or first responders are the ones to treat the patient. In such a situation, any security mechanism must not deny access to the medical professional seeing the patient. Techniques such as key distribution or authorization can act as burdens in this situation and possibly lead to server consequences, even death. The main trouble with such a system lies in determining when an emergency occurs and distinguishing between a legitimate medical professional and a malicious attacker in both normal situations and emergencies. Proposed solutions that are too lenient are liable to be abused by malicious attackers, and too strict solutions are liable to refuse access to first responders in the event of an emergency.

CLASSIFICATION OF ATTACKS

Traditionally, attacks on IMDs are classified into two categories: passive attacks and active attacks. Passive attacks primarily include eavesdropping attacks, which listen in on the communication between IMDs and programmers. Considering the limitations discussed earlier, many IMDs do not implement any form of encryption when communicating with other devices, either by design or necessity. This fault in security, along with things such as lack of authentication or access control mechanisms, can lead to the attacker discovering not only who among a crowd has an IMD, but also potentially disclose information such as the device's make, model, and the patient name, age, current condition, ID, and health records (Hei et al., 2013). Valuable information can be inferred using passive attacks, such as the device's relationship with the patient, the device's capacities, or the device's settings. For example, it has been shown that with an oscilloscope and software radio, an attacker could obtain personal information using an ICD along with information on the ICD itself (Halperin et al., 2008). This information can potentially be used to calculate a plan of attack to use against the patient.

While these attacks are dangerous in their own right, their true potential lies when used in conjunction with active attacks. Active attacks are malicious attacks that modify, impersonate, or replay messages between IMDs and programmers, with the end goal of performing some action or set of activities that would detriment the patient. These attacks are much more frequent and dangerous than passive attacks, but passive attacks are often used as a forefront to active attacks, to get their foot in the door, so to speak. Active attacks can include Man-In-The-Middle attacks, DoS or battery draining attacks, performing unauthorized or potentially harmful actions, jamming communication between the device and the programmer, holding the device ransom, or completely shutting off the device. Though the range of possible actions included under the tag of active attack is broad, all of these attacks have the potential to be devastating or even fatal to the patient. (Halperin et al., 2008).

CLASSIFICATION OF PROPOSED SOLUTIONS

Solutions proposed to counter attacks on IMDs are as varied as IMDs and the patients who trust their health. However, most of these proposed solutions share some commonalities, allowing them to fit into broad classifications. Most proposed solutions to security issues in wireless IMD systems fall into the following categories: Key Management, Communication Control through Proxy, Attack Detection/Reaction, and general Access Control/Authentication. These classifications are intentionally broad, as there are many different techniques presented in the literature, with many other methods designed around overcoming the many limitations of IMDs. You may notice that the first two categories could potentially fall under the umbrella of access control. Though potentially arbitrary, this distinction is intentional, as these are two of the more heavily researched areas among the proposed solutions and deserve to be explored independently.

COMMUNICATION CONTROL

External devices typically handle control of communication between IMDsand programmers. These WEDs are well known throughout wireless medical device security literature. These devices are the IMDGuard, IMDShield, and Cloaker. The IMDGuard intercepts all communication with the IMD and acts as a man in the middle. ECG signals are used to authenticate the IMD and IMDGuard. The IMDShield offers one-way confidentiality by way of jamming. The IMDShield will jam the IMD's frequency to communicate, blocking all traffic to the device. The Shield knows the method for jamming, so it can reverse the technique to retrieve messages from the IMD and transfer them to a caregiver. Lastly, we have the Cloaker. The Cloaker is simple in that it blocks all communication to the IMD except to an authorized caregiver. While the cloaker is active, nothing can communicate with the IMD except the authorized caregiver, but simply removing the Cloaker allows full access in the event of an emergency.

ATTACK DETECTION AND REACTION

The main solution proposed for detecting and responding to a malicious attack comes from (Hei et al., 2011) in the form of a machine learning technique that uses patient access models that contain various dimensions of access, such as access location and time, day, etc. The patient's cell phone is used to offload storage and computation, preventing the use of precious resources on the IMD. When the IMD attempts to interface with a programmer, it will send a verification message to the patient's phone. The patient's phone will run a classification algorithm to determine if access is malicious or not. If the phone decides the access is normal, then the IMD continues with the access as planned. Should the phone determine that the access is abnormal or malicious, it will send a blocking command to the IMD, which will then go to sleep, saving power and rejecting any access attempt. Lastly, if the phone is unsure of the validity of the access request, it will prompt the user to intervene, trusting their judgment.

Another technique is presented in MedMon, which can detect adversarial attacks that deviate from legitimate transmissions by some measurable physical characteristic such as signal strength, time of arrival, or angle of arrival. Upon receiving a new command, MedMon will compare this new data with the records of historical data to decide whether there exists some anomaly. Upon detection, MedMon can either respond passively by alerting the patient or actively by jamming transmissions.

GENERAL ACCESS CONTROL

There exist a small section of techniques that do not fall under the categories listed above. They primarily deal with proximity-based solutions, but unlike the ones described earlier, they do not share keys. Examples include magnetic field solutions, such as a magnetic switch within the IMD which a powerful magnet can trigger to switch on the device's wireless communication module. These techniques have some shortcomings. Because they can be activated by any strong magnet, not just the ones intended for such use, and is less secure than other options. The last example includes Near Field Communication, or NFC, technology. In this method, a smartphone is given a key at IMD insertion and cannot be regenerated. A use case for this technique involves an in-vivo NFC chip additionally implanted in the patient, which is used to communicate with the smartphone. Because NFC technology draws power from the reader, it requires no power from the IMD. However, in the event of a lost phone, the data stored on the IMD becomes irretrievable. This technique also does not qualify as a key sharing technique because the key is shared once and can never be shared again, so sharing keys is not a part of the technique's normal operation.

CASE STUDIES: INTRODUCTION ON PACEMAKERS

With thousands of pacemakers implanted into people a year, and millions already in circulation, ensuring the security of medically implanted pacemakers is paramount to the long-term survival and longevity of the people that rely on them. With a pacemaker, someone who has a debilitating heart problem can live a long and fulfilling life and can even be alerted to complications or issues quickly, possibly before they are even aware of difficulties, thanks to in-home monitoring technology. However, these life-saving devices create a unique problem: Their livelihood, safety, and even their own lives are only as secure as the measures put in place to protect against malicious intent. This chapter aims to analyze the different attack vectors, attack symptoms, known security issues, and other vulnerabilities of implanted pacemakers in patients.

HOW PACEMAKERS WORKS

To fully understand how a hacker could interfere with a pacemaker, one must understand how the pacemaker functions, communicates, and interfaces with other technology. The purpose of a pacemaker is to treat arrhythmia in the heart, which is any irregularity of the heartbeat. This is detected by the electrodes surgically placed in one to three of the heart's chambers. These electrodes are where a pacemaker will assist the patient by sending an electric jolt into the heart's muscular tissue, forcing a contraction. The electrodes are attached to a pulse generator via wires placed in the patient's veins. The pulse generator creates the electric pulse by pulling on power from the battery within its system. The device must be replaced approximately every ten years, as the battery is not rechargeable internally without serious danger to a patient. There are non-implantable pacemakers, but they limit the patient's maneuverability and freedom, often do not come with network-enabled features and are traditionally seen as a temporary solution.

Many of the newest models of pacemakers come packed with networking functions, known as "telemetry," that can allow medical personnel to both access the data from the pacemaker on-demand and wirelessly reconfigure the rate of impulse and capabilities of the device (Halperin et al., 2008).

ATTACK VECTORS

Figure 1. Network vectors for attacks

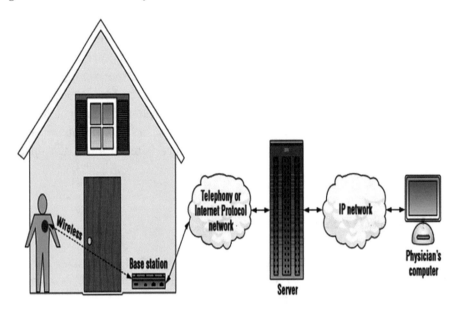

As shown in Figure 1 from (Halperin et al., 2008) and mentioned previously, major pacemaker manufacturers can now acquire data from implanted devices and relay it to a central repository over either a Wi-Fi signal or a dial-up connection. This data repository is available to medical professionals via a website utilizing SSL protocols. The visible connections in the diagram are our attack vectors for this communication system. The attack vectors are the user's device to the network, the user's home network to the data repository, the data repository to the user's network, and the user's network to the user's device. This chapter primarily focuses on the network communications between the user and their surrounding network.

THE DANGER OF IMPROPER SECURITY

The most important and terrifying type of hack that a hacker can perform concerning Implanted Medical Devices (IMDs) like pacemakers is the attack on the user and the device itself. If one needs an example, they would only need to Google "Barnaby Jack", a renowned gray hat hacker. At conferences in 2011 and 2012, Barnaby Jack was able to show that he could hack into any pacemaker with an RF communication. The hack would cause the device to either withhold therapy that the device would deliver, which would cause extreme discomfort or pain or directly deliver a potentially lethal 830-volt shock to a person's heart (Sen et al., 2020). He was able to accomplish this by having the devices disclose their serial and model numbers and alter the transmitter's code while simultaneously extracting data that would identify that person and their medical healthcare provider, as often crucial medical information stored on these devices is not encrypted. The encryption of this data is usually handled by either the base station that is associated with the device or via a cellular device before the upload to the network. Barnaby Jack also stated in an interview that this type of attack could be turned into a worm-based style attack. This worm-based style attack can then be broadcasted to any internet-connected pacemaker, allowing nearly anyone with a pacemaker to become a victim of a large-scale cyber-attack suddenly, held hostage by the devices keeping them alive.

NETWORK TO HOSPITAL

The tradeoff between allowing emergency system access to healthcare providers and ensuring that the device avoids unauthorized access is a significant issue in pacemaker protection (Pinisetty et al., 2018). The comprehensive survey discusses certain tradeoffs for cyber-physical systems (CPS), such as a pacemaker (a cyber-component) regulating the rhythmic beating of the human heart (a physical system). This can be referred to as an "Internet of Bodies" network. People are becoming increasingly reliant on IMDs such as pacemakers, insulin pumps, etc. being able to communicate with external devices such as smartwatches, cellular devices, and each other for ease of use and quick, reliable access data. (Sen et al., 2020). Cyber-security in IMDs is hampered by three major issues (Puat et al., 2020): Most embedded devices lack the memory and processing power needed to support cryptographic security, encryption, and access control. Doctors and patients value convenience and accessibility over protection. The ability to control embedded devices remotely is a good function, but it also renders them vulnerable. Power versus security: Most embedded medical devices lack the memory, processing power, or battery life needed to support cryptographic protection (Puat et al., 2020), encryption, or access control. Using HTTPS instead of HTTP (a method of encrypting web traffic to prevent eavesdropping) is an example. Cryptography suites (the algorithms and keys used to prove identity and keep transmissions secret) are designed for computers, and they require complex mathematical operations that are beyond the capabilities of small, low-cost IoT devices. Moving cryptography into dedicated hardware chips is an emerging solution, but this increases the cost.

- **Convenience vs. Security:** Doctors and patients do not anticipate having to log into these medical devices regularly. The prospect of remembering usernames, passwords, and encryption keys are incompatible with how they want to use them. Likewise, no one anticipates having to log into their toaster or refrigerator. Fortunately, the pervasiveness of mobile phones and their use as interfaces to "smart" IoT computers are altering users' expectations. Often, communications between devices in the body of things happen through either a Radio Frequency (RF) connection or a Bluetooth Low Energy (BLE) connection. BLE can easily be used to connect to a smartphone or other external device, which then can be sent to the patient monitoring system in the hospital if required (Heydari et al., 2020). BLE connection's greatest strength is a low-energy communication type that is easily discoverable and accessible. However, this is also the greatest weakness, as those with the knowledge on how to exploit this connection can efficiently utilize it in an unethical and dangerous way.
- **Remote Monitoring vs. Security:** When surgical implants need to be removed or replaced, they pose an immediate medical risk. As a result, remote monitoring is unquestionably a lifesaving technology for patients who are using these devices. Patients are no longer dependent on the low battery "buzz" sound, and doctors may easily upgrade the device's software if it malfunctions. Regrettably, this remote control feature introduces a whole new level of danger. Others will upgrade the program remotely if your doctor can.

Cyber security Attacks (Kaschel et al., 2019) are divided into two categories. Attacks that aren't focused on a particular objective but instead terminate and disable items are known as blind attacks. Targeted attacks aim to ruin everything by focusing on specific individual details. Targeted attacks are a form of intentional attack. If the information is not encrypted, an attacker may insert false data or steal it during the communication phase. In addition, the attacker may install malicious software on the computers.

USER TO NETWORK ATTACK

A modern pacemaker will gather information about a patient and send it over Wi-Fi to an access point or medical equipment used during hospital visits. The data is sent to remote servers by the access point systems (Pinisetty et al., 2018), which collect information about the patient's health when they are at home. Patients with mobility issues can benefit from pacemakers that can send data over the internet.

However, the communications protocols to send data to remote servers are very simple and vulnerable to hacking. As healthcare facilities increasingly rely on devices that communicate with each other, hospital medical record systems, and the internet, concerns about the vulnerability of medical devices such as pacemakers, ICDs, insulin pumps, defibrillators, fetal monitors, and scanners are growing. Using brute-force attacks and hard-coded logins, these are simple to break. Failures may include disclosing sensitive patient information, mishandling, inadequate supervision, gaining access to the equipment system, changing computer scheduled tasks, causing battery swings, or even delivering unwanted stimuli or disabling alarms.

The most common method of attack is to use Wi-Fi communication to avoid having to be close to the victim (Longras et al., 2020). With the ease with which backdoors can be installed in hospital networks and with medical devices linked to the same network, several systems can be compromised with malware, including the likelihood of twenty-four insulin pumps and pacemaker failures that can be controlled remotely.

A forced authentication attack, also known as a resource exhaustion attack, is a denial of service attack (DoS). IMDs that communicate wirelessly with external readers or monitors are vulnerable to this attack. When an external reader tries to bind to an IMD, the first move is for the IMD and the reader to authenticate each other (Longras et al., 2020). If the authentication fails, the reader's contact with the IMD will be terminated. However, the authentication process necessitates IMD communications, which consume a significant amount of power. If an unauthorized reader tries to connect to an IMD multiple times, the IMD will perform multiple authentications, consuming a substantial amount of the necessary battery power.

Furthermore, this form of attack produces many security logs, which causes IMD storage to become overburdened. This type of attack can be repeated nearly infinitely while in range of the signal and attacks two resources of the IMD simultaneously, causing a pacemaker that may not need to be replaced for almost a decade to need to be surgically repaired and replaced in a matter of weeks. (Hei et al., 2010). When contact is blocked, and interference is made, this form of DoS occurs. By repeatedly sending true or false messages, the attacker exploits machine resources. This is Radio Jamming. Man-in-the-middle attack: To gain access to confidential health information (Longras et al., 2020), the intruder listens without interrupting or changing the conversation. Another scenario is for an intruder to intercept data or code from a medical device when radio frequencies are working and then transmit the altered data to the monitor or warning system. Replay Attack: The intersection and representation of the medical device or monitoring system, represented by a network attack in which real data is manipulated, are also part of this attack. Such an attack may be used to avoid receiving care, for example, by mucking up the order in which packets arrive at IMD or, even worse, by sending the same message to medical equipment and the monitoring system repeatedly. Code Injection: When an intruder modifies the source code on a medical device, monitor, or even a potential warning system to perform an undefined function, such as changing the pacemaker program to deliver electric shocks regularly, this is known as a medical device compromise.

COUNTER MEASURES

Many of these attacks, however, have had proposed alterations and system changes occur as a result. Many new security ideas, such as having an application that creates a trusted connection jam the emitted BLE signal from the pacemaker to make the device more secure and less targetable from Bluetooth-based attacks. (Heydari et al., 2020). Security methods have been recommended that utilize a patient's daily schedules and times and necessary locations for access to determine if the attempt to authorize should be allowed or is likely an attack (Hei et al., 2010). This would help reduce the number of requests the pacemaker would have to handle in an RD attack. The following security properties must be considered to secure patients who use IMDs. Authentication: Before conducting any procedure, the identities of the communicating parties must be verified. The lack of proper authentication in the case of IMDs may be used to launch an elevation of privileges attack (EoP). Authorization Both users' use and management should be clearly stated and tracked. Only those with the appropriate privileges may perform each procedure. Reprogramming the IMD, for example, requires the collaboration of a doctor and a technician. Availability the service provided by the IMD must be accessible at all times. Because of the vital role that IMDs perform, their availability is a must. Active jamming can be used to block the radio channel, making the IMD inoperable. The intruder may also overload the system with network traffic, preventing access and draining the battery. Non-Repudiation In the access log, the system must record and validate all user activities. No log-in is used in current IMDs due to memory limitations. If logging is used, an alarm may be set off to notify the user if a malicious incident occurs. To hide their tracks, attackers will try to remove access logs. The device should be able to detect and prevent parameter manipulation and protect against tampering and reverse engineering. During transmission, IMD data may be intercepted and changed. The IMD could also allow malicious input, which could carry out attacks such as code injection. The lack of integrity checking allows data stored on the IMD memory to be altered. Confidentiality Only approved parties should have access to data. Since the various components of the IMDs (Tabasum et al., 2018) interact over the network, they are vulnerable to eavesdropping. Private patient data will be exposed if the data is not encrypted, putting the patients' privacy at risk. Possession (or control) to avoid unauthorized control, coercion, or intervention, protect the design (Tabasum et al., 2018), installation, service, and maintenance of systems and associated processes. Before being deployed, IMDs are subjected to extensive security monitoring. However, the systems must be modified to combat emerging security threats (Tabasum et al., 2018). The framework is protected from malicious updates by allowing changes in a highly restricted and validated environment.

- **Anomaly Detector:** If an attack is detected, the patient can be notified (for example, via a warning mechanism), or the system can be made unavailable by turning off the communications (or jamming the channel) while the medical functions continue to operate. The use of the wireless communication channel makes it difficult to avoid these types of attacks (Kaschel et al., 2019). The reader's communication with the IMD begins with the IMD authenticating the reader. The contact is disrupted if the reader fails the authentication stage. Failure to authenticate may use up resources in the IMD, which can be abused by an opponent who, for example, tries to connect with the IMD repeatedly. The result would be a classic Denial-of-Service (DoS) attack, in which the battery level would be significantly reduced, and memory/storage would be impacted. Some registers are used to store security values, including session tokens and logs in each authentication. This type of attack is known as a Resource Depletion (RD) attack since it focuses on wasting the IMD's resources. They are straightforward to enforce, and the effects can be very harmful, as sending dummy requests can reduce the battery life of the IMD from many years to a few weeks.
- **Access Control:** Unauthorized and improper use of the IMD functions was prevented by access control mechanisms (Kaschel et al., 2019). Before performing a specific action (e.g., entry, reading, reprogramming, etc.), the requester's rights are assessed to determine whether or not it is allowed to perform that action. Permitted and prohibited operations, in particular, are regulated by access control policies that define who may do what, depending on the context in which the access request is made. Access control is completely compatible with other security measures such as cryptographic protocols to secure the communication channel. Furthermore, access control typically necessitates prior authentication because decisions about whether or not an operation is allowed are taken based on the requester's identity, which must be identified beforehand.
- **Cryptographic Measures:** Cryptography-based security solutions (Kaschel et al., 2019), (Tabasum et al., 2018) are heavily reliant on cryptographic primitives, which fall into three categories. Hash functions and one-way permutations are examples of unkeyed primitives. We may differentiate between symmetric-key and public-key primitives in keyed cryptographic

tools. A hidden key is exchanged between the trusted entities in symmetric-key primitives. Symmetric key ciphers solutions (Kaschel et al., 2019), (Tabasum et al., 2018) (block and stream ciphers), message authentication codes (MACs), pseudorandom sequences, and identification primitives are among the primitives in this group. Asymmetric-key primitives, on the other hand, include public-key ciphers and signatures. Two keys are used in this form of an algorithm, one of which is public, and the other must be kept secret. However, the main disadvantage of this approach is its high energy consumption.

- **Biometric Access:** Using biometrics to access the IMD (Tabasum et al., 2018), (Hei et al., 2011), such as fingerprints, iris, and speech, will alleviate the urgent access restriction. A two-level access control system is proposed (Hei et al., 2011). The first level uses the patients' fingerprints, iris color, and height as biometrics, and the second level uses an effective iris authentication scheme. Thus, in an emergency, medical personnel can access data using the patient's biometrics, which does not require anything from the patient. It also eliminates the need for the patient to recall passwords or bring authentication tokens.

SECURITY WITH RUNTIME VERIFICATIONS

Pacemaker security threats are life-threatening, turning a life-saving system into a possible killer. Existing pacemaker monitoring solutions necessitate wireless contact with the device. This adds to the security risks, mainly when encryption and key distribution are complex. We suggest a monitoring system that does not rely on contact with the pacemaker or any other external device. The monitor is a wearable system that uses an individual's ECG to detect events of interest. The cardiologist programs the system with strong pacemaker timing values. We believe that no wireless protocol is used to link this device to any other device, including the pacemaker. We adapt a timed automata runtime verification method to build a monitor that detects anomalous events in real-time. An alarm is heard to warn the patient if any anomaly is observed. Approaches to runtime verification (RV) (Pinisetty et al., 2018) are concerned with monitoring and verifying if a device's run under inspection satisfies or violates a particular desired property. Since RV is only concerned with runs of the machine, which is called a black-box, it is an excellent match for pacemaker security. As a result, there will be no need to modify the current pacemaker, and no new wireless protocols or key distribution will be needed. There will be no extra certification costs as well. RV is a lightweight, formally based verification approach. One of the key focuses of formally based RV approaches is to produce RV monitors from a formal high-level specification of a collection of properties. The system's execution is unaffected by RV monitors. They are used to check whether a system's stored performance (offline verification) or its current live execution (online confirmation) meets the desired correctness property. An externally wearable system that continuously tracks the body's ECG signals using runtime verification techniques to verify essential safety properties specified for heart-pacemaker operation, adding an extra layer of protection and safety.

Figure 2. Wearable devices

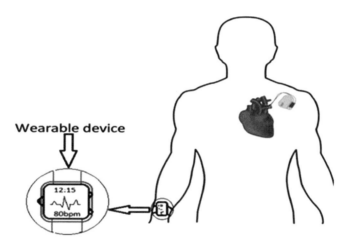

The RV (Pinisetty et al., 2018) monitor (externally worn device) is expected to have more power and computational resources than the pacemaker and measure ECG signals. The pacemaker is supposed to stay inside the body for a long time after it is implanted. The doctor programs it with the assistance of a programming unit (outside controller) with a direct connection before being implanted. If the pacemaker has to be reprogrammed after implantation, it should be done wirelessly. Doctors may use the programming unit to communicate with the pacemaker via radio frequency transmission to change running parameters (timers), change operating modes, or retrieve stored data. The doctor will consult with the patient to determine the right pacemaker for them. The doctor sets the pacing mode (e.g., DDD), the threshold voltage value of the pacing pulse, the pacemaker's sensitivity, and, most importantly, the timers such as AVI and AEI when programming. If a hacker gains access to the pacemaker, they can attempt to alter either of these timers.

- **An External Device:** After the pacemaker is implanted, the patient receives the wearable unit (Pinisetty et al., 2018), (Tabasum et al., 2018). Any computing device with an ECG sensor and an accelerometer, such as a smartwatch, may be used as this external wearable device. The doctor also sets the timing values for the external wearable system. Both of the values of the set timers are stored in the memory of the wearable computer. It also knows the normal heart rate at which the pacemaker is set to pace (for example, 60–120 BPM) and the pacing pulses' characteristics such as voltage, current, and impedance. In addition, the software includes an accelerometer that tracks the user's movement.

Figure 3. External device

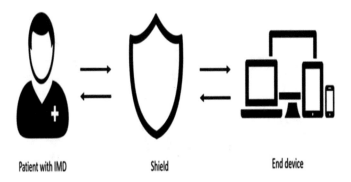

Patient with IMD   Shield   End device

The diagram above depicts a general explanation of how external devices function. End-system requests (Tabasum et al., 2018) are routed via an external device rather than directly to the IMD. The external computer is in charge of authenticating all incoming requests and safeguarding the IMD against various attacks. The external unit can be recharged and has fewer size restrictions than the IMD. In an emergency, medical personnel may remove the external monitor and communicate with the IMD directly. However, the patient must still be near the external system, which is a disadvantage of this approach. This approach is also appropriate if the IMD is already implanted in the patient's body and protection is needed later.

CONCLUSION

In this chapter, the description of the restrictions placed on security mechanisms for IMDs, including the purpose or reasons for such restrictions is discussed in detail. As well as some manner of classification for both security attacks and security solutions are also discussed. Attacks can be split into the categories of passive and active attacks. At the same time, solutions can be classified as either key management, communication control, attack detection and reaction, or general access control techniques. This chapter also addressed the security of medical device communications, focusing on the security of communications with other systems, such as the monitoring system, which is critical because it affects people's health, if not their lives. As a result, it's critical to put "security" first. Finally, a number of flaws in these systems and potential attack types and how to mitigate them are analyzed.

REFERENCES

Halperin, D., Heydt-Benjamin, T. S., Fu, K., Kohno, T., & Maisel, W. H. (2008). Security and privacy for implantable medical devices. *IEEE Pervasive Computing*, *7*(1), 30–39. doi:10.1109/MPRV.2008.16

Halperin, D., Heydt-Benjamin, T. S., Ransford, B., Clark, S. S., Defend, B., Morgan, W., ... Maisel, W. H. (2008). Pacemakers and Implantable Cardiac Defibrillators: Software Radio Attacks and Zero-Power Defenses. *2008 IEEE Symposium on Security and Privacy*. 10.1109/SP.2008.31

Hei, X., & Du, X. (2011). Biometric-based two-level secure access control for Implantable Medical Devices during emergencies. *2011 Proceedings IEEE INFOCOM*. 10.1109/INFCOM.2011.5935179

Hei, X., & Du, X. (2011). Biometric-based two-level secure access control for Implantable Medical Devices during emergencies. *Proceedings - IEEE INFOCOM*, 346–350. doi:10.1109/INFCOM.2011.5935179

Hei, X., & Du, X. (2013). IMD Access Control during Emergencies. *SpringerBriefs in Computer Science Security for Wireless Implantable Medical Devices*, 19-35. doi:10.1007/978-1-4614-7153-0_4

Hei, X., Du, X., Wu, J., & Hu, F. (2010). Defending Resource Depletion Attacks on Implantable Medical Devices. *2010 IEEE Global Telecommunications Conference GLOBECOM 2010*. 10.1109/GLOCOM.2010.5685228

Hei, X., Du, X., Wu, J., & Hu, F. (2010, December). *Defending resource depletion attacks on implantable medical devices. In 2010 IEEE global telecommunications conference GLOBECOM 2010*. IEEE.

Heydari, V. (2020). A New Security Framework for Remote Patient Monitoring Devices. *2020 International Symposium on Networks, Computers and Communications (ISNCC)*, 1-4. 10.1109/ISNCC49221.2020.9297214

Kaschel, H., & Ahumada, C. (2019). Security Mechanism to Protect the Privacy and Security of Patients Who have cardiovascular Diseases (ECG). *2019 IEEE CHILEAN Conference on Electrical, Electronics Engineering, Information and Communication Technologies (CHILECON)*, 1-7. doi: 10.1109/CHILECON47746.2019.8987984

Longras, A., Oliveira, H., & Paiva, S. (2020). Security Vulnerabilities on Implantable Medical Devices. *2020 15th Iberian Conference on Information Systems and Technologies (CISTI)*, 1-4. doi: 10.23919/CISTI49556.2020.9141043

Pacemakers. (n.d.). *National Heart Lung and Blood Institute*. Available: https://www.nhlbi.nih.gov/healthtopics/pacemakers

Pinisetty, S., Roop, P. S., Sawant, V., & Schneider, G. (2018). Security of Pacemakers using Runtime Verification. *2018 16th ACM/IEEE International Conference on Formal Methods and Models for System Design (MEMOCODE)*, 1-11. doi: 10.1109/MEMCOD.2018.8556922

Puat, H. A. M., & Abd Rahman, N. A. (2020, December). IoMT: A Review of Pacemaker Vulnerabilities and Security Strategy. *Journal of Physics: Conference Series, 1712*(1), 012009.

Radcliffe, J. (2011). Hacking medical devices for fun and insulin: Breaking the human SCADA system. Black Hat Conference presentation slides.

Rios, B., & Butts, J. (2017). *Security evaluation of the implantable cardiac device ecosystem architecture and implementation interdependencies*. Available: http://blog.whitescope.io/2017/05/understanding-pacemaker-systems.html

Rostami, M., Burleson, W., Koushanfar, F., & Juels, A. (2013). Balancing security and utility in medical devices? *Proceedings of the 50th Annual Design Automation Conference on - DAC 13*. 10.1145/2463209.2488750

Rostami, M., Juels, A., & Koushanfar, F. (2013). Heart-to-heart (H2H). *Proceedings of the 2013 ACM SIGSAC Conference on Computer & Communications Security - CCS 13*. 10.1145/2508859.2516658

Sen, Maity, & Das. (2020). The body is the network: To safeguard sensitive data, turn flesh and tissue into a secure wireless channel. *IEEE Spectrum, 57*(12), 44-49. doi:10.1109/MSPEC.2020.9271808

Tabasum, A., Safi, Z., AlKhater, W., & Shikfa, A. (2018). Cybersecurity Issues in Implanted Medical Devices. *2018 International Conference on Computer and Applications (ICCA)*, 1-9. doi: 10.1109/COMAPP.2018.8460454

Zheng, G., Zhang, G., Yang, W., Valli, C., Shankaran, R., & Orgun, M. A. (2017). From WannaCry to WannaDie: Security trade-offs and design for implantable medical devices. *2017 17th International Symposium on Communications and Information Technologies (ISCIT)*. 10.1109/ISCIT.2017.8261228

Conclusion

This book discussed the security-related issues present in smart devices and the latest technologies. Many of the emerging technologies can be vulnerable to various approaches. The book discussed the security holes, the attacks that can be performed on these technologies, and the countermeasures to those attacks. The book's first chapter discussed challenges in designing efficient Internet of Things Search Engines (IoTSE) and proposed the NDN-based approach for IoTSE. To validate the feasibility of the presented approach, a simple simulation environment to compare the performance of NDN and TCP/IP is designed. Then four scenarios and settings developed in ns-3 to demonstrate the feasibility of NDN improving network performance is proposed. The second chapter discussed IoT from a legal perspective. The chapter sheds light on the concern about personal data protection in the IoT sphere to help the IoT stakeholders properly comply with data protection law. Chapter three of the book emphasized the importance of biometric usage in smart devices and thus, discussed the need to keep biometric information safe. The chapter discussed presentation attacks since this type of attack is more appropriate to the sensors and the software used to interpret the information. This chapter focused on fingerprint fabrication attacks for the fingerprint sensor and the preventative measures to thwart this type of attack. Different ways to attack the voice assistant systems are presented in chapter four. This chapter discussed spoofing attacks, hardware nonlinearity-based attacks, obfuscated commands attacks, adversarial commands attacks, and the defending mechanisms to those attacks. Chapter five outlined the security issues in cyber-physical systems in the context of automobiles. It is observed through the survey in this chapter that studies already done on automotive CPS Security are headed in the right direction. With the development and advent of the latest cutting-edge technologies, automotive systems are supposed to become more complex. As a result, more threats are bound to appear for automotive CPS systems. Following secured protocols to design the vehicles will help mitigate this. The work in chapter six demonstrated the effectiveness of a CGAN model to generate fake, handwritten signatures. Chapter seven discusses the ubiquity of LEDs in commodity devices and uses this advantage to extract fingerprints and use it in device pairing.

Convolutional neural networks are employed to classify the images of different LEDs due to the high accuracy of this network. Smart voice assistant systems are the target for attack due to their wide adaptability in households. Chapter eight demonstrated a deep learning-based method to detect malicious signals intended to attack voice assistant systems. Although amplitude modulated laser signals were defended in this chapter, other attacks can also be detected by applying deep learning models for identification. Due to the accuracy and its capability to perform surgeries remotely, teleoperated robots have gradually made their way into the surgical room to replace and reduce the number of human surgeons. Chapter nine discusses the security issues present in teleoperated robots and the efforts to mitigate them to enhance security. Chapter ten presented the attack surface analysis of the brain-computer interface (BCI) system currently under development at Neuralink. The research focus should assess the potential for misusing the recharging periphery in induction-based EMI attacks, as this unknown power-transfer source may be vulnerable to manipulation. The current BLE standard has been shown to be vulnerable to numerous active and passive attacks, which may severely impact implant recipient privacy and safety. Given the attack vectors assessed in the chapter, the most effective recommendation for minimum acceptable security should be for all user applications that process data related to the Neuralink implant to employ robust authentication and encryption of all recorded device information and all communications to the implant device that passes through the OS. In chapter eleven, the security risks involved with Implantable Medical Devices (IMDs) are discussed in detail. The chapter presented different types of attacks that can be mounted on IMDs and the defending measures. Then a case study with pacemakers is presented in detail. The security risks and attack methods discussed in this book are intended to provide a general idea of the security risks associated with the technologies discussed. The attack methods and countermeasures will give the readers the idea to prevent the attacks and improve the security of personal devices.

Compilation of References

Abdullah, H. (2019). *Practical Hidden Voice Attacks against Speech and Speaker Recognition Systems*. Academic Press.

Abdullah, H., Garcia, W., Peeters, C., Traynor, P., Butler, K. R., & Wilson, J. (2019). *Practical hidden voice attacks against speech and speaker recognition systems*. arXiv preprint arXiv:1904.05734. doi:10.14722/ndss.2019.23362

Abdullah, H., Rahman, M. S., Garcia, W., Blue, L., Warren, K., Yadav, A. S., Shrimpton, T., & Traynor, P. (2019). *Hear no evil, see kenansville: Efficient and transferable black-box attacks on speech recognition and voice identification systems*. arXiv preprint arXiv:1910.05262.

Abdullah, H., Warren, K., Bindschaedler, V., Papernot, N., & Traynor, P. (2007). *The Faults in our ASRs: An Overview of Attacks against Automatic Speech Recognition and Speaker Identification Systems*. arXiv preprint arXiv:2007.06622.

Abdullah, H., Warren, K., Bindschaedler, V., Papernot, N., & Traynor, P. (2020). *The Faults in Our ASRs: An Overview of Attacks against Automatic Speech Recognition and Speaker Identification Systems*. arXiv preprint arXiv:2007.06622.

Abdul-Qawy, A. S., J., P. P., Magesh, E., & Srinivasulu, T. (2015). The Internet of Things (IoT): An Overview. *Journal of Engineering Research and Applications*, *5*(12), 71–82.

Abdur-Razzaq, M., Gill, S. H., Qureshi, M. A., & Ullah, S. (2017). Security Issues in the Internet of Things (IoT): A Comprehensive Study. *International Journal of Advanced Computer Science and Applications*, *8*(6), 383–388.

Abomhara, M., & Køien, G. M. (2015). Cyber Security and the Internet of Things: Vulnerabilities, Threats, Intruders and Attacks. *Journal of Cyber Security*, *4*, 65–88. doi:10.13052/jcsm2245-1439.414

African Union. (2014, June 27). *African Union Convention on Cyber Security and Personal Data Protection*. African Union. https://au.int/en/treaties/african-union-convention-cyber-security-and-personal-data-protection

Compilation of References

Agarwal, A., Dowsley, R., McKinney, N. D., Wu, D., Lin, C.-T., De Cock, M., & Nascimento, A. C. (2019). Protecting privacy of users in brain-computer interface applications. *IEEE Transactions on Neural Systems and Rehabilitation Engineering*, *27*(8), 1546–1555. doi:10.1109/TNSRE.2019.2926965 PMID:31283483

Ahmed, M. E., Kwak, I.-Y., Huh, J. H., Kim, I., Oh, T., & Kim, H. (2020). Void: A fast and light voice liveness detection system. *29th USENIX Security Symposium (USENIX Security 20)*, 2685–2702.

Ahmed, S. M., & Zulhuda, S. (2019). Data Protection Challenges in the Internet of Things Era: An Assessment of Protection Offered by PDPA 2010. *International Journal of Law, Government and Communication, 4*(17), 1-12. doi:10.35631/ijlgc.417001

Ahmed, S. M. (2019). Identity Crime in the Digital Age: Malaysian and Mauritanian Legal Framework. *International Journal of Law, Government, and Communication*, *4*(15), 154–165. doi:10.35631/ijlgc.4150016

Ahmed, S. M., & Mohamed, D. (2020). Data in the Internet of Things Era: The Propertization of Data In Light of Contemporary Business Practices. *International Journal of Business and Society*, *21*(1), 81–94.

Ahmed, S. M., & Zulhuda, S. (2015). The Concept of Internet of Things and Its Challenges to Privacy. *South East Asia Journal of Contemporary Business, Economics and Law*, *8*(4), 1–6.

Alcaraz, C., Lopez, J., & Wolthusen, S. (2017). *OCPP protocol: Security threats and challenges* (Vol. 8). IEEE.

Alegre, F., Vipperla, R., Evans, N., & Fauve, B. (2012). On the vulnerability of automatic speaker recognition to spoofing attacks with artificial signals. In *Proceedings of the 20th European signal processing conference (EUSIPCO)*. IEEE.

Alemzadeh, Chen, Lewis, Kalbarczyk, Raman, Leveson, & Iyer. (2015). *Systems-theoretic safety assessment of robotic telesurgical systems*. Academic Press.

Alemzadeh, H., Chen, D., Li, X., Kesavadas, T., Kalbarczyk, Z. T., & Iyer, R. K. (2016). Targeted attacks on teleoperated surgical robots: Dynamic model-based detection and mitigation. *2016 46th Annual IEEE/IFIP International Conference on Dependable Systems and Networks (DSN)*, 395–406.

Alepis, E., & Patsakis, C. (2017). Monkey Says, Monkey Does: Security and Privacy on Voice Assistants. *IEEE Access: Practical Innovations, Open Solutions*, *5*, 17841–17851. doi:10.1109/ACCESS.2017.2747626

Ali, I., Sabir, S., & Ullah, Z. (2016). Internet of Things Security, Device Authentication and Access Control: A Review. *International Journal of Computer Science and Information Security*, *14*(8), 1–11.

Alzantot, M., Balaji, B., & Srivastava, M. (2018). *Did you hear that? adversarial examples against automatic speech recognition*. arXiv preprint arXiv:1801.00554.

Alzantot, M., Balaji, B., & Srivastava, M. (2018). *Did You Hear That? Adver-Sarial Examples against Automatic Speech Recognition.* arXiv preprintarXiv:1801.00554.

Amodei, D. (2016). Deep Speech 2: End-to-End Speech Recognition in English and Mandarin. *33rd International Conference on Machine Learning, ICML 2016.*

Android developers: Bluetooth low energy. (2021). Available: https://developer.android.com/guide/topics/connectivity/bluetooth-le

Antonioli, D., Tippenhauer, N. O., & Rasmussen, K. (2020). Key negotiation downgrade attacks on bluetooth and bluetooth low energy. *ACM Transactions on Privacy and Security, 23*(3), 1–28.

Apple core bluetooth programming guide. (n.d.). Available: https://developer.apple.com/library/archive/documentation/NetworkingInternetWeb/Conceptual/CoreBluetoothconcepts/CoreBluetoothOverview/CoreBluetoothOverview.html#//appleref/doc/uid/TP40013257-CH2-SW1

Article 29 Data Protection Working Party. (2013, February 27). *Opinion 02/2013 on Apps on Smart Devices.* Pdpjournals. https://www.pdpjournals.com/docs/88097.pdf

Article 29 Data Protection Working Party. (2014, September 16). *Opinion 8/2014 on the on Recent Developments on the Internet of Things.* Pdp. https://www.pdpjournals.com/docs/88440.pdf

Asia-Pacific Economic Cooperation. (2017, August). *APEC Privacy Framework [2015].* APEC Secretariat.

Barbry, E. (2012). The Internet of Things, Legal Aspects: What Will Change (Everything). *Communications & Stratégies, 1*(87), 83–100.

Benesty, Chen, & Huang. (2008). *Automatic speech recognition: a deep learning approach.* Academic Press.

Bernal, S. L., Celdran, A. H., Pérez, G. M., Barros, M. T., & Balasubramaniam, S. (2021). Security in brain-computer interfaces: State-of-the-art, opportunities, and future challenges. *ACM Computing Surveys, 54*(1), 1–35. doi:10.1145/3427376

Bernardini, C., Asghar, M., & Crispo, B. (2017). Security and privacy in vehicular communications: Challenges and opportunities. *Vehicular Communications, 10*, 13–28.

Bojinov, H. (2014). *Mobile device identification via sensor fingerprinting.* arXiv preprint arXiv:1408.1416.

Burkert, H. (2000). Privacy-Data Protection: A German/ European Perspective. In E. Christoph & H. K. Kenneth (Eds.), *Governance of Global Networks in the Light of Differing Local Values* (pp. 44–48). Nomos Verlagsgesellschaft.

Cai, Wang, & Zhang. (2019). *0-days and mitigations: roadways to exploit and secure connected bmw cars.* Academic Press.

Compilation of References

Camara, C., Peris-Lopez, P., & Tapiador, J. E. (2015). Security and privacy issues in Implantable medical devices: A comprehensive survey. *Journal of Biomedical Informatics*, *55*, 272–289. doi:10.1016/j.jbi.2015.04.007 PMID:25917056

Carlini, N., & Wagner, D. (2018). Audio Adversarial Examples: Targeted Attacks on Speech-to-Text. *Proceedings - 2018 IEEE Symposium on Security and Privacy Workshops, SPW 2018.* 10.1109/SPW.2018.00009

Carlini, N., Mishra, P., Vaidya, T., Zhang, Y., Sherr, M., Shields, C., Wagner, D., & Zhou, W. (2016). Hidden voice commands. *25th USENIX Security Symposium (USENIX Security 16),* 513–530.

Carlini, N. (2016). Hidden Voice Commands This Paper Is Included in the Proceedings of the Hidden Voice Commands. *USENIX Security Symposium.*

Carlini, N., & Wagner, D. (2018). *Audio adversarial examples: Targeted attacks on speech-to-text. In 2018 IEEE Security and Privacy Workshops (SPW).* IEEE.

Carsten, P., Yampolskiy, M., Andel, T. R., & Mcdonald, J. T. (2015). In-vehicle networks: Attacks, vulnerabilities, and proposed solutions. CISR, 1, 1–8.

Celosia, G., & Cunche, M. (2019). Fingerprinting bluetooth-low-energy devices based on the generic attribute profile. *Proceedings of the 2nd International ACM Workshop on Security and Privacy for the Internet of-Things*, 24–31. 10.1145/3338507.3358617

Cerf, V. G., Ryan, P. S., Senges, M., & Whitt, R. S. (2016). IoT Safety and Security as Shared Responsibility. *Business Info*, *1*(35), 7–19. doi:10.17323/1998-0663.2016.1.7.19

Chang, Raheem, Rha. (2018). Novel robotic systems and future directions. *Indian Journal of Urology*, *34*, 110.

Chattopadhyay, A., & Lam, K. (2017). Security of autonomous vehicle as a cyber-physical system. *2017 7th International Symposium on Embedded Computing and System Design (ISED)*, 1–6.

Chen, S. (2017). You Can Hear but You Cannot Steal: Defending Against Voice Impersonation Attacks on Smartphones. *Proceedings - International Conference on Distributed Computing Systems.* 10.1109/ICDCS.2017.133

Chen, Y., Yuan, X., Zhang, J., Zhao, Y., Zhang, S., Chen, K., & Wang, X. (2020). Devil's whisper: A general approach for physical adversarial attacks against commercial black-box speech recognition devices. *29th USENIX Security Symposium (USENIX Security 20)*, 2667–2684.

Chen, Y., Zhang, J., Yuan, X., Zhang, S., Chen, K., Wang, X., & Guo, S. (2021). *SoK: A Modularized Approach to Study the Security of Automatic Speech Recognition Systems.* arXiv preprint arXiv:2103.10651.

Chen, T., Shangguan, L., Li, Z., & Jamieson, K. (2020). Metamorph: Injecting inaudible commands into over-the-air voice controlled systems. *Proceedings of NDSS.* 10.14722/ndss.2020.23055

Choi, W., Joo, K., Jo, H., Park, M., & Lee, D. (2018). *Voltageids: lowlevel communication characteristics for automotive intrusion detection system* (Vol. 13). IEEE.

Cisse, A. Neverova, & Keshet. (2017). Houdini: Fooling deep structured visual and speech recognition models with adversarial examples. Advances in Neural Information Processing Systems, 30. doi:10.14722/ndss.2021.24551

Cisse, M., Adi, Y., Neverova, N., & Keshet, J. (2017). *Houdini: Fooling Deep Structured Visual and Speech Recognition Models with Adversarial Examples.* Advances in Neural Information Processing Systems.

Coble, Wang, Chu, & Li. (2010). Secure software attestation for military telesurgical robot systems. *MILCOM 2010 Military Communications Conference*, 965–970.

Convention for the Protection of Individuals with regard to Automatic Processing of Personal Data, ETS No.108 (The Council of Europe 01 28, 1981) .

Cyber security and resilience of smart cars. (2016). Available: https://www.enisa.europa.eu/publications/cyber-security-and-resilience-of-smart-cars

Cyber-physical systems (CPS). (n.d.). Available: https://www.nsf.gov/pubs/2021/nsf21551/nsf21551.htm

Dak, A. Y., Yahya, S., & Kassim, M. (2012). A literature survey on security challenges in vanets. *International Journal of Computer Theory and Engineering*, *4*(627).

Dang, T. A. (2020, October 13). *Facial Recognition: Types of Attacks and Anti-Spoofing Techniques.* Retrieved from https://towardsdatascience.com/facial-recognition-types-of-attacks-and-anti-spoofing-techniques-9d732080f91e

Data Protection Act (Ghana 2012).

Data Protection Act, Chapter 12 (UK 2018).

De Graeve, F., De Jonghe, O., & Vander Vennet, R. (2007). Competition, transmission and bank pricing policies: Evidence from Belgian loan and deposit markets. *Journal of Banking & Finance*, *31*(1), 259–278. doi:10.1016/j.jbankfin.2006.03.003

De Leon, P. L., Pucher, M., Yamagishi, J., Hernaez, I., & Saratxaga, I. (2012). Evaluation of speaker verification security and detection of hmm-based synthetic speech. *IEEE Transactions on Audio, Speech, and Language Processing*, *20*(8), 2280–2290. doi:10.1109/TASL.2012.2201472

Dean. (2011). Microfibrous metallic cloth for acoustic isolation of a MEMS gyroscope. In *Proceedings of Industrial and Commercial Applications of Smart Structures Technologies.* Society of Photo-Optical Instrumentation Engineers.

Deng, J., Yu, L., Fu, L., Oluwakemi, H., & Brooks, R. (2017). *Security and data privacy of modern automobiles, in: Data analytics for intelligent transport systems.* Elsevier.

Compilation of References

DeVries, W. T. (2003). Protecting Privacy in the Digital Age. *Berkeley Technology Law Journal*, *18*(19), 283–311.

Diao, W., Liu, X., Zhou, Z., & Zhang, K. (2014). Your Voice Assistant Is Mine: How to Abuse Speakers to Steal Information and Control Your Phone. *Proceedings of the ACM Conference on Computer and Communications Security*. 10.1145/2666620.2666623

Drew. (2019). The ethics of brain-computer interfaces. *Nature, 571*(7766), S19–S19.

Edwards, L. (2016). Privacy, Security and Data Protection in Smart Cities: A Critical EU Law Perspective. *European Data Protection Law Review*, *2*(1), 28–58. doi:10.21552/EDPL/2016/1/6

Eiza, M. H., & Ni, Q. (2017). Driving with sharks: rethinking connected vehicles with vehicle cybersecurity. IEEE.

El-Rewini, Sadatsharan, Selvaraj, Plathottam, & Prakash. (2019). Cybersecurity challenges in vehicular communications. *Vehicular Communications*, *23*.

El-Rewini, Sadatsharan, Sugunaraj, Selvaraj, Plathottam, & Ranganathan. (2020). Cybersecurity attacks in vehicular sensors. *IEEE Sensors Journal*, *20*(22), 752–767.

EskensS. J. (2016, February 29). *Profiling the European Citizen in the Internet of Things: How Will the General Data Protection Regulation Apply to this Form of Personal Data Processing, and How Should It?* https://papers.ssrn.com/sol3/papers.cfm?abstract_id=2752010 doi:10.2139/ssrn.2752010

Esteves, J. L., & Kasmi, C. (2018). *Remote and silent voice command injection on a smartphone through conducted IEMI: Threats of smart IEMI for information security*. Wireless Security Lab, French Network and Information Security Agency (ANSSI), Tech. Rep.

Facial recognition technology explained. (2019, February 8). Retrieved from https://www.androidauthority.com/facial-recognition-technology-explained-800421/

Ferrer, M. A., Diaz-Cabrera, M., & Morales, A. (2013). *Synthetic off-line signature image generation. In 2013 international conference on biometrics (ICB)*. IEEE.

Fries & Falk. (2012). Electric vehicle charging infrastructure-security considerations and approaches. *INTERNET 2012*.

Gady, F.-S. (2014). EU/U.S. Approaches to Data Privacy and the "Brussels Effect": A Comparative Analysis. *Georgetown Journal of International Affairs,* 12-23.

Galbally, J. (2009). Synthetic generation of handwritten signatures based on spectral analysis. In *Optics and Photonics in Global Homeland Security V and Biometric Technology for Human Identification VI* (Vol. 7306). International Society for Optics and Photonics.

Gartner. (2017, February 7). *Gartner Says 8.4 Billion Connected "Things" Will Be in Use in 2017, Up 31 Percent From 2016*. Gartner-Newsroom. https://www.gartner.com/en/newsroom/press-releases/2017-02-07-gartner-says-8-billion-connected-things-will-be-in-use-in-2017-up-31-percent-from-2016

Gavison, R. (1980). Privacy and the Limits of Law. *The Yale Law Journal, 89*(3), 421–471. doi:10.2307/795891

Giechaskiel, I., & Rasmussen, K. (2019, November 12). Taxonomy and challenges of out-of-band signal injection attacks and defenses. *IEEE Communications Surveys and Tutorials, 22*(1), 645–670.

Giechaskiel, I., & Rasmussen, K. (2020). Taxonomy and Challenges of Out-of-Band Signal Injection Attacks and Defenses. *IEEE Communications Surveys and Tutorials, 22*(1), 645–670. doi:10.1109/COMST.2019.2952858

Gong, Y., & Poellabauer, C. (2018). An Overview of Vulnerabilities of Voice Controlled Systems. *1st International Workshop on Security and Privacy for the Internet-of-Things.*

Goodfellow, I. (2014). Generative adversarial nets. *Advances in Neural Information Processing Systems.*

Greengard, S. (2015). *The Internet of Things*. Massachusetts Institute of Technology. doi:10.7551/mitpress/10277.001.0001

Guidelines for the Regulation of Computerized Personal Data Files, Resolution 45/95 (United Nations December 14, 1990).

Halperin, D., Heydt-Benjamin, T. S., Fu, K., Kohno, T., & Maisel, W. H. (2008). Security and privacy for implantable medical devices. *IEEE Pervasive Computing, 7*(1), 30–39. doi:10.1109/MPRV.2008.16

Halperin, D., Heydt-Benjamin, T. S., Ransford, B., Clark, S. S., Defend, B., Morgan, W., ... Maisel, W. H. (2008). Pacemakers and Implantable Cardiac Defibrillators: Software Radio Attacks and Zero-Power Defenses. *2008 IEEE Symposium on Security and Privacy.* 10.1109/SP.2008.31

Han, J. (2018). Do you feel what I hear? Enabling autonomous IoT device pairing using different sensor types. In *2018 IEEE Symposium on Security and Privacy (SP).* IEEE. 10.1109/SP.2018.00041

Hannaford, B., Rosen, J., Friedman, D., King, H. I., Roan, P., Cheng, L., Glozman, D., Ma, J., Kosari, S. N., & White, L. W. (2013). Raven-ii: An open platform for surgical robotics research. *IEEE Transactions on Biomedical Engineering, 60*(4), 954–959. doi:10.1109/TBME.2012.2228858 PMID:23204264

Hautamaki, Kinnunen, Hautamaki, Leino, & Laukkanen. (2013). I-vectors meet imitators: on vulnerability of speaker verification systems against voice mimicry. Interspeech, 930–934.

He, Y., Bian, J., Tong, X., Qian, Z., Zhu, W., Tian, X., & Wang, X. (2019). Canceling inaudible voice commands against voice control systems. *The 25th Annual International Conference on Mobile Computing and Networking*, 1–15. 10.1145/3300061.3345429

Compilation of References

Hei, X., & Du, X. (2011). Biometric-based two-level secure access control for Implantable Medical Devices during emergencies. *2011 Proceedings IEEE INFOCOM*. 10.1109/INFCOM.2011.5935179

Hei, X., & Du, X. (2013). IMD Access Control during Emergencies. *SpringerBriefs in Computer Science Security for Wireless Implantable Medical Devices*, 19-35. doi:10.1007/978-1-4614-7153-0_4

Hei, X., Du, X., Wu, J., & Hu, F. (2010). Defending Resource Depletion Attacks on Implantable Medical Devices. *2010 IEEE Global Telecommunications Conference GLOBECOM 2010*. 10.1109/GLOCOM.2010.5685228

Hei, X., Du, X., Wu, J., & Hu, F. (2010, December). *Defending resource depletion attacks on implantable medical devices. In 2010 IEEE global telecommunications conference GLOBECOM 2010*. IEEE.

Henniger, O., Apvrille, L., Fuchs, A., Roudier, Y., Ruddle, A., & Weyl, B. (2009). *Security requirements for automotive on-board networks*. ITST.

Hensler, C., & Tague, P. (2019). Using bluetooth low energy spoofing to dispute device details. *Proceedings of the 12th Conference on Security and Privacy in Wireless and Mobile Networks*, 340–342.

Heydari, V. (2020). A New Security Framework for Remote Patient Monitoring Devices. *2020 International Symposium on Networks, Computers and Communications (ISNCC)*, 1-4. 10.1109/ISNCC49221.2020.9297214

Internet Society. (2019, September). *Policy Brief: IoT Privacy for Policymakers. Internet Society*. https://www.internetsociety.org/wp-content/uploads/2019/09/IoT-Privacy-Brief_20190912_Final-EN.pdf

InvenSense MPU-6500 datasheet. (2013). https://store. invensense.com/datasheets/invensense/MPU_6500_ Rev1.0.pdf

Iqbal, S., Farooq, S., Shahzad, K., Malik, A. W., Hamayun, M. M., & Hasan, O. (2019). Securesurginet: A framework for ensuring security in telesurgery. *International Journal of Distributed Sensor Networks*, *15*(9), 1550147719873811.

Iter & Jermann. (2017). *Generating adversarial examples for speech recognition*. Stanford Technical Report.

Jadoon, Wang, Li, & Zia. (2018). Lightweight cryptographic techniques for automotive cybersecurity. *Wireless Communications and Mobile Computing*, 1–15.

Jaisingh, R. A. K., & El-Khatib, K. (2016). Paving the way for intelligent transport systems (its): Privacy implications of vehicle infotainment and telematics systems. DIVANet, 25–31.

Jang, Y. (2014). A11y Attacks: Exploiting Accessibility in Operating Systems. *Proceedings of the ACM Conference on Computer and Communications Security*. 10.1145/2660267.2660295

Janocha, K., & Czarnecki, W. M. (2016). *On Loss Functions for Deep Neural Networks in Classification*. Schedae Informaticae.

Jo, H., Choi, W., Na, S., Woo, S., & Lee, D. (2017). Vulnerabilities of android os-based telematics system. *Wireless Personal Communications*, 1512–1530.

Kamrani, F., Wedlin, M., & Rodhe, I. (2016*). Internet of Things: Security and Privacy Issues*. Docplayer. http://docplayer.net/50469759-Internet-of-things-security-and-privacy-issues.html

Kaschel, H., & Ahumada, C. (2019). Security Mechanism to Protect the Privacy and Security of Patients Who have cardiovascular Diseases (ECG). *2019 IEEE CHILEAN Conference on Electrical, Electronics Engineering, Information and Communication Technologies (CHILECON)*, 1-7. doi: 10.1109/CHILECON47746.2019.8987984

Kasmi, C., & Esteves, J. L. (2015). IEMI Threats for Information Security: Remote Command Injection on Modern Smartphones. *IEEE Transactions on Electromagnetic Compatibility*, *57*(6), 1752–1755. doi:10.1109/TEMC.2015.2463089

Kasmi, C., & Esteves, J. L. (2015, August 13). IEMI threats for information security: Remote command injection on modern smartphones. *IEEE Transactions on Electromagnetic Compatibility*, *57*(6), 1752–1755.

Kereliuk, C., Sturm, B. L., & Larsen, J. (2015). Deep Learning and Music Adversaries. *IEEE Transactions on Multimedia*, *17*(11), 2059–2071. doi:10.1109/TMM.2015.2478068

Khaitan, S. K., & McCalley, J. D. (2015). Design techniques and applications of cyberphysical systems: A survey. *IEEE Systems Journal*, *9*(2), 350–365.

King, H. H., Hannaford, B., Kwok, K.-W., Yang, G.-Z., Griffiths, P., Okamura, A., Farkhatdinov, I., Ryu, J.-H., Sankaranarayanan, G., Arikatla, V., Tadano, K., Kawashima, K., Peer, A., Schauß, T., Buss, M., Miller, L., Glozman, D., Rosen, J., & Low, T. (2010). Plugfest 2009: Global interoperability in telerobotics and telemedicine. *2010 IEEE International Conference on Robotics and Automation*, 1733–1738. 10.1109/ROBOT.2010.5509422

Kinnunen, Sahidullah, Delgado, Todisco, Evans, Yamagishi, & Lee. (2017). *The asvspoof 2017 challenge: Assessing the limits of replay spoofing attack detection*. Academic Press.

Kinnunen, T., Wu, Z.-Z., Lee, K. A., Sedlak, F., Chng, E. S., & Li, H. (2012). Vulnerability of speaker verification systems against voice conversion spoofing attacks: The case of telephone speech. In *2012 IEEE International Conference on Acoustics, Speech and Signal Processing (ICASSP)*. IEEE. 10.1109/ICASSP.2012.6288895

Korolova, A., & Sharma, V. (2018). Cross-app tracking via nearby Bluetooth low energy devices. *Proceedings of the Eighth ACM Conference on Data and Application Security and Privacy*, 43–52. 10.1145/3176258.3176313

Kovelman. (2017). *A remote attack on the bosch drivelog connector dongle-argus cyber security*. Academic Press.

Compilation of References

Kranz, M., Whitley, M., Rudd, C., Craven, J. D., Clark, S. D., Dean, R. N., & Flowers, G. T. (2017). Environmentally isolating packaging for MEMS sensors. In *International Symposium on Microelectronics*. International Microelectronics Assembly and Packaging Society.

Kune, D. F. (2013). Ghost Talk: Mitigating EMI Signal Injection Attacks against Analog Sensors. *Proceedings - IEEE Symposium on Security and Privacy*. 10.1109/SP.2013.20

Kune. (2013). Ghost Talk: Mitigating EMI Signal Injection Attacks against Analog Sensors. *Proceedings - IEEE Symposium on Security and Privacy*.

Lavner, Y., Cohen, R., Ruinskiy, D., & IJzerman, H. (2018). Baby Cry Detection in Domestic Environment Using Deep Learning. SSRN *Electronic Journal*.

Lavrentyeva, G., Novoselov, S., Malykh, E., Kozlov, A., Kudashev, O., & Shchemelinin, V. (2017). Audio replay attack detection with deep learning frameworks. Interspeech, 82–86. doi:10.21437/Interspeech.2017-360

Lee, Choi, & Lee. (2019). Securing ultrasonic sensors against signal injection attacks based on a mathematical model. *IEEE Access*, 7, 716–729.

Lee, S., Park, Y., Lim, H., & Shon, T. (2014). Study on analysis of security vulnerabilities and countermeasures in iso/iec 15118 based electric vehicle charging technology. *International Conference on IT Convergence and Security*.

Lee, Y., Zhao, Y., Zeng, J., Lee, K., Zhang, N., Shezan, F. H., Tian, Y., Chen, K., & Wang, X. (2020). Using sonar for liveness detection to protect smart speakers against remote attackers. *Proceedings of the ACM on Interactive, Mobile, Wearable and Ubiquitous Technologies*, 4(1), 1–28. doi:10.1145/3380991

Lei, X. (2018). The Insecurity of Home Digital Voice Assistants - Vulnerabilities, Attacks and Countermeasures. *2018 IEEE Conference on Communications and Network Security, CNS 2018*. 10.1109/CNS.2018.8433167

Leloglu, E. (2017). A Review of Security Concerns in Internet of Things. *Journal of Computer and Communications*, 5(1), 121–136. doi:10.4236/jcc.2017.51010

Li, H., Yu, L., & He, W. (2019). The Impact of GDPR on Global Technology Development. *Journal of Global Information Technology Management*, 22(1), 1–6. doi:10.1080/1097198X.2019.1569186

Lim, B., Keoh, S., & Thing, V. (2018). Autonomous vehicle ultrasonic sensor vulnerability and impact assessment. *2018 IEEE 4th World Forum on Internet of Things (WF-IoT)*, 231–236.

Lindberg, J., & Blomberg, M. (1999). Vulnerability in speaker verification-a study of technical impostor techniques. *Sixth European Conference on Speech Communication and Technology*.

Liu, J., & Zhang, S. (2017). In-vehicle network attacks and countermeasures: Challenges and future directions. *IEEE Systems Journal*, 31(5), 50–58.

Li, W. (2018). A tale of two rights: Exploring the potential conflict between right to data portability and right to be forgotten under the General Data Protection Regulation. *International Data Privacy Law*, *8*(4), 309–317. doi:10.1093/idpl/ipy007

Li, X., & Wang. (2018). Rainbowlight: Towards low cost ambient light positioning with mobile phones. *Proceedings of the 24th Annual International Conference on Mobile Computing and Networking*.

Logan, B. (2000). Mel Frequency Cepstral Coefficients for Music Modeling. *International Symposium on Music Information Retrieval*.

Longras, A., Oliveira, H., & Paiva, S. (2020). Security Vulnerabilities on Implantable Medical Devices. *2020 15th Iberian Conference on Information Systems and Technologies (CISTI)*, 1-4. doi: 10.23919/CISTI49556.2020.9141043

Lopez, A., Malawade, A. V., Al Faruque, M. A., Boddupalli, S., & Ray, S. (2019). Security of emergent automotive systems: A tutorial introduction and perspectives on practice. *IEEE Design Test*, *36*(6), 10–38.

Lu, Z., Qu, G., & Liu, Z. (2019). A survey on recent advances in vehicular network security, trust, and privacy. IEEE.

Lum, Friedman, Sankaranarayanan, King, Fodero, Leuschke, Hannaford, & Rosen. (2009). The raven: Design and validation of a telesurgery system. *I. J. Robotic Res.*, *28*, 1183–1197.

Maheshwari, S. (2017). *Burger King 'O.K. Google' Ad Doesn't Seem O.K. With Google*. www.nytimes.com/2017/04/12/business/burger-king-tv-ad-google-home.html

Malaysian Personal Data Protection Act [PDPA], 709 (2010).

Mardonova, M., & Choi, Y. (2018). Review of Wearable Device Technology and Its Applications to the Mining Industry. *Energies*, *11*(3), 1–14. doi:10.3390/en11030547

Marin, E., Singelee, D., Yang, B., Volski, V., Vandenbosch, G. A., & Nuttin, B. (2018). Securing wireless neurostimulators. *Proceedings of the Eighth ACM Conference on Data and Application Security and Privacy*, 287–298.

Mark Heyink. (2018). *Protection of Personal Information for South African Law Firms*. Mark Heyink.

Martin. (n.d.). *72% Want Voice Control In Smart-Home Products*. https://www.mediapost.com/publications/article/292253/72-want-voice-control-in-smart-home-products.html?edition=993

Martin, E. A. (Ed.). (2003). *Oxford Dictionary of Law*. Oxford University Press.

Masunaga, S. (2017). A quick guide to elon musk's new brain-implant company, neuralink. *Los Angeles Times*.

Mauritanian Personal Data Protection Law, 020 (2017).

Mayrhofer, R., & Gellersen, H. (2009). Shake well before use: Intuitive and secure pairing of mobile devices. *IEEE Transactions on Mobile Computing*, *8*(6), 792–806. doi:10.1109/TMC.2009.51

Mazloom, S., Rezaeirad, M., Hunter, A., & Mccoy, D. (2016). *A security analysis of an in-vehicle infotainment and app platform*. WOOT.

Melo. (2019). Deep learning approach to generate offline handwritten signatures based on online samples. *IET Biometrics*, *8*(3), 215-220.

Moller, D., Jehle, I. A., & Haas, R. E. (2018). Challenges for vehicular cyber-security. *2018 IEEE International Conference on Electro/Information Technology (EIT)*, 428–433.

Mueck, M., & Karls, I. (2018). *Networking vehicles to everything: evolving automotive solutions*. Walter de Gruyter Inc.

Munir, A. B., & Yasin, S. H. (2010). *Personal Data Protection in Malaysia: Law and Practice*. Sweet & Maxwell Asia.

Musk. (2019). An integrated brain-machine interface platform with thousands of channels. *Journal of Medical Internet Research, 21*(10).

Mustafa, M., Zhang, N., Kalogridis, G., & Fan, Z. (2013). *Smart electric vehicle charging: Security analysis*. IEEE PES.

Narain, S., Ranganathan, A., & Noubir, G. (2019). Security of gps/ins based on-road location tracking systems. *2019 IEEE Symposium on Security and Privacy (SP)*, 587–601.

Newitz. (2017). Elon musk is setting up a company that will link brains and computers. *Ars Technica.*

Nowak, M., Januszewski, K. M., & Hofstätter, T. (Eds.). (2012). *All Human Rights for All – Vienna Manual on Human Rights*. NWV Neuer Wissenschftlicher Verlag.

O'Rourke & Daleyn. (2017). *Front, back or side: Where should a fingerprint sensor be located?* https://mobilesyrup.com/2017/07/14/front-back-or-side-where-should-a-smartphone-fingerprint-sens or-be-located/

Ortega-Garcia, J. (2003). MCYT baseline corpus: A bimodal biometric database. *IEE Proceedings. Vision Image and Signal Processing*, *150*(6), 395–401.

Pacemakers. (n.d.). *National Heart Lung and Blood Institute*. Available: https://www.nhlbi.nih.gov/healthtopics/pacemakers

Pan, S. (2018). Universense: Iot device pairing through heterogeneous sensing signals. *Proceedings of the 19th International Workshop on Mobile Computing Systems & Applications.* 10.1145/3177102.3177108

Parkinson, Ward, Wilson, & Miller. (2017). Cyber threats facing autonomous and connected vehicles: Future challenges. *IEEE Transactions on Intelligent Transportation Systems*, *18*, 1–18.

Pennacchi, G. (2006). Deposit insurance, bank regulation, and financial system risks. *Journal of Monetary Economics*, *53*(1), 1–30. doi:10.1016/j.jmoneco.2005.10.007

Peppet, S. R. (2014). Regulation of the Internet of Things: First Steps Toward Managing Discrimination, Privacy, Security, and Consent. *Texas Law Review*, *93*, 85–166.

Personal Data Protection Act, 26 (Singapore 2012).

Petit & Shladover. (2014). Potential cyberattacks on automated vehicles. *Intelligent Transportation Systems, IEEE Transactions on.*

Petit, Stottelaar, & Feiri. (2015). *Remote attacks on automated vehicles sensors: Experiments on camera and lidar.* Academic Press.

Petit, S. S. J. (2015). *Potential cyberattacks on automated vehicles.* IEEE.

Petracca, G., Sun, Y., Jaeger, T., & Atamli, A. (2015). AuDroid: Preventing Attacks on Audio Channels in Mobile Devices. *ACM International Conference Proceeding Series.* 10.1145/2818000.2818005

Pike, L., Sharp, J., Tullsen, M., Hickey, P. C., & Bielman, J. (2017, May). Secure automotive software: The next steps. *IEEE Software*, *34*(03), 49–55.

Pinisetty, S., Roop, P. S., Sawant, V., & Schneider, G. (2018). Security of Pacemakers using Runtime Verification. *2018 16th ACM/IEEE International Conference on Formal Methods and Models for System Design (MEMOCODE)*, 1-11. doi: 10.1109/MEMCOD.2018.8556922

Poellabauer, Y., & Gong, C. (2017). *Crafting Adversarial Examples for Speechparalinguistics Applications.* arXiv preprint arXiv:1711.03280.

Poullet, Y. (2010). About the E-Privacy Directive: Towards a Third Generation of Data Protection Legislation? In G. Serge, P. Yves, & D. Paul (Eds.), Data Protection in a Profiled World (pp. 3-30). SpringerScience+Business Media B.V.

Privacy International. (2018). *The Keys to Data Protection.* Privacy International.

Protection of Personal Information Act, Act No. 4 (South Africa 2013).

Puat, H. A. M., & Abd Rahman, N. A. (2020, December). IoMT: A Review of Pacemaker Vulnerabilities and Security Strategy. *Journal of Physics: Conference Series*, *1712*(1), 012009.

Pugh, J., Pycroft, L., Sandberg, A., Aziz, T., & Savulescu, J. (2018). Brainjacking in deep brain stimulation and autonomy. *Ethics and Information Technology*, *20*(3), 219–232. doi:10.100710676-018-9466-4 PMID:30595661

Purwins, H. (2019). Deep Learning for Audio Signal Processing. *IEEE Journal of Selected Topics in Signal Processing.*

Radcliffe, J. (2011). Hacking medical devices for fun and insulin: Breaking the human SCADA system. Black Hat Conference presentation slides.

Rahimpour, S., Kiyani, M., Hodges, S. E., & Turner, D. (2021). Deep brain stimulation and electromagnetic interference. *Clinical Neurology and Neurosurgery*, *203*, 106577. doi:10.1016/j.clineuro.2021.106577 PMID:33662743

Ramirez, J. J. M., & J. C. (2007). Voice Activity Detection. Fundamentals and Speech Recognition System Robustness. Robust Speech Recognition and Understanding.

Rasmussen, K. B., Castelluccia, C., Heydt-Benjamin, T. S., & Capkun, S. (2009). Proximity-based access control for implantable medical devices. *Proceedings of the 16th ACM conference on Computer and communications security*, 410-419.

Rasmussen, K. B., Castelluccia, C., Heydt-Benjamin, T. S., & Capkun, S. (2009). Proximity-Based Access Control for Implantable Medical Devices. *Proceedings of the ACM Conference on Computer and Communications Security*. 10.1145/1653662.1653712

Regulation (EU) 2016/679 on the protection of natural persons with regard to the processing of personal data and on the free movement of such data, and repealing Directive 95/46/EC (General Data Protection Regulation), 2016/679 (The European Parliament and of the Council April 27, 2016).

Rios, B., & Butts, J. (2017). *Security evaluation of the implantable cardiac device ecosystem architecture and implementation interdependencies*. Available: http://blog.whitescope.io/2017/05/understanding-pacemaker-systems.html

River Publishers Series in Communication. (2014). *Internet of Things- From Research and Innovation to Market Development* (V. Ovidiu & F. Peter, Eds.). River Publisher.

Rodriguez Lera, Fernandez, Guerrero, & Matellan. (2017). *Cybersecurity of Robotics and Autonomous Systems: Privacy and Safety*. Academic Press.

Roman, R., Zhou, J., & Lopez, J. (2013). On the Features and Challenges of Security and Privacy in Distributed Internet of Things. *Computer Networks*, *57*(10), 2266–2279. doi:10.1016/j.comnet.2012.12.018

Rostami, M., Burleson, W., Koushanfar, F., & Juels, A. (2013). Balancing security and utility in medical devices? *Proceedings of the 50th Annual Design Automation Conference on - DAC 13*. 10.1145/2463209.2488750

Rostami, M., Juels, A., & Koushanfar, F. (2013). Heart-to-heart (H2H). *Proceedings of the 2013 ACM SIGSAC Conference on Computer & Communications Security - CCS 13*. 10.1145/2508859.2516658

Rouf, I., Miller, R., Mustafa, H., Taylor, T., Oh, S., Xu, W., Gruteser, M., Trappe, W., & Seskar, I. (2010). Security and privacy vulnerabilities of in-car wireless networks: A tire pressure monitoring system case study. In *Proceedings of the 19th USENIX Conference on Security*. USENIX Association.

Rowland, D., Kohl, U., & Charlesworth, A. (2012). Information Technology Law (4th ed.). Routledge.

Roy, N., Shen, S., Hassanieh, H., & Choudhury, R. R. (2018). Inaudible voice commands: The long-range attack and defense. *15th USENIX Symposium on Networked Systems Design and Implementation (NSDI 18)*, 547–560.

Roy, N. (2018). "naudible Voice Commands : The Long-Range Attack and Defense. *Proceedings of the 15th USENIX Symposium on Networked.*

Roy, N. (2018). Inaudible Voice Commands : The Long-Range Attack and Defense. *Proceedings of the 15th USENIX Symposium on Networked.*

Roy, N., Hassanieh, H., & Roy Choudhury, R. (2017). Backdoor: Making microphones hear inaudible sounds. *Proceedings of the 15th Annual International Conference on Mobile Systems, Applications, and Services*, 2–14. 10.1145/3081333.3081366

Scalas, M., & Giacinto, G. (2019). Automotive cybersecurity: Foundations for next-generation vehicles. Academic Press.

Schonherr, L., Kohls, K., Zeiler, S., Holz, T., & Kolossa, D. (2018). *Adversarial ¨attacks against automatic speech recognition systems via psychoacoustic hiding.* arXiv preprint arXiv:1808.05665.

Schwart, P. M. (2004). Property, Privacy and Personal Data. *Harvard Law Review*, *117*(7), 2056–2128. doi:10.2307/4093335

Schwartz, P. M., & Solove, D. J. (2011). The PII Problem: Privacy and a New Concept of Personally Identifiable Information. *New York University Law Review*, *86*, 1814–2011.

Selvaraj, J., Dayanıklı, G. Y., Gaunkar, N. P., Ware, D., Gerdes, R. M., & Mina, M. (2018). Electromagnetic induction attacks against embedded systems. *Proceedings of the 2018 on Asia Conference on Computer and Communications Security*, 499–510. 10.1145/3196494.3196556

Sen, Maity, & Das. (2020). The body is the network: To safeguard sensitive data, turn flesh and tissue into a secure wireless channel. *IEEE Spectrum, 57*(12), 44-49. doi:10.1109/MSPEC.2020.9271808

Seo, J., Kim, K., Park, M., Park, M., & Lee, K. (2018). An Analysis of Economic Impact on IoT Industry under GDPR. *Mobile Information Systems*, 1-6. doi:10.1155/2018/6792028

Shin, H., Kim, D., Kwon, Y., & Kim, Y. (2017). Illusion and dazzle: Adversarial optical channel exploits against lidars for automotive applications. In W. Fischer & N. Homma (Eds.), *Cryptographic Hardware and Embedded Systems – CHES 2017* (pp. 445–467). Springer International Publishing.

Shin, J., Rahim, M. A., Islam, M. R., & Yun, K. S. (2020). A novel approach of cursive signature generation for personal identity. *International Journal of Computer Applications in Technology*, *62*(4), 384.

Shoukry, Y., Martin, P., Tabuada, P., & Srivastava, M. (2013). Non-invasive spoofing attacks for anti-lock braking systems. *Cryptographic Hardware and Embedded Systems - CHES 2013*, 55–72.

Simacsek, B. (n.d.). *Can we trust our cars?* Available: https: //www.nxp.com/docs/en/white-paper/AUTOSECWP.pdf

Compilation of References

Singh, P. M., & Gandhi, K. (2014). Interconnected Smart Objects: Era of Internet of Things. *IJARCET*, *3*(6), 2041–2046.

Smith, D. (2018). *Forwards for "Preparing for General Data Protection Regulation"*. Allenovery. https://www.allenovery.com/SiteCollectionDocuments/Radical%20changes%20 to%20European%20data%20protection%20legislation.pdf

Smithies & Newman. (1996). *Method and system for the capture, storage, transport and authentication of handwritten signatures*. U.S. Patent No. 5,544,255.

Soobramaney, P., Flowers, G., & Dean, R. (2015). Mitigation of the effects of high levels of high002Dfrequency noise on MEMS gyroscopes using microfibrous cloth. *ASME 2015 International Design Engineering Technical Conferences and Computers and Information in Engineering Conference*.

Stephenson, H. (n.d.). *UX design trends 2018: From voice interfaces to a Need to Not Trick People*. https://www.digitalartsonline.co.uk/features/interactive-design/ux-design-trends-2018-from-voice-interfaces-need-not-trick-peop

STMicroelectronics L3G4200D datasheet. (2011). https://www. elecrow.com/download/ L3G4200_AN3393.pdf

STMicroelectronics L3GD20 datasheet. (2013). http://www.st.com/en/mems-and-sensors/ l3gd20.html

STMicroelectronics LSM330 datasheet. (2012). www.st.com/ resource/en/datasheet/dm00037200. pdf

Stottelaar, B. G. (2015). *Practical cyber-attacks on autonomous vehicles*. Available: http://essay. utwente.nl/66766/

Studnia, I., Nicomette, V., Alata, E., Deswarte, Y., Kaaniche, M., & Laarouchi, Y. (2013). Survey on security threats and protection mechanisms in embedded automotive networks. *2013 43rd Annual IEEE/IFIP Conference on Dependable Systems and Networks Workshop (DSN-W)*, 1–12.

Sugawara, T., Cyr, B., Rampazzi, S., Genkin, D., & Fu, K. (2020). Light commands: laser-based audio injection attacks on voice-controllable systems. *29th USENIX Security Symposium (USENIX Security 20)*, 2631-2648.

Sugawara, T. (2020). Light Commands: Laser-Based Audio Injection Attacks on Voice-Controllable Systems. *Proceedings of the 29th USENIX Security Symposium*.

Sun, X., Xia, L., & Jia, S. (2015). *Enhancing location privacy for electric vehicles by obfuscating the linkages of charging events*. IEEE.

Symantec. (2018, Murch). *Internet Security Threat Report*. Symantec. https://www.symantec. com/content/dam/symantec/docs/reports/istr-23-2018-en.pdf

Tabasum, A., Safi, Z., AlKhater, W., & Shikfa, A. (2018). Cybersecurity Issues in Implanted Medical Devices. *2018 International Conference on Computer and Applications (ICCA)*, 1-9. doi: 10.1109/COMAPP.2018.8460454

The Commonwealth. (2017). *Model Bill on the Protection of Personal Information*. The Commonwealth. https://thecommonwealth.org/sites/default/files/key_reform_pdfs/P15370_9_ROL_Model_Privacy_Bill_0.pdf

The European Data Protection Board. (2018, November 16). *Guidelines 3/2018 on the territorial scope of the GDPR (Article 3)*. Edpb. https://edpb.europa.eu/sites/edpb/files/files/file1/edpb_guidelines_3_2018_territorial_scope_after_public_consultation_en_1.pdf

The European Union (EU) General Data Protection Regulation [GDPR], 679 (2016).

The Federal Trade Commission Staff Report. (2015, January). *Internet of Things Privacy & Security in a Connected World*. ftc.gov.https://www.ftc.gov/system/files/documents/reports/federal-trade-commission-staff-report-november-2013-workshop-entitled-internet-things-privacy/150127iotrpt.pdf

The Federal Trade Commission. (2019, July 2). D-*Link Agrees to Make Security Enhancements to Settle FTC Litigation*. FTC Gov. https://www.ftc.gov/news-events/press-releases/2019/07/d-link-agrees-make-security-enhancements-settle-ftc-litigation

The Organisation for Economic Co-operation and Development. (2013, July 11). *Recommendation of the Council concerning Guidelines governing the Protection of Privacy and Transborder Flows of Personal Data*. oecd.org. https://www.oecd.org/sti/ieconomy/2013-oecd-privacy-guidelines.pdf

Tom, F., Jain, M., & Dey, P. (2018). End-to-end audio replay attack detection using deep convolutional networks with attention. Interspeech, 681–685. doi:10.21437/Interspeech.2018-2279

Torrey, L., & Shavlik, J. (2010). Transfer Learning. In *Handbook of Researchon Machine Learning Applications and Trends: Algorithms, Methods,and Techniques* (pp. 242–26). IGI Global. doi:10.4018/978-1-60566-766-9.ch011

Tozal, M. E., Wang, Y., Al-Shaer, E., Sarac, K., Thuraisingham, B., & Chu, B.-T. (2011). On secure and resilient telesurgery communications over unreliable networks. *IEEE Conference on Computer Communications Workshops (INFOCOM WKSHPS)*, 714–719. 10.1109/INFCOMW.2011.5928905

Tozal, M. E., Wang, Y., Al-Shaer, E., Sarac, K., Thuraisingham, B., & Chu, B.-T. (2013, October). Adaptive information coding for secure and reliable wireless telesurgery communications. *Mobile Networks and Applications, 18*(5), 697–711.

Trippel, T., Weisse, O., Xu, W., Honeyman, P., & Fu, K. (2017). Walnut: Waging doubt on the integrity of MEMS accelerometers with acoustic injection attacks. *Proceedings of IEEE European Symposium on Security and Privacy*.

Tu, Y. (2018). Injected and delivered: Fabricating implicit control over actuation systems by spoofing inertial sensors. *27th USENIX Security Symposium (USENIX Security 18)*.

Tu, Y. (2019). *Trick or Heat?* Academic Press.

Tu, Y., Lin, Z., Lee, I., & Hei, X. (2018). Injected and delivered: Fabricating implicit control over actuation systems by spoofing inertial sensors. *27th USENIX Security Symposium (USENIX Security 18),* 1545-1562.

Tu, Y., Rampazzi, S., Hao, B., Rodriguez, A., Fu, K., & Hei, X. (2019). Trick or heat? Manipulating critical temperature-based control systems using rectification attacks. *Proceedings of the 2019 ACM SIGSAC Conference on Computer and Communications Security*, 2301-2315.

Tu, Y., Tida, V. S., Pan, Z., & Hei, X. (2021). Transduction Shield: A Low-Complexity Method to Detect and Correct the Effects of EMI Injection Attacks on Sensors. *Proceedings of the 2021 ACM Asia Conference on Computer and Communications Security*, 901-915.

Tu, Y., Lin, Z., Lee, I., & Hei, X. (2018). *Injected and delivered: Fabricating implicit control over actuation systems by spoofing inertial sensors. In 27th USENIX Security Symposium (USENIX Security 18)*. USENIX Association. Available https://www.usenix.org/conference/usenixsecurity18/presentation/tu

Tu, Y., Lin, Z., Lee, I., & Hei, X. (2018). Injected and Delivered: Fabricating Implicit Control over Actuation Systems by Spoofing Inertial Sensors. *Proceedings of the 27th USENIX Security Symposium.*

Tu, Y., Tida, V. S., Pan, Z., & Hei, X. (2021). Transduction Shield: A Low-Complexity Method to Detect and Correct the Effects of EMI Injection Attacks on Sensors. *Proceedings of the 2021 ACM Asia Conference on Computer and Communications Security*. 10.1145/3433210.3453097

Ueda, Kurachi, Takada, Mizutani, Inoue, & Horihata. (2015). Security authentication system for in-vehicle network. *SEI*, *81*.

United Nations Conference on Trade and Development. (2016). *Data Protection Regulations and International Data Flows: Implications for Trade and Development*. United Nations Publication.

Vaidya, T., Zhang, Y., Sherr, M., & Shields, C. (2015). Cocaine noodles: exploiting the gap between human and machine speech recognition. *9th USENIX Workshop on Offensive Technologies (WOOT 15).*

Vaidya, T., Zhang, Y., Sherr, M., & Shields, C. (2015). Cocaine Noodles: Exploiting the Gap between Human and Machine Speech Recognition. *9th USENIX Workshop on Offensive Technologies, WOOT 2015.*

Valasek & Miller. (2014). *Adventures in automotive networks and control units.* Technical Report.

Van Goethem, T. (2016). Accelerometer-based device fingerprinting for multi-factor mobile authentication. In *International Symposium on Engineering Secure Software and Systems*. Springer. 10.1007/978-3-319-30806-7_7

Venugopalan, S. (2015). Translating Videos to Natural Language Using Deep Recurrent Neural Networks. *NAACL HLT 2015 - 2015 Conference of the North American Chapter of the Association for Computational Linguistics: Human Language Technologies, Proceedings of the Conference.* 10.3115/v1/N15-1173

Vera-Diaz, J. M., Pizarro, D., & Macias-Guarasa, J. (2018). *Towards End-to-End Acoustic Localization Using Deep Learning: From Audio Signals to Source Position Coordinates.* Sensors.

Villalba, J., & Lleida, E. (2011). Detecting replay attacks from far-field recordings on speaker verification systems. In *European Workshop on Biometrics and Identity Management.* Springer. 10.1007/978-3-642-19530-3_25

Vrabec, H. U. (2019). *Uncontrollable: Data Subject Rights and the Data-driven Economy.* Universiteit Leiden.

Wachter, S. (2018). The GDPR and the Internet of Things: A Three-Step Transparency Model. *Law, Innovation and Technology, 10*(2), 266–294. doi:10.1080/17579961.2018.1527479

Wang, C., Daneshmand, M., Dohler, M., Mao, X., Hu, R. Q., & Wang, H. (2013). Guest Editorial-Special issue on internet of things (IoT): Architecture, protocols and services. *IEEE Sensors Journal, 13*(10), 3505–3510. doi:10.1109/JSEN.2013.2274906

Wang, Y., Attebury, G., & Ramamurthy, B. (2006). A survey of security issues in wireless sensor networks. *IEEE Communications Surveys and Tutorials, 8*(2), 2–23.

Weiss, M. A., & Archick, K. (2016). *U.S.-EU Data Privacy: From Safe Harbor to Privacy Shield.* FAS. https://fas.org/sgp/crs/misc/R44257.pdf

Winkler, R. (2017). Elon musk launches neuralink to connect brains with computers. *The Wall Street Journal.*

Wu, Z., & Li, H. (2013). Voice conversion and spoofing attack on speaker verification systems. In *2013 Asia-Pacific Signal and Information Processing Association Annual Summit and Conference.* IEEE. 10.1109/APSIPA.2013.6694344

Xu, M. (2004). HMM-Based Audio Keyword Generation. Lecture Notes in Computer Science (including subseries Lecture Notes in Artificial Intelligence and Lecture Notes in Bioinformatics). doi:10.1007/978-3-540-30543-9_71

Xu, Yan, Jia, Ji, & Liu. (2018). Analyzing and enhancing the security of ultrasonic sensors for autonomous vehicles. *IEEE Internet of Things Journal.*

Xu, Z., Hua, R., Juang, J., Xia, S., Fan, J., & Hwang, C. (2021). Inaudible Attack on Smart Speakers with Intentional Electromagnetic Interference. *IEEE Transactions on Microwave Theory and Techniques, 69*(5), 2642–2650. doi:10.1109/TMTT.2021.3058585

Yan, C. (2020). SoK: A Minimalist Approach to Formalizing Analog Sensor Security. *Proceedings - IEEE Symposium on Security and Privacy.* 10.1109/SP40000.2020.00026

Yan, Q. (2020). *SurfingAttack: Interactive Hidden Attack on Voice Assistants Using Ultrasonic Guided Waves.* Academic Press.

Yan. (2016). *Can you trust autonomous vehicles: Contactless attacks against sensors of self-driving vehicle.* Academic Press.

Yan, C., Shin, H., Bolton, C., Xu, W., Kim, Y., & Fu, K. (2020). Sok: A minimalist approach to formalizing analog sensor security. In *2020 IEEE Symposium on Security and Privacy (SP)* (pp. 233-248). IEEE.

Yang, N., Dey, N., Shcrratt, R. S., & Shi, F. (2020). Recognize Basic Emotional Statesin Speech by Machine Learning Techniques Using Mel-Frequency Cepstral Coefficient Features. *Journal of Intelligent & Fuzzy Systems*, *39*(2), 1925–1936. doi:10.3233/JIFS-179963

Yuan, X., Chen, Y., Zhao, Y., Long, Y., Liu, X., Chen, K., Zhang, S., Huang, H., Wang, X., & Gunter, C. A. (2018). Commandersong: A systematic approach for practical adversarial voice recognition. *27th USENIX Security Symposium (USENIX Security 18)*, 49–64.

Yuan, X. (2018). CommanderSong: A Systematic Approach for Practical Adversarial Voice Recognition. *Proceedings of the 27th USENIX Security Symposium.*

Yunker. (2013). Sound attenuation using microelectromechanical systems fabricated acoustic metamaterials. *Journal of Applied Physics.*

Zhang, G., X. L. G. Q. W. X., & Ji, X. (2011). Eararray: defending against dolphinattack via acoustic attenuation. *The Network and Distributed System Security Symposium (NDSS).*

Zhang, Y., & Rasmussen, K. (2020). Detection of Electromagnetic Interference Attacks on Sensor Systems. *Proceedings - IEEE Symposium on Security and Privacy.* 10.1109/SP40000.2020.00001

Zhang, G. (2017). DolphinAttack: Inaudible Voice Commands. *Proceedings of the ACM Conference on Computer and Communications Security.*

Zhang, G., Yan, C., Ji, X., Zhang, T., Zhang, T., & Xu, W. (2017). Dolphin attack: Inaudible voice commands. *Proceedings of the 2017 ACM SIGSAC Conference on Computer and Communications Security*, 103–117. 10.1145/3133956.3134052

Zhang, L., Tan, S., & Yang, J. (2017). Hearing your voice is not enough: An articulatory gesture based liveness detection for voice authentication. *Proceedings of the 2017 ACM SIGSAC Conference on Computer and Communications Security*, 57–71. 10.1145/3133956.3133962

Zhang, Y., & Rasmussen, K. (2020). Detection of electromagnetic interference attacks on sensor systems. In *2020 IEEE Symposium on Security and Privacy (SP)* (pp. 203-216). IEEE.

Zhang, Y., Shi, P., Dong, C., Liu, Y., Shao, X., & Ma, C. (2018). Test and evaluation system for automotive cybersecurity. *2018 IEEE International Conference on Computational Science and Engineering (CSE)*, 201–207.

Zheng, G., Zhang, G., Yang, W., Valli, C., Shankaran, R., & Orgun, M. A. (2017). From WannaCry to WannaDie: Security trade-offs and design for implantable medical devices. *2017 17th International Symposium on Communications and Information Technologies (ISCIT)*. 10.1109/ISCIT.2017.8261228

Zhou, W., Jia, Y., Peng, A., Zhang, Y., & Liu, P. (2019). The Effect of IoT New Features on Security and Privacy: New Threats, Existing Solutions, and Challenges Yet to Be Solved. *IEEE Internet of Things Journal*, 6(2), 1606–1616. doi:10.1109/JIOT.2018.2847733

Zhu, S., & Zhang, X. (2017). Enabling high-precision visible light localization in today's buildings. *Proceedings of the 15th Annual International Conference on Mobile Systems, Applications, and Services*.

Zue, V. W. (1980). Digital Processing of Speech Signals, by L. R. Rabiner and R. W. Schafer. *The Journal of the Acoustical Society of America*, 67(4), 1406–1407. doi:10.1121/1.384160

About the Contributors

Sidi Mohamed Sidi Ahmed is an independent researcher who recently obtained a PhD in laws from International Islamic University Malaysia (IIUM). He specialises in cyberlaw, particularly, privacy, data protection, data security and related issues. In addition to his PhD thesis which focused on Data in the IoT environment from some legal aspects, Dr. Sidi Mohamed also published articles related to cyberlaw various scientific journals.

Michael Arienmughare is a Master's student at the University of Louisiana at Lafayette (ULL) Computer Science Department.

Lauren Burgess is a doctoral student at Towson University. Her research interests include networking and data analytics.

Md Imran Hossen is a PhD candidate at the University of Louisiana at Lafayette, USA. His research interest includes Web security and Machine learning security. He obtained his bachelor's degree in Electronics and Communication Engineering in 2016 from Khulna University of Engineering and Technology, Khulna, Bangladesh.

Hengshuo Liang is a doctoral student. His research interests include networking, machine learning and big data.

Weixian Liao is an assistant professor at Towson University. His research interests include cyber-physical system and machine learning.

Chao Lu is a professor at Towson University. His research interests include networking and distributed computing.

Raghabendra Shah recently completed his MS in Computer Science from Louisiana at Lafayette in May 2021. He received a BE degree in electrical engineering from Tribhuvan University, Nepal, in 2014. His BE final year project on remote low-cost smart energy meter earned a government fund for further research. From 2018 to 2021, he was an exemplary teaching assistant for operating system courses. His research interests include systems architecture, GPU, and machine learning.

Vijay Srinivas Tidawas was born in Guntur, Andhra Pradesh, India in 1993. He received the B.S. from the KL University India in 2015 and Master's degree in Computer engineering from Illinois Institute of Technology, Chicago, IL, in 2018. From 2018, he was a Research and Teaching Assistant in University of Louisiana at Lafayette. His research interests include approximate computing, Deep Learning and Low power VLSI Design.

Anthony Triche is a doctoral candidate at the University of Louisiana at Lafayette focusing on research spanning the fields of cognitive science and machine learning.

Wei Yu is a professor in Towson University. His research area is Internet of Things, Networking and Big Data Analytics.

Index

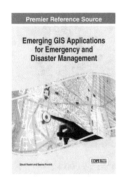 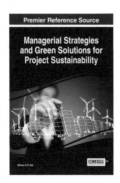  

Printed in the United States
by Baker & Taylor Publisher Services